Alan Kendall

Vivaldi

PANTHER
GRANADA PUBLISHING
London Toronto Sydney New York

Published by Granada Publishing Limited
in Panther Books 1979

ISBN 0 586 050655

First published in Great Britain by
Chappell & Co. Ltd 1978
Copyright © Alan Kendall 1978

Granada Publishing Limited
Frogmore, St Albans, Herts AL2 2NF
and
3 Upper James Street, London W1R 4BP
866 United Nations Plaza, New York, NY 10017, USA
117 York Street, Sydney, NSW 2000, Australia
100 Skyway Avenue, Rexdale, Ontario, M9W 3A6, Canada
PO Box 84165, Greenside, 2034 Johannesburg, South Africa
CML Centre, Queen & Wyndham, Auckland 1, New Zealand

Set, printed and bound in Great Britain by
Cox & Wyman Ltd, Reading
Set in Intertype Times

Granada ®
Granada Publishing ®

To the memory of SIDNEY SCHOLFIELD CAMPBELL

Alan Kendall was educated at Barnard Castle School, County Durham, and King's College, Cambridge, continuing his musical education in Paris where he lived and worked for four years. On his return to England he decided to pursue a career as a musician and writer. He has had considerable teaching experience, and has translated four books from French. As a professional musician he sings regularly for the BBC, and as a writer his works include – in addition to a number of historical books for children – a book on musical instruments and biographies of Benjamin Britten, Nadia Boulanger and Beethoven. He is currently writing a biography of Handel.

Contents

List of Illustrations

Acknowledgements

I am indebted to many people for the very practical help they gave me with this book, notably the directors of the State Archives in Venice, Florence and Ferrara, and of the Conservatory, Civic Museums and Galleria Querini Stampalia in Venice, together with the staffs of the Fondazione Cini and Biblioteca Marciana in that city, and those of the Biblioteca Nazionale in Turin and the Liceo Musicale in Bologna. In England I must thank the staffs of: the Italian Institute in London, and especially Antonio Spallone; Sir John Soane's Museum; the Royal College of Music, and especially Watkins Shaw; in Oxford the Bodleian Library (music department); and last, but by no means least, in Cambridge the Fitzwilliam Museum, the library of King's College, and the University Library, especially the Anderson and Rare Books rooms.

I owe particular thanks to Richard Andrewes of the Pendlebury Music Library, Cambridge; Roger Blanchard, whose transcriptions of Vivaldi's vocal music have been of enormous help; Lady Egremont, Werner Forman, Raymond Leppard and Michael Talbot.

Finally, my thanks are due to Peter Locke for his generous hospitality in Venice on several occasions, and to the Council of King's College, Cambridge, for permission to reside there for long periods; to Andrew Whitehouse, who was a patient and considerate companion on my travels; to Lidia Dingley, who inspired in me a love for her native language; to Simon Scott for his enthusiasm for the project, and to Brenda Holt who, as always, typed the manuscript with care and efficiency.

For permission to quote copyright material, thanks are due to: Messrs Faber & Faber for a quotation from T. S. Eliot's *Murder in the cathedral*; H. Honour and Messrs Collins for a quotation from *The companion guide to Venice* (1965 ed.); M. Talbot for a quotation from his Ph.D. thesis *The instrumental music of Tomaso Albinoni*, Cambridge University Library (1968), and D. Maxwell White and Manchester University Press for a quotation from *Zaccaria Angelo Seriman*.

Attempts were made to contact all holders of copyright material, and failure to include acknowledgement here is no indication of intent to avoid such acknowledgement. Any omissions notified to the publishers will be included in future editions.

Preface

The music of Antonio Vivaldi enjoys enormous popularity today, and not simply because of a handful of works, but through an ever increasing repertoire as more of his compositions are made available to musicians in modern performing editions, and to the public at large through concerts and gramophone records. Soon we shall be celebrating the tercentenary of his birth, and yet, despite his remarkable popularity, there has never been a book devoted entirely to him in the English language. The two previously available, by Marc Pincherle and Walter Kolneder, were translated from French and German respectively.

Since the first of these books was written, the date of Vivaldi's birth has been confirmed by documentary evidence (though the news still does not seem to have reached the ears of some writers of programme and record sleeve notes), and since the second was published more of Vivaldi's letters have come to light. Also, Peter Ryom has published his invaluable catalogue of the works known to us so far, which will hopefully put an end to the confusion that has hitherto obtained in that field.

Even so, the would-be biographer of Vivaldi is faced with a daunting task. Unlike so many of his contemporaries, Vivaldi wrote no theoretical treatise or memoirs, nor did he keep a diary or write an autobiography (for one thing he was much too busy, even if he had been temperamentally disposed to consider such a thing). Even the letters that we have were occasioned solely by business matters, and in any case they relate only to a very short period of his life, and to a specific part of his activity during that period.

The fact that we now know with certainty the dates of

his birth and death have not, moreover, made him any more accessible as a person. Despite his international reputation, he moves across the European scene as a somewhat shadowy character for much of his life, and we are forced to rely on the tantalizing glimpses given us by such people as Goldoni, or Abate Conti in his letters to Madame de Caylus, or the eye-witness accounts of such visitors to Venice as the Frenchman Charles de Brosses, the German Johann von Uffenbach and the Englishman Edward Wright. Luckily those glimpses are wonderfully vivid at times, and with patience and assistance from passages in his own letters, and details taken from the account books and minutes of the governors' meetings of the Venetian orphanage where Vivaldi was employed for much of his working life (with frequent and often pro-longed absences), a picture emerges of the strange man known to his contemporaries as the Red Priest.

Of fundamental importance in any consideration of Vivaldi both as a person and as a musician is the nature of Venetian society and culture in the last two decades of the seventeenth century and the first half of the eighteenth century, and the enormous part played by music in that society and culture.

It is perhaps difficult for us today to imagine to what extent music mattered to Venetians. Hardly a single ceremony, whether sacred or secular, was complete without it, and the very slightest pretext seemed to be sufficient for the composition of a new work. To the many foreign visitors, the very air seemed to be heavy with music, and it is little wonder that the Venetians seem to have had an insatiable appetite for it. Nowhere is this more apparent than in the Venetian consumption of opera, which combined music with another, almost equally strong appetite, that for spectacle. Vivaldi responded to this medium with extraordinary stamina, writing almost fifty operas of which we have record, and possibly almost twice that number if we are to take one of his letters at face value. As to the other vocal works, and the vast amount of purely instrumental compositions, we may never know exactly how many there were. What we do have, however, is a voice that speaks to us over the centuries in terms that are clear and direct because they treat of a common humanity that we share with Vivaldi.

For its pathetic element, we may well equate his life story with that of many creative artists throughout history – Mozart at once springs to mind. Yet at the same time it has a very contemporary flavour. There was a strong element of the survivalist in Vivaldi. In his own day his popularity only lasted as long as he appealed to popular taste, and in the composers' league he is by way of being something of an anti-hero. Nobility is not a word one would readily associate with his character as it is revealed to us in his letters. At times he was positively deceptive in his dealings, if not downright dishonest. He fought against illness, financial problems and waning popularity with amazing determination and yet died in poverty and obscurity far from the place of his birth.

In the wider context, one can see several parallels between the state of Venetian civilization as it launched itself upon the last century of its independent existence, and certain aspects of our own – at times somewhat weary – civilization today. The concern here, then, is both with the man who – through his music – has given such enormous pleasure to the world, and the society and culture that produced him. The paradox is that whereas the culture that produced him lionized, and then abandoned him, has decayed to vanishing point, and indeed the very city itself now seems in danger of physical collapse, Vivaldi's music – the very essence of the man – will survive as long as there are people to play and hear it.

THE CLOISTERS, WINDSOR CASTLE
January 1977

ALAN KENDALL

1. Beginnings

Antonio Lucio Vivaldi was born in Venice in 1678. Despite the numerous variants still to be found on record sleeves, in programme notes, and even in reference books, the year had been deduced with reasonable certainty almost fifty years ago,[1] though no confirmation was possible until the record of his baptism – which took place on 6 May 1678 – was discovered in the 1960s in the registers of the church of S. Giovanni in Bràgora, Venice.[2] From this we learn that Antonio was born on 4 March 1678 and was baptized by a midwife, Madama Margarita, who was originally from Verona, because she was afraid that he might die.

Vivaldi's mother Camilla, the daughter of a Venetian tailor Camillo Calicchio, married Gianbattista Vivaldi on 6 August 1677, after an 'engagement' of more than a year, for which the document – the declaration of *stato libero*, or being free from any impediment to matrimony – is still in existence.[3] Antonio was therefore presumably born prematurely, since he was not baptized in church until two months after his birth. The baptism with water by the midwife may have had something to do with an earthquake which Remo Giazotto claims shook Venice on 4 March 1678.[4] On the other hand, Antonio was always afflicted with illness throughout his life, and he may have been such a sickly child at birth that the midwife took it upon herself to baptize him in case he died before he could have a proper baptism.

As we see from the declaration of *stato libero*, the Vivaldi family at that time lived in the *contrada* or parish of S. Martino in the *sestiere* or district of Castello, between the Arsenale and the Riva degli Schiavoni, and Antonio's Venetian life was always centred on this part of the city. *Sestiere* means sixth part, and to this day Venice retains the same six districts. There were other brothers:[5] Bonaventura

13

Tomaso and Francesco Gaetano, and three sisters: Margherita Gabriela, Cecilia Maria and Zanetta Anna. Francesco followed his father's original calling as a barber, but was banished from Venice in 1721 for having insulted a patrician who mistook him for a doctor. He was back in Venice in 1727, however, since there is a mention of him as having been involved in the new paving of the Piazza S. Marco, which had been started in 1722, abandoned, and then started up again. In 1731 he became a printer. There may also have been a third brother, Iseppo, who also fell foul of the law, and was banished for three years in 1729. On 9 November 1728 he had injured an errand boy in a brawl, and one of the witnesses identified him in a way which reveals the standing of Antonio at this time: 'Iseppo, non so il cognome, fratelle de Prete rosso famoso che sona il violin.' ('Iseppo, I don't know his surname, brother of the famous Red Priest who plays the violin.')

The red hair of the Vivaldis seems to have stood instead of a surname, and indeed one of the earliest references to the father, in the registers of S. Marco, identifies him as G. B. Rossi. Furthermore, one of the chief reasons for identifying the portrait in the Liceo Musicale in Bologna as that of Antonio is the fact that an auburn curl is peeping out from under the sitter's wig at the left temple.

Despite many references to Vivaldis as far back in history as the thirteenth century – and those, incidentally, were citizens of Genoa who were seafarers – it has not been possible to trace this particular branch of the Vivaldi family back further than the composer's paternal grandparents, who lived in Brescia. Their son Giovanni Battista or Gianbattista was born there in 1665, and when he was ten his mother took him to Venice, presumably on the death of his father. Initially Gianbattista became a barber by trade, but he was also an accomplished violinist, and gradually this came to assume more importance, for in 1685 he was one of the founder members of the *Sovvegno dei musicisti di Santa Cecilia*, a musical fraternity whose director was Giovanni Legrenzi, and whose headquarters were at the local parish church of S. Martino. There is still a side chapel there

14

dedicated to S. Cecilia. Membership was limited to one hundred, and it included singers, as well as instrumentalists. Its charter is in the Biblioteca Marciana in Venice.[6]

In his capacity as *maestro di cappella* of S. Marco, Legrenzi was the successor to such distinguished composers as Willaert, Cipriano de Rore, the Gabrielis, Monteverdi and Cavalli. Less well known, but also important in the process of improving the standard of the music in S. Marco was Legrenzi's immediate predecessor Natale Monferrato (*c.* 1603–1685). In a way almost the whole of Monferrato's life was devoted to S. Marco, and he was steeped in its traditions.[7] He was a pupil of Rovetta, or Roveta, who was Monteverdi's successor as *maestro di cappella* at S. Marco, and became cantor there in 1640, second *maestro di cappella* (to Cavalli) in 1647, and finally first *maestro* on the death of Cavalli in 1676. He was also, incidentally, *maestro di coro* at the Ospedale dei Mendicanti. Monferrato did much to improve the conditions at S. Marco, particularly by having fairly rigorous trials for prospective entrants. He also collaborated with Giuseppe Sala to found a printing firm in 1675, and it was this firm that printed Vivaldi's Op. I. His pupil Legrenzi succeeded him both as *maestro di cappella* at S. Marco and *maestro di coro* at the Mendicanti.

Giovanni Legrenzi himself was born at Clusone near Bergamo in 1626, and died in Venice on 27 May 1690. He studied in Venice with Rovetta, but returned to Bergamo to take up an appointment as organist of the church of S. Maria Maggiore there, in 1654. Three years later he went to Ferrara, where he was *maestro di cappella* at the Accademia dello Spirito Santo until 1665. It was in Ferrara that his first operas were performed, to libretti by Marquis Ippolito Bentivoglio, whose brother Guido was to become Vivaldi's patron. By 1672 Legrenzi was back in Venice, and at the beginning of 1681 was appointed Antonio Sartorio's successor as second *maestro di cappella* at S. Marco. In 1685, as we have already seen, he became first *maestro* on the death of Monferrato. From then on he devoted himself mainly to church music and oratorios, wrote some instrumental music, and organized concerts at his house of his own music and

15

that of his pupils Lotti and Caldara, and the two Gasparinis Francesco and Michelangelo. It is possible that they were brothers, since they both came from Lucca.

When Legrenzi became *maestro di cappella* at S. Marco, one of the first things he did was re-organize the orchestra there. Under Legrenzi there were thirty-four members: eight violins, eleven violette (possibly a treble or alto viol),[8] two viole da braccio, three violoni (double-bass viols), four theorboes (large lutes), two cornetts, one bassoon and three trombones. The balance then would seem to have been in favour of the upper strings, but in 1708, according to Caffi,[9] this had been redressed, the forces reduced, and the composition then was: ten violins, three violette, one viola da braccio, one violone, three theorboes, one cornett, two trumpets, one trombone and one oboe. The sort of sound that the young Vivaldi heard in S. Marco was therefore still undergoing a certain amount of change all through his formative years.

Gianbattista Vivaldi became a regular performer there, and in a foreigners' guide to Venice published in 1713, Gianbattista, along with his son Antonio, was mentioned as one of the best violinists in the city. In August 1689, Gianbattista, another violinist and a viola player were given extra pay because of an increase in the amount of work they had to do through the greater use of instruments and organs.[10] Legrenzi had obviously made some headway in his reforms at S. Marco, then. Because of the association with Legrenzi, it has been assumed that Antonio would naturally have studied with him, but in view of the fact that Legrenzi died in 1690, this does not seem very probable. There is a *Laetatus sum* (RV Anhang 31),[11] with the date of 1691, in Turin, which may be a fruit of such a period of study, though however celebrated Antonio may have become later in life, he was not known as a child prodigy such as Mozart was to be.

As far as the violin itself was concerned, however, one need look no further for an instructor than his own father, who was obviously a performer of considerable skill. Moreover the continual mixing with other musicians, and the visits Antonio must have made to S. Marco with his father, and then eventually deputizing for him, provided a strong musical atmosphere in which his talents developed. It may nevertheless seem somewhat strange that he never became a member of the staff of S. Marco. However, it was by no means a foregone conclusion that Antonio would take up music as a profession. In fact what happened was that he embarked upon a career in the church, and on 18 September 1693 he received the tonsure from the Patriarch of Venice and the next day took the first of the minor orders, that of porter. On this occasion he was described as of the parish of S. Geminiano. On 21 September he became a lector, but after that it was more than two years before he moved on to the next stage of exorcist – on 25 December 1695 – and almost another year again before he completed the minor orders when he became an acolyte on 21 September 1696.

Nowadays the minor orders are usually conferred on the same day, often during a student's career at a seminary, and even in Vivaldi's day it was unusual for a candidate for the priesthood to take quite so long to complete all the stages. When next presented, he was described as of the parish of S. Giovanni in Oleo. He became a sub-deacon on 4 April 1699, a deacon on 18 September 1700, and finally a priest on 23 March 1703 – in other words some nine-and-a-half years after he embarked on the process.[12] Once again his health may have been a problem, and indeed we have his own testimony that not long after he became a fully fledged priest, able to say Mass himself, illness forced him to abandon the practice. The information comes from a letter to his patron, the Marquis Guido Bentivoglio, dated 16 November 1737, which runs as follows:

I have not said Mass now for twenty-five years, and I shall never do so again, not because of any veto or order ... but on my own account, and this because of an illness I have suffered from since I was born, which oppresses me very much. After I had been ordained priest I said Mass for a year or more and then renounced doing so because I had to leave the altar three times without finishing Mass through this same illness.[13]

It may well be this abandoning of the altar that led to the much repeated story that if a musical theme came into his head, Vivaldi would leave the sanctuary in the middle of Mass and dash off to the sacristy to jot it down. In the same letter to the marquis, however, he maintained that everyone in Venice knew about his illness:

This is why I almost always live at home, and only go out in a gondola or carriage, since I cannot walk because of my chest complaint, more precisely chest constriction [*stretteza di petto*]. None of the nobility invites me to his house, not even our prince [doge], because they all know about my illness. I can usually go out straight after lunch, but I never walk. This, then, is why I do not say Mass.

And yet from somewhere Vivaldi found the energy necessary to compose at a seemingly impossible rate, rehearse hundreds of works for performance, play the violin exquisitely, and act as his own opera impresario. It was perfectly understandable, therefore, that some should have expressed incredulity about the real state of his health. Be that as it may, the fact remains that within a year of being ordained priest, Vivaldi had embarked on an entirely different career, and one that was to make him one of the most famous of all Venetian composers. In September 1703 he began to teach violin at the orphanage and conservatory known as the Ospedale della Pietà, and his name first appears on the accounts for 17 March 1704, when he received the sum of thirty ducats for the preceding term – i.e. from 1 September 1703 to 28 February 1704. In this modest way began an association that was to last – intermittently – for almost the rest of Vivaldi's life.[14]

If it seems strange to us that a priest should suddenly abandon his vocation for the life of a professional musician, one must remember that in the eighteenth century things were very different, and certainly in Venice at that time. Initially, obviously, the fact that Vivaldi was a priest would facilitate, to some degree, his entry into an establishment such as the Pietà where there were a number of single women, some of whom were quite young, and some of whom were possibly there against their will. We shall look at the life in the four *ospedali* presently, suffice it to say here that the religious orders played an extremely large part in the educational and musical life of the city, and were much more in evidence than they are today. In fact the whole attitude to the religious calling was very different. It has been estimated that in 1766 there was one ecclesiastic to every twenty-three members of the population. Pompeo Molmenti said that, in order to escape the boredom of their public duties, some young patricians even went so far as to assume the clerical garb, often without giving themselves the trouble of ever saying Mass.[15] In support he quotes a letter from Del Teglia, the Tuscan Resident in Venice, dated 8 January 1697,[16] in which he accuses Giovanni Francesco Barbarigo, Venetian Ambassador to France, of this practice. Certainly it was a recurring problem, because an Act of State dated 27 February 1749 deplored the fact that nobles were avoiding their public duties by donning clerical garb.

Then as far as priests practising a musical profession went, François Misson had something to say about that in a letter dated 14 February 1688 – i.e. when Vivaldi was ten years old: 'They have found a mean[s?] to accommodate the affair, and have concluded that a priest fitted for musick may exercise the priesthood as well as another; provided he hath his *necessities*, or, if you will, his *superfluities* in his pocket.'[17] This of course refers to the fact that priests had to be sound in body before being ordained – hence the reference to testicles as '*necessities*'. On the other hand, since priests were bound to a life of celibacy – at least in theory – then the testicles were also '*superfluities*'. This may well have been the reason for the Englishman Edward Wright's statement that Vivaldi was a eunuch,[18] since presumably he automatically assumed that any single man let loose among so many young women must perforce be rendered harmless. Misson admitted that he had no authority for his assertion, however: 'I will not be bound to produce the act for this regulation, which certainly was only given *viva voce*. But let that be as it will,

I can positively assure you from my own certain knowledge, that what I have told you is truth.'

One might have thought that such a large number of clergy would tend to constitute a threat to the State, but Venetians were always Venetians first, and dutiful children of the pope second, so that their loyalty to their homeland came before any loyalty to the Papacy, and the body that was directly under the pope's command, the Jesuits, never had a great deal of success in Venice, despite their excessively opulent and flamboyant church there, built with money given by the Manin family. In fact it was customary to hear, in the streets of Venice, Jesuits being followed by the cry of: 'Andate, andate, niente pigliate e mai ritornate!' ('Go away, go away, take nothing with you and never return!') Misson revealed, however, a more subtle estimation of the State's attitude, which was probably fairly accurate: 'In a word, it is certain that Messieurs of Venice suffer themselves to be governed neither by the priests nor the monks. Those fathers are permitted to wear masks during the Carnival, to treat their concubines, sing on the stages, and do what they please, but they dare not thrust their noses into affairs of state'.[19]

There was little danger, then, from a scheming priesthood. Freschot, writing early in the eighteenth century, maintained that the ordinary parish clergy came from the lower strata of society, and therefore it was no wonder that they were poorly educated and badly behaved.[20] In fact he wondered that the parishioners would receive instruction and the sacraments at their hands. He reproached the government for their failure to take action, since the Patriarch of Venice seemed virtually powerless, but he felt that the official line in Venice was that the government was only responsible for remedying that which might trouble the State and private individuals. In the case of incontinent clergy, neither the individual nor the public at large were liable to be harmed in any way, so that the Senate did not include cognizance of it amongst their obligations, and left it to the conscience of each one to adjust his conduct, and to God to administer what punishment He thought fit. A very satisfactory state of affairs, in other words, since by a piece of masterly inactivity the Senate ensured that the clergy were not encouraged to reform themselves too far, lest they became a focal point of any potential popular movement, and yet on the other hand by allowing a considerable degree of licence, the clergy had nothing to react against. Even so, from time to time the government made the right sort of noises to indicate that they were not totally unconcerned, as for example on 23 March 1724, when they officially deplored the fact that the clergy were dressing and behaving improperly. Even this had its point, however, in the control the State exercised over its citizens, since it was always easier to see what the clergy were up to when they were instantly recognizable as such.

Some parishes seemed more reprehensible than others in this matter, as the archives of the Inquisitors (still preserved in Venice) reveal, and S. Geminiano was at one point particularly notorious. The church now no longer exists, demolished on the orders of Napoleon to improve the symmetry of what he regarded as the best drawing-room in Europe, but its vulnerable position at the opposite end of the Piazza to S. Marco was probably more the reason for its appearance on the files of the Inquisition than the behaviour of its clergy. Even so, basing himself on the fact that Vivaldi was presented for the various stages of ordination at one time and another, as we have seen, by the clergy of S. Geminiano and S. Giovanni in Oleo (another 'notorious' church), Giazotto concludes that the clergy were rather lax at both places.[21] Roland de Candé (as with much else in his book) echoes Giazotto – though since both their books have had subsequent editions it is difficult to know who influences whom – and takes this a step further, building up a portrait of Vivaldi as part of a very dubious circle almost tantamount to a Venetian underworld.[22] As we shall see, the evidence is almost entirely circumstantial, though the world of Venetian opera was, and still is, riddled with intrigue.

The monks and nuns probably came in for even more abuse than the secular clergy, especially from foreign visitors. In fact volume II of Misson's book [23] opens with a

21

series of replies to individual points raised in criticism of his first volume, published as a series of letters, and it would appear that one reader took him to task for failing to provide enough lurid details:

In my former letters I said nothing, or very little, concerning the libertinism and debauchery that reigns in the monasteries, because I am not particularly acquainted with the fashions of those places . . . I leave you to judge of their private employments, for I am resolved not to pry into them. As for the bouncing Brothers of the Cowle, they are such horrible debauchees, that 'tis impossible to fancy any excess of which they are not guilty.

The nuns of S. Lorenzo were particularly famous for their escapades, partly because many of them were high-spirited daughters of the nobility who had certainly not chosen the religious life of their own accord, and therefore determined to continue enjoying life to the full. They were in the habit of receiving masked visitors to their parlour during the Carnival, but the Patriarch of Venice – for once trying to make a show of his authority – ordered them to close it, at least between the hours of noon and three in the afternoon. When they failed to comply, he put a bolt on the door on the outside. Thereupon the nuns climbed on the roof and threw lighted faggots and strips torn from their plentiful supply of shrouds, which they dipped in oil, down against the door, which was totally burnt, along with a marble statue of St Laurence which was over the doorway, which meant that the poor saint was grilled all over again, and totally reduced to ashes.

It was the way in which the nuns so openly chatted with their guests, as we see from the paintings by Guardi and the Master of the Ridotto (formerly attributed to Pietro Longhi), as well as their garb, which most seems to have shocked visitors, especially those from northern and western European countries. As Edward Wright put it:

On their feast-days the door of their convent is flung

22

open, and they stand in crowds at the entrance, where I observed them talking to their acquaintance with great freedom. Nor do these noble vestals at any time confine themselves to such close restrictions as others of their order are obliged to do. Those I saw at the Celestia were dressed in white; no veil over their faces; a small transparent black covering goes round their shoulders; their heads were very prettily dressed; a sort of small thin coif went round the crown, and came under the chin; their hair was seen at the forehead, and nape of the neck: the covering on their neck and breast was so thin, that 'twas next to nothing at all.[24]

From this it was but a small step to imputing loose morals to the nuns, and indeed it is certain that by our standards their behaviour at times left much to be desired. Whether the sort of scandal that was retailed by such writers as President Charles de Brosses, however, is totally worthy of credence, is open to doubt.[25] For example, he wrote from Venice on 13 August 1739:

This current practice of the ladies [of using gondolas in which to receive their lovers] has much diminished the profits of the nuns, who were previously in the possession of *galanterie*. Even so, there are still a good number of them who come out of it today with distinction, I might say with emulation, since, even as I talk to you, there is a furious dispute amongst three convents of the city to decide which will have the advantage of giving a mistress to the new nuncio who has just arrived. In truth, it would be towards the nuns that I would turn most willingly if I had to stay here for long. All those that I have seen at Mass, through the grille, talking the whole of the time and laughing together, have seemed pretty to me and got up in such a way to set off their beauty. They have a charming little hairstyle, a simple habit but, of course, almost entirely white, which uncovers their shoulders and throat no more nor less than the Roman costumes of our actresses.

Whatever the moral problems, however, it was the Church that was responsible for providing so much employment for musicians, and provided the setting for such a large part of the musical life of the city at this time. In fact it seemed at one point as if music constituted almost all the life of Venice. It was Nietzsche who said: 'When I search for a word to replace that of music, I can think only of Venice', and it is true that for generations of travellers – both serious musicians and avid tourists – music has been an almost integral part of the lure of the city.

One of the first English visitors of the seventeenth century to record his impressions was Thomas Coryate (1577?–1617) who travelled through France, Italy and Switzerland, Germany and Holland – mostly on foot – in 1608. He published the narrative of his travels three years later, in 1611, under the titles of *Coryats crudities* and *Coryats cramb*. It is the first of these that deals with Venice. After visiting S. Marco and S. Lorenzo, he then came to Scuola di S. Rocco on 16 August, the saint's feast day,[26] where he heard: 'the best musicke that ever I did in all my life both in the morning and the afternoone, so good that I would willingly goe an hundred miles a foote at any time to heare the like'.

Coryate always wrote with enthusiasm and in a somewhat highly coloured way, and even at this distance – happily for us – we are able to enter into the spirit of the times, and experience something of what he felt:

This feast consisted principally of musicke, which was both vocall and instrumentall, so good, so delectable, so rare, so admirable, so super excellent, that it did even ravish and stupifie all those strangers that never heard the like. But how others were affected with it I know not; for mine owne part I can say this, that I was for the time even rapt up with Saint Paul into the third heaven.

This is the sort of reaction we encounter time and time again from visitors to Venice, except for the most jaded of palates, and music is what most frequently seems to carry them into these transports of delight. A notable exception

24

was Lady Mary Wortley Montagu, whom Mrs Thrale referred to as 'our luxurious Lady Mary'. In a letter to Francesco Algarotti on 12 March 1757 she wrote (in French): 'You do not know, perhaps, that I love music to the point of hate. I could not listen to it with impunity; I am as sensitive as Alexander, and another Timotheus would make me run, torch in hand, and set fire to the city.'

For most people, however, the very air seemed to be heavy with music, as another English visitor, John Evelyn, recorded when he went there in June 1645:

> It was evening, and the canal where the Noblesse go to take the air, as in our Hyde-Park, was full of ladies and gentlemen . . . Here they were singing, playing on harpsichords, and other music, and serenading their mistresses; in another place, racing, and other pastimes on the water, it being now exceeding hot . . .
>
> At our return to Venice [from Murano], we met several gondolas full of Venetian ladies, who come thus far in fine weather to take the air, with music and other refreshments.[27]

This was twenty years before the Vivaldi family settled in Venice, and more than thirty years before Antonio was born. Here is the Frenchman Charles de Brosses, writing almost a century later, on 29 August 1739, when Antonio Vivaldi was at the height of his powers: 'It's not that I lack music; there is hardly an evening when there is not *académie* somewhere; the people rush along the canal to hear it with as much ardour as if it were for the first time. The infatuation of the nation for this art is inconceivable.'[28]

But the love of music was not principally the preserve of the upper classes. P. J. Grosley, writing in 1764, said:

> We also had the pleasure of hearing, in S. Mark's Square, a man of the dregs of the people, a shoemaker, a blacksmith, in the dress of his trade, begin an aria: other people of the same sort joined him, singing this aria in several parts, with an exactness, precision and taste that

one scarcely encounters among the best people in our northern countries.[29]

When Charles Burney visited Italy six years later, music seemed around him from the very first (3 August): 'The instant I got to the inn a band of musicians consisting of two good fiddles, a violoncello and female voice stopt under the windows and performed in such a manner as would have made people stare in England, but here they were as little attended to as coalmen or oyster women are with us.' And then, six days later (9 August): 'The canals are crowded with musical people at night – bands of music – French horns – duet singers in every gondola.'[30]

Within fourteen or fifteen years, however, Mrs Thrale for one was of the opinion that the standard had deteriorated – though of course she was not referring to the general musical propensities of the Venetians at large: 'The state of music in Italy, if one may believe those who ought to know it best, is not what it was. The manner of singing is much changed, I am told; and some affectations have been suffered to encroach upon their natural graces.'[31]

One of the chief reasons for this was the gradual incursion of operatic style, with a resultant mingling of manner. By 1709, when Freschot was writing, and Vivaldi was launched upon his career, there was a feeling that the distinction between church music and opera had somehow been lost:

I do not know whether it is to cheer the saints' days up even more and for the special satisfaction of those who only go to church as they go to the theatres, that they do scarcely ever fail in this noisy music to mingle the same that one has heard at the operas, and which have pleased more, and that with no scandal to the favour of the words which one changes and which, instead of expressing, for example, the loves of Pyramus and Thisbe, say something of the life of the saint whose feast day it is.[32]

Grosley, writing in 1764, gives a more perceptive account of things.[33] He saw that there was a distinction between the

26

music of the parish churches, and that of the monasteries, convents and *ospedali*: 'On feast-days and Sundays, the parochial morning office in Venice is only attended by a few good souls whose confidence the priest possesses entirely. The *scuole* and the monks share the rest of the people ... The oratorios given by the conservatories serve for all as the afternoon service.'

Even so, according to the author of *Le brigandage de la musique italienne* of 1770: 'The music of the ordinary churches did not fail to participate in this new corruption. A sung Mass became a spectacle for the faithful, one found there all the fashionable ariettas. The Kyrie was composed of a *kyrielle* of notes, and nothing was more gay than an Elevation [of the Host].'[34]

It was really no wonder that things reached this point, since the various establishments vied with one another as to who should have the best music, as Wright tells us:

> The nuns of S. Lorenzo, and those of S. Maria Celestia, have on their feast-days, one the 10th, the other the 15th of August, a great concert of musick in their several churches. The nuns of both these convents are noble ladies; and they vie for superiority with each other, which shall have the best musick; and therefore each obliges the chief of their musicians, when they engage them to be at their feast, not to be employed at the other. So that which ever of the two gets the best of the home musicians first for their feast, puts the other under a necessity of sending to Bologna, or some such distant place, for others.[35]

There are two concertos by Vivaldi marked *Per la solennità di S. Lorenzo*, the first a violin concerto (RV 286) and the second a concerto for two oboes, two *claren* (see p. 104), two recorders, two violins and bassoon, with orchestra and basso continuo (RV 556), and he may well have been commissioned to compose them for just such a feast day. This was where places like the *ospedali* and S. Marco, with a resident musical establishment, had the advantage, since they could always rely on the 'home team'. Nevertheless,

27

the others evidently went to a great deal of trouble. As Wright continues:

> At the Celestia there was an occasional portico, and a colonnade on the bridge that leads to the church, with extempore statues, made up of pasteboard and stiffened linen cloth; both without the church and within. The churches on these occasions are adorned with the richest hangings they can get. Without doors these viragoes have guns firing, with trumpets and hautboys sounding, to make all the noise they can. Their guns are a little sort of mortars stuck in the ground, which are so hard rammed, that they make a report like a cannon.

No wonder then, that Venice was such an amazing and exciting place for her visitors.

In the predominantly agricultural society of western Europe before the Industrial Revolution, almost any large town caused a certain amount of amazement to strangers, and even today a city such as Paris, with its monumental conception, can overwhelm the first time one sees it, even for a person used to living in London where, despite its overall size, everything is on a much more homely scale. Imagine then the impact of the city of Venice, poised between sky and sea, between East and West, a glittering palimpsest of ethnic and cultural splendours set down on the edge of the Adriatic. There was everything to charm the eye and captivate the senses, and if one had to choose only one word to describe what Venice most held out to those who flocked to her, it was exoticism. Here is Evelyn once again:

> I passed through the Mercera, one of the most delicious streets in the world for the sweetness of it, and is all the way on both sides tapestried as it were with cloth of gold, rich damasks and other silks, which the shops expose and hang before their houses from the first floor, and with that variety that for near half the year spent chiefly in this city, I hardly remember to have seen the same piece twice

exposed; to this add the perfumes, apothecaries' shops, and the innumerable cages of nightingales which they keep, that entertain you with their melody from shop to shop, so that shutting your eyes, you would imagine yourself in the country, when indeed you are in the middle of the sea. It is almost as silent as the middle of a field, there being neither rattling of coaches nor trampling of horses. This street, paved with brick, and exceedingly clean, brought us through an arch into the famous piazza of St Mark.[36]

Here, in the shape of S. Marco itself, is the most characteristic Venetian palimpsest of all, almost swamped with the booty brought back by centuries of Venetian imperialism, set to adorn the doge's chapel (it only became the cathedral in 1807, on the orders of Napoleon). It was, and still is, a kind of icon, which may be retouched from time to time, but never appreciably modified. Already in Vivaldi's day it was that, as it had been almost two centuries earlier, when Giovanni Bellini (1430–1516) painted the view of it that is now in the Accademia, except that then its sprockets and pinnacles were all gilded, making it an even more glittering sight. Vivaldi lived here, and saw it all. This is one of the most compelling things about Venice. So much of what is there would have been familiar to him. We can look at buildings that were already old for him, as well as ones that were relatively new, such as the Ospedaletto church, with the deliberately overwhelming statuary on its façade, designed by Baldassare Longhena (1598–1682), begun in 1662 and finished in 1674, only four years before Vivaldi was born. Longhena was also responsible for the less surprising, but no less ponderous, mass of Ca' Rezzonico on the Grand Canal.

Or there was the Gesuiti church (S. Maria Assunta) near the Fondamente Nuove, which was built between 1714 and 1729, designed by Domenico Rossi (1678–1742), almost an exact contemporary of Vivaldi, who also designed the façade of S. Stae (Eustace) on the Grand Canal. What must the fantastic interior of the Gesuiti have seemed like to the people of the time, with marble walls made to look as if they

29

were hung with damask, even to the marble curtains that billow around the pulpit, and what can its row of ecstatic statues on the pediment have seemed like, when even today they are striking enough, especially as one returns from Torcello by boat and sees them from the rear, their bleached white forms exploding into the sky. Perhaps Venice had its effect on Rossi, too, for despite the fact that he was a nephew of Giuseppe Sardi, he was a Swiss by birth. Such is the power of the stones of Venice.

And then there is the water, everywhere, lapping against the stones, giving a curious feeling of insubstantiality, and accentuating the effects of the light, whether it be on the still waters of a quiet canal or the dazzling reflections set up by the waves out in the *bacino*. There were other cities with canals – Amsterdam, for example – but it is typical of the Venetians to make them such an integral part of the life of Venice, and develop the gondola and all the concomitant panoply. As De Brosses wrote:

A procession in gondolas is, to my mind, a divine morsel, even more so since they are not ordinary gondolas, but those of the Republic, superbly carved and gilded, accompanied by those of the ambassadors, even more rich and more gallant, above all that of ours. They are the only ones in the State to whom it is permitted to own other than black ones. The gondoliers of the Republic are all in capes of red velvet, decked with gold, with huge Albanian bonnets [*à l'albanaise*]. They are too proud of this equipage to give themselves the trouble to row. So they have themselves towed by little boats filled with musical instruments.[37]

In 1736 one of Lotti's madrigals was sung as the doge's great barge of state, the Bucintoro, went out to the lagoon for the annual Ascension Day ceremony of 'wedding the sea'.[38] As we shall see, Antonio Lotti's career ran alongside that of Vivaldi.

To use a somewhat anachronistic analogy, Venice in particular, but Italy in general, was to some extent the

30

Hollywood of Europe for many decades. One feels this in Shakespeare's plays; indeed it is of paramount importance to appreciating his contemporaries' approach to such plays as *Romeo and Juliet* and *The merchant of Venice*. Even the Illyria of *Twelfth night* owes more than a passing glance to Venice and the Italian convention, one feels, at least in the portrayal of Orsino and the main-plot characters, however English the rest may be. And where one finds a whole city consciously playing a role, whether it be eighteenth-century Venice or twentieth-century Hollywood, and all the citizens are permanently 'on set', then at times the border between fact and fiction is extremely hard to discern.

Not content with the ordinary run of Christian saints, for example, Venice chose to canonize Moses, Zaccariah, Samuel, Job, and even the Archangel Raphael. Of course there was a Byzantine precedent for this, but in Venice it went a stage further. Then there was a habit of running two saints' names together, so that Gervasius and Protasius became Trovaso; Giovanni and Paolo became Zanipolo (this aided and abetted by Venetian dialect), and Ermagora and Fortunato became Marcuola. Of course people no doubt knew if they were asked, or at least the more educated members of society did, but did the majority of the people? And in any case did it really matter? This was, after all, Venice. Everything was that much larger than life, and exaggeration was almost taken for granted, both by the Venetians themselves and those who came to visit.

Edward Wright, who visited France and Italy in 1720–2, almost accepted it as a matter of course: 'The Arsenal of Venice they call three miles in compass; but we must allow somewhat for their usual exaggeration.'[39] De Brosses also, writing from Venice on 13 August 1739, records the marvels, whilst apparently taking a large pinch of salt at the same time: 'They say that there are more of them [paintings] in Venice than in the rest of Italy, as they pretend that in lighting the three floors of the Procuratie with flambeaux of white wax, on Christmas Night, they burn more wax here, on that night, than in the whole of the rest of Italy during the course of a year.'[40]

Wright also records the wax tapers, though he saw them for himself, and was content to register the fact that he was impressed – almost as if he, too, was falling in with the tendency to marvel:

The Venetians are excessively lavish of their white wax tapers in their processions, at their night-litanies, and at the *quaranta hore*; i.e. the exposition of the host for forty hours, for the gaining of indulgences. I have seen near five hundred lighted up at once over one altar, rising pyramid-wise, almost to the top of the church; and a glorious show it makes. The host is seen through a circular plate of crystal set in gold, or silver gilt; adorned richly with jewels, and rays of silver, as shooting from it. In some churches, upon such an occasion, we have seen jewels set in stars, and other figures, and rays of silver coming from them placed among the candles; which made such a glittering, there was scarce any looking upon them. The solemn music playing, and incense wafting all the while, entertaining several senses at once, after the most agreeable manner.[41]

The Venetian love of colour and spectacle is still to be seen today, albeit on a different level. The Venetians are fond of bright colours, and the women wear a good deal of jewellery – often of exceptional quality. They are also still a very pious people, and S. Giovanni Grisostomo, a church well known to Vivaldi from its nearby theatre, is always a blaze of votive candles as people pass to and from nearby Rialto. In S. Marco, on high days such as Christmas, the huge gold Pala d'Oro or reredos, encrusted with enamels, pearls and semi-precious stones, is turned round to face the congregation, and sparkles and gleams in the candlelight on the high altar. It was in S. Marco that Wright saw a typically Venetian effect:

One night in S. Mark's church, besides the vast illumination of the great altar, a row of candles went round the whole body of the great nave, and they were all lighted in a minute's time, by the means of a line of loose flax, extended all along their wicks, which were ready prepared by being dipped in oil of turpentine . . . It is generally said, that more wax candles are spent at festivals and processions in Venice, than in any other city of Italy. I heard a Venetian carry it so far once, as to say, more than in all Italy besides. But, that I know not whether I am in the right to repeat.[42]

The Venetians adored ceremonies and processions, as we see from the paintings left to us by Bellini, Carpaccio and Canaletto, and as the Republic grew older, the ceremonies grew even longer. When St Peter Orseolo was canonized in May 1731, the ceremonies lasted three days.[43] When his relics had been translated earlier that year, Vivaldi's music had been performed. All sorts of anniversaries were observed, and were the excuse for a display of state panoply. In Venice for the Feast of the Assumption in 1608, Coryate saw: 'the Duke [Doge] in some of his richest ornaments, accompanyed with twenty six couples of senators, in their damask-long-sleeved gownes come to Saint Marks'.[44] On 25 March 1721 the doge paid a special visit to S. Marco to celebrate 1,300 years of the city's existence. Events that were of a much more domestic nature originally, however, were elevated into anniversaries that had to be observed with due solemnity by the doge.

In the church of S. Maria Formosa, for example, was the chapel of the Scuola dei Casselleri, who made marriage chests. Apparently one day in 944, when a party of girls were going to the cathedral (at that time S. Pietro di Castello, right at the eastern end of Venice) for their marriage ceremony, some marauding Slavs appeared and abducted them, with the intent of taking them to Dalmatia. It was the Casselleri who were the heroes of the day, since they pursued the Slavs and rescued the girls. When it came to a question of a reward – and in this the Venetians were almost as canny as Scots – it was decided that the doge himself would visit them at their chapel every year. To the doge's question 'What if it rains?' the Casselleri replied 'We shall give you a hat'; and to the question 'What if I am thirsty?' they answered 'We shall give you wine'. So it happened that every Candlemas Day (2 February) until the end of the Republic in 1797, the doge went in state to S. Maria Formosa, and was presented with a straw hat and a glass of wine. One of the hats is still visible in the Museo Correr in Venice, along with a straw basket presented when the doge attended another such ceremony in S. Zaccaria.

Always at these ceremonies music was an essential part of the proceedings. Grosley, writing in the 1760s, described the lavishness of the ceremonial at one of the convents – albeit one of the most famous in Venice – that of S. Lorenzo:

The patronal feasts of the almost innumerable convents of Venice are celebrated with great musical services, mostly composed for each feast. On St Laurence's day we followed one of these offices in the church of the nuns whose monastery bears the name of this saint. Four hundred voices or instruments chosen from the virtuosi of Italy who flock to Venice for this feast, made up the orchestra directed by the famous *Sassone* [Hasse], who composed the music.[45]

Thomas Coryate had attended the same feast more than 150 years previously, and he had been struck by its magnificence even then. By Grosley's day it had all become much more commercial. It was obviously a good annual engagement for musicians, and the music seems to have become much more important than the Mass. Also, we see the Venetians' insatiable demands for more and more new music which eventually appeared to conspire to drive Vivaldi from Venice towards the end of his life. As Grosley continued:

This orchestra was behind the door facing the altar and took up the whole width of the church which, in its entirety, forms a kind of large hall wider than it is long: it was above twelve feet off the ground, and divided into interconnecting compartments decorated tastefully, as well as the columns that carried the whole affair, with ribbons and garlands and swagged linen. The church was garnished with several rows of chairs with their backs to the altar, and which kept this singular position even during High Mass, which lasted five mortal hours, as hot as it was possible to have them in Venice in the month of August.

The church of S. Lorenzo is still there, though it is now deconsecrated and looks rather sad. In the 1976 Biennale, for example, it housed an exhibition of Fascist architecture. The shape is basically much the same as it was in Grosley's day, however, and one gets some impression of what it must have looked like from a painting in the Galleria Querini Stampalia which shows a nun being vested with her habit. The convent of S. Lorenzo was much favoured by noble families, who found that one way to try and prevent unsuitable marriages for their daughters was by putting them behind a grille. This had only varying degrees of success, but it ensured that the nuns of the convent of S. Lorenzo were always full of high spirits, rather like a Venetian St Trinians. At the Pietà things cannot be very different, and one wonders whether Vivaldi had problems in dealing with such lively and potentially exhausting pupils.

2. Venetian Carnival

It was Palladio's declared intent that he wanted to give Venice the most beautiful church in the world and with it a theatre worthy of the gods – an aim with which the Venetians themselves readily identified, though from a totally different standpoint, for the Venetian love of splendour was not only confined to ceremonial and churches. The riches of the Venetian aristocracy were legendary, and gave rise to such stories as the oft-repeated one of the member of the Labia family who threw all his gold plate out of the window into the canal after a banquet, saying: 'L'abia o non l'abia, sarò sempre Labia' ('Whether I have it or not, I will always be Labia'). It sounds rather as if the possibility of the pun was too good to miss, and so the event was carefully staged, especially since the second part of the story tells how the servants were then ordered to retrieve the discarded plate. The sumptuous palace, begun in 1720 to designs by Andrea Cominelli, was not completed until thirty years later, when Tiepolo added the famous frescoes.

Others took their wealth more in their stride, and Molmenti gives several examples of this.[1] When the jewels of Polissena Contarini were inventoried, for example, she possessed 487 oriental pearls, 54 emeralds and 192 rubies. When Pisana Corner married Giovanni Alvise Mocenigo on 5 October 1739, her trousseau included, amongst other things, an outfit made of lace worth almost 700 ducats, and one of fur worth 5,412 lire. She also had eighteen pairs of shoes, some of which were white, embroidered with gold and silver thread, and others with lace from Spain and Burano, yet others were of embroidered cloth of gold and silver. Another inventory of 1744 mentions a brocade dress decorated with flowers made out of brilliants, with gold ornaments and one of cloth of 'Isabella' colour, all decorated with finest silver lace, with enamels of various colours and little silver flowers. In 1766, for the trousseau of Francesca Grimani, who married another member of the Mocenigo family, the sum of 456,487 lire was spent.

Mrs Thrale, who eventually deserted her Doctor Johnson and married an Italian, was nevertheless somewhat dismissive of the women of Venice:

> Like all sensualists, however, they fail of the end proposed, from hurry to obtain it; and consume those charms which alone can procure them continuance or change of admirers; they injure their health too irreparably, and that in their earliest youth; for few remain unmarried till fifteen, and at thirty have a wan and faded look. *On ne goute pas ses plaisirs icy, on les avale* (They do not taste their pleasures here, they swallow them whole), said Madame la Presidente yesterday, very judiciously.[2]

In fact the Venetians were much more aware of themselves than Mrs Thrale was willing to allow, or apparently even able to perceive. It was much more complex than that. Under this façade of sensuality, even frivolity, there was a strongly Puritan streak, and a great deal of pragmatism, certainly among the aristocracy, and despite the excesses of ceremony in the churches, there was a genuine underlying piety, as indeed there still is today. There were stringent sumptuary laws, for example, so that, despite the rich jewels and clothes of the patrician women, the occasions on which they were allowed to wear them were relatively few. Moreover, the laws were continually being revised or brought up to date. On 18 March 1732 a law was passed forbidding the use of fans that were too luxurious, and on 26 July 1750 ladies exchanging visits were not to serve each other refreshments worth more than a ducat. It seems odd that in the midst of so much external profligacy, the lives of individuals might be regulated to such a degree, but as we shall see, this was one of the most fundamental premises of the Venetian state.

De Brosses could scarcely believe what he encountered when he paid a visit to a patrician home, and was inclined to put it down to mere parsimony:

37

That is enough talk about public matters; I would be hard put to it to say as much about private houses. Here foreigners do not have much chance on that score. My lords the nobles come in the evening to the cafe where they talk with us in great friendliness; but, to introduce us into their houses is quite another matter. Moreover, there are very few houses here where they hold assemblies, and these assemblies are neither numerous nor amusing for foreigners. One does not even have the facility of gaming there; for one would have to be worse than a sorcerer to know their cards, which have neither the names nor the pictures of ours. With all their splendour and their palaces, the Venetians do not know what it is to give a chicken to a person. On occasion I have been to *conversazione* at the home of the Procuratessa Foscarini, a house of immense richness, and a very gracious lady, moreover; the only *régal* there was, on the stroke of three, that is to say at eleven o'clock at night in France, twenty valets brought in, on a vast silver salver, a huge pumpkin cut into quarters, to which they give the name of *angouri* or water melon, a detestable dish if ever there was one. A pile of silver plates accompanied it; everyone threw himself on a portion, took also a little cup of coffee, and went away at midnight to eat at home, his head free and his stomach hollow.[3]

In part he was right, but the Venetians had a great sense of form, and did their utmost to uphold appearances. For example, they looked after the destitute members of the aristocracy, the Barnabotti, and when they saw that they themselves were too fond of gambling, the patricians outlawed games of chance, and in particular *biribis*, on 13 July 1734. In 1774 they even ordered the *ridotti*, or gambling houses, to be closed, which shows, however, that the malady had persisted until then.

The pragmatism in the Venetian character was doubtless intensified in the centuries after her power and wealth had evaporated, but during which she managed to live on, like some elderly dowager, at least giving the impression of being as affluent as ever. Until the sixteenth century, as part of their coronation oath, the doges undertook to make a New Year's present of five ducks to every nobleman. By 1521, however, the vast total of 9,000 was needed, so with typical Venetian ingenuity the doge petitioned the Senate to permit him to distribute medals instead, and these became known as *oselle* (birds). As with the saints' portmanteau names, what did it really matter if the birds were turned into medals that were still called birds – everyone knew what was really intended. But it was more fundamental than this. Given the nature of the Venetian state, it was essential that people conformed. If only from a practical point of view this was necessary when there were so many visitors to the city, and Carnival held sway for so much of the year.

Grosley tells the story of an Englishman who would not genuflect at the Elevation of the Host in S. Marco on an occasion when the Senate attended.[4] A senator sent him a message to do so, and when the Englishman still failed to comply, the senator went over to him and spoke to him about it. The Englishman said that he did not believe in transubstantiation, to which he received the retort: 'Ne anche io, però ginocchione, o fuor di chiesa' which may be translated as: 'Neither do I, but down on your knees or get out of the church'.

Then the Venetians also have a strong sense of humour, which might well be at their own expense – a sure sign of well-balanced personalities – which is more than one can say for the French. When the word got around that Cecilia Zeno Tron had sold her box at the S. Benedetto theatre for some great occasion, a rhyme was made up: 'Brava la Trona/Le vende il palco/Più caro della . . .' which might be translated loosely as: 'Well done la Trona; she sells her box for more than she sells her . . .' to which she replied, when it was reported to her: 'You're quite right, for sometimes I make a present of the latter!'[5]

One must not ignore either the fact that there was a flourishing intellectual life in the city, though naturally the government looked with alarm on those who were too closely interested in 'French' ideas as the events leading up to 1789 pursued their inexorable way. For this reason the house of the artist Rosalba Carriera was regarded with suspicion by the authorities. In 1706, for example, there were public lectures in moral philosophy, law, medicine, notarial procedure, rhetoric and geography which were established in the library of S. Marco.[6] The University of Padua alone cost the state 30,000 ducats at this time.[7] Then on 13 November 1710 Apostolo Zeno founded his *Giornale de' Letterati d'Italia*, which lasted until 1740, and several Venetians were in correspondence with intellectuals throughout Europe.

The Venetians were a charitable people. In April 1734 a lottery was held to benefit the orphanages and distressed women, and in 1755 13,412·10 ducats were set aside for poor relief. Of these, 8,103·5 went to public charity, and 6,642·5 to one institution, Vivaldi's place of work, the Pietà.[8] They were also a hospitable people, and despite the cynics who commented on the amount of money the city made out of its visitors, the Venetians genuinely cared about orphans and exiles. One of the more famous of the latter to whom they gave refuge was the Scots financier John Law who, after the failure of his bank in France, found refuge in Venice, where he died in penury in 1729. He was originally buried in S. Geminiano, and when Napoleon ordered the church to be demolished in 1807 his bones were removed to S. Moisè, where a tablet just inside the main door still keeps his memory alive. With his usual love of the sententious, Henry James describes it all very well in *Italian hours* (1909):

... almost everyone interesting, appealing, melancholy, memorable, odd, seems at one time or another, after many days and much life, to have gravitated to Venice by a happy instinct, settling in it and treating it, cherishing it, as a sort of repository of consolations; all of which today, for the conscious mind, is mixed with its air and constitutes its unwritten history. The deposed, the defeated, the disenchanted, or even only the bored, have seemed to find there something that no other place could give.

From the historical point of view it might be argued that

this was the only possible role left for Venice to play, but only to say that is seriously to underestimate – by implication – the amazing degree to which Venice has inspired artists over the centuries, and still inspires today. It has always held something special – as for example in individual cases such as the sight of Titian's *Assumption* in the Frari, which suddenly released all Wagner's creative energies (so he maintained) and inspired him to produce *Die Meistersinger* – or as a symbol in itself of a past that is still alive and meaningful. If one may mis-apply some words of T. S. Eliot from *Murder in the cathedral*:

There is holy ground, and the sanctity shall not depart from it
Though armies trample over it, though sightseers come with guide-books looking over it;
From such ground springs that which forever renews the earth.

By the time Vivaldi was born, however, Venice had long since had her heyday – that had been in the fifteenth century. True, she had defeated the Turks at Lepanto in the sixteenth century (1571), but then two years later she lost Cyprus. True, she won back the Morea (the Peloponnesus) in the seventeenth century (1684), but had to surrender it at the Treaty of Passarowitz in 1718. The sands of time were running out, and by the time Vivaldi was ten years old, the Republic had already embarked upon the last century of her existence as an independent state. For a long time she was able to conceal the fact, and by playing a waiting game she managed to keep up the illusion of strength and power, but everything was against her.

Whilst Venice waited, the world flocked to see her, and the eighteenth century saw a succession of the rich and the famous, on whom the State and the nobility lavished entertainment, almost until the end of the Republic. On 7 April 1705, for example, official presents were made to the Dowager Queen of Poland and the Duchess of Bavaria, a visit which followed an earlier one in January 1698, during the course of which the queen paid a visit to the Church of S. Lorenzo. Lucrezia Basadonna Mocenigo – known as Mocenigo of the Pearls for the ring and pendants of magnificent pearls which were heirlooms in the Mocenigo family, and which Rosalba Carriera included in her portrait of her in Dresden – wanted to see the Queen of Poland, so put on a veil and stationed herself in the church in such a position where she might see without being seen. However, the queen was informed of her presence, went up to Lucrezia, and with her own hands lifted her veil, exclaiming that she had never seen a more beautiful woman.[9]

Pearls were the focal point of another royal visit, that of Frederick IV of Denmark and Norway who, as we shall see, became a patron of Vivaldi. The king came to Venice on 29 December 1708, and despite the fact that he was officially incognito, he was '*pomposamente festeggiato*'. Part of the festivities included a ball at the house of the Procurator Sebastiano Foscarini, whose wife Caterina Quirina possessed a magnificent pearl necklace.[10] Whilst dancing with the king of Denmark, a buckle of the king's clothing caught the string of his hostess's pearls, which snapped, scattering them across the ballroom floor. With patrician composure the lady never even glanced at them, nor did her husband move from his seat. The king, however, was so embarrassed that he began to try and recover the pearls. At this his host rose, and pretending not to notice the pearls, walked across the floor, crushing them as if they were not there. The hostess, we are told, continued the dance as if nothing had happened, though by this time the king must have been doubly mortified. We shall see later what specifically musical events the king attended during his visit, and we are extremely lucky that they were recorded, for they give us valuable insights into the musical practices of the time, and also first-hand accounts of Vivaldi himself in operation. All in all the king must surely have enjoyed himself, and was so taken with the Venetian ladies that he commissioned Rosalba Carriera to paint miniatures of twelve of the most beautiful of them to take home with him.

In February 1712 the State gave a banquet at the Arsenale

for the Prince of Poland and Saxony, and four years later it was the turn of the Elector of Bavaria. The Venetians obviously entered into these occasions with zest. In a letter to the Abate Conti, dated from Verona on 28 February 1716, Scipione Maffei, who was to provide the libretto for Vivaldi's opera *La fida ninfa*, wrote: 'All my studies have been dormant for ages. Over and above other interruptions, the arrival in Italy of the Prince Elector of Bavaria has almost made me forget the business I had in hand'.[11] In May 1716 it was again the turn of the Prince of Poland and Saxony, in whose honour a regatta was given. These regattas, once more in vogue in Venice today, brought the whole city to fever pitch. For the splendour of such occasions we have Canaletto's painting in the Royal Collection at Windsor. Another foreign visitor to be fêted in the same way was the Crown Prince of Modena, on 17 April 1720.

The list goes on: on 2 June 1738 the Queen of the Kingdom of the Two Sicilies sailed down the Grand Canal, which was lavishly decorated for the occasion. On 30 December 1739 the Prince of Poland and Saxony – yet again – was in Venice, and was presented with gifts. Possibly the grandest of all visits, however, came towards the end of the century, when the Crown Prince and Princess of Russia came to Venice in January 1782. There was a concert given by the girls of the orphanages, a dinner at the Arsenale, and a gala evening in the S. Benedetto theatre, which was transformed into a ballroom for the occasion by throwing a bridge across the orchestra pit and making stage and auditorium into one large room. The throng of the crowds was the only thing to mar the occasion; until it was time for the dignitaries to depart, that is. They only wanted to pay half the bill at their hotel, so the owner had to have recourse to the government, and the guests did not even leave a tip.

Apart from the state visits, the Carnival in Venice annually drew hundreds of visitors. Evelyn witnessed it in the middle of the seventeenth century, for example:

In January, Signor Molino was chosen Doge of Venice, but the extreme snow that fell, and the cold, hindered my going to see the solemnity, so as I stirred not from Padua till Shrovetide, when all the world repair to Venice, to see the folly and madness of the Carnival; the women, men and persons of all conditions disguising themselves in antique dresses, with extravagant music and a thousand gambols, traversing the streets from house to house, all places being then accessible and free to enter. Abroad, they fling eggs filled with sweet water, but sometimes not over-sweet. They also have a barbarous custom of hunting bulls about the streets and piazzas, which is very dangerous, the passages being generally narrow. The youth of several wards and parishes contend in other masteries and pastimes, so that it is impossible to recount the universal madness of this place during this time of license. The great banks are set up for those who will play at basset; the comedians have liberty, and the operas are open; witty pasquils are thrown about, and the mountebanks have their stages at every corner.[12]

Then Wright left us his account from the 1720s, telling a story which seems to have done the round of visitors. Since Carnival ended on Shrove Tuesday, followed by the sprinkling of ashes on Ash Wednesday, it seemed to outsiders that it was all some sort of collective folly:

This puts me in mind of a remark I have somewhere read or heard, said to be made by some remote Indian, who was in Venice, during the time of the Carnival; that the people of Venice, about the beginning of the New Year, are seized with a sort of frenzy or madness; which goes on still increasing, till a certain day, on which a grave person, by sprinkling a sort of powder on their head, brings 'em all to their senses again.[13]

At all events, Mrs Thrale has the same story, though she attributes it to a Turkish sailor.

Another feature that drew people to Venice, though it was one of which the Venetians themselves were inordinately fond, was the gaming room known as the *ridotto*. Originally these *ridotti* (there were several at one stage) were annexes to the theatres, as side attractions where clients might gamble and take refreshments. Soon, however, they had become an end in themselves, and the government became quite concerned on several occasions at the effect they were having. Edward Wright paints the *ridotto* in a somewhat sombre tone: 'The place is dark and silent, a few glimmering tapers with a half light shew a set of beings, stalking along with their pale faces, which look like so many death's heads poking out through black pouches; so that one would almost imagine himself in some enchanted place, or some region of the dead.'[14]

Indeed, when one looks at the masks (*baùtte*) and hoods and three-cornered hats peering out from the paintings that have come down to us, there is something faintly chilling about the spectacle. Certainly the impression communicated is not one of unalloyed pleasure, by any means, and there seems but little distance from a *baùtta* to a skull. It certainly gave some of the visitors food for thought. In theory the masks gave anonymity to all, they lowered the social barriers, and the Venetian government, in its wisdom, thought that this was a good thing. The *ridotto* was the place where patricians were allowed to go unmasked, and one of them usually acted as banker. Was it simply an example of bread and circuses on a vast scale, or was the whole population involved in a colossal money-making operation? François Misson, who published *A new voyage to Italy* as early as 1695, speculated on the matter:

> Since it is true, that everything must be attributed to the policy of Venice, you must suppose there are particular reasons for the [*sic*] permitting this licentiousness of the Carnival . . . I imagine . . . that the nobility, who otherwise are not well beloved, are very glad to find some cunning ways to please and amuse the people. There is yet another thing which seems to me of some moment. I am credibly informed, that at the last Carnival, there was an account of seven sovereign princes, and thirty thousand other foreigners. Consider how much money all this multitude must have brought to Venice.[15]

45

Whether the money question was all that important to Venice is a matter for discussion. Where Misson was perfectly accurate in his speculation, however, was that the government – for one reason or another – knew exactly what it was doing, though as he tartly observed, that still did not prevent the ultimate catastrophe: 'the wonderful policy of Venice hath not hindered the many declensions into which that republic hath fallen'. And yet the Republic managed to survive for almost another century in this way. Indeed, had the Corsican never crossed the Alps, it might even have survived for another two. Mrs Thrale, nearly a century after Misson, took a much more rosy view:

> It was therefore not an ill saying, though an old one perhaps, that the government of Venice was rich and consolatory like its treacle, being compounded nicely of all the other forms: a grain of monarchy, a scruple of democracy, a dram of oligarchy, and an ounce of aristocracy ... Indeed, the longevity of this incomparable commonwealth is a certain proof of its temperance, exercise, and cheerfulness, the great preservatives in every body, politic as well natural.[16]

The other side to this particular coin is the fact that it has been estimated that between 1741 and 1762 some 73,000 people were either executed or sent to the galleys for life,[17] and the State controlled the life of an individual to a degree that those brought up under Western democracy in this century find difficult to appreciate. It certainly gave one eighteenth-century Venetian, Zaccaria Angelo Seriman, food for thought, and inspired him to write a very entertaining, though none the less bitter, satire on Venice, published in 1764, and entitled *I viaggi di Enrico Wanton alle terre incognite australi ed ai regni delle scimmie e dei cinocefali*. About the book D. Maxwell White has written:

> In eighteenth-century Venice, as in modern Russia, the unrestricted development of individuality was firmly discouraged in the interests of homogeneity and the preser-

vation of the *status quo*. Zaccaria Seriman, it would seem, was greatly troubled by the implications of this state of affairs, and in the *Viaggi* he explored the moral problems involved. On a number of occasions for instance, Enrico Wanton takes Signor Faggio to task for the uncritical manner in which he accords '*la sua stima, o la sua disapprovazione secondo le leggi: dell'uso, e del preguidizio*' [His esteem or disapproval, according to the laws of usage and prejudice] Vol. II p. 608.[18]

It is all too easy to revel in the splendours and diversions when contemplating eighteenth-century Venice, and to ignore such problems completely. Just as artists have problems in Iron Curtain countries today, so did their Venetian counterparts, and it is as well to bear this in mind, even with someone like Vivaldi, whose music appears totally free from any sort of tension.

Wright, who saw Vivaldi in Venice, was under no illusions about the state of affairs, certainly as far as public figures were concerned:

. . . ' tis as fatal to deserve too well of them, as to deserve ill. And we saw a nobleman of their own, who lost a hand in their service, concerning whom it was debated in council, whether he should be brought home in chains, or be made Procurator of St Mark (the second highest office in the Republic after the Doge). The latter, as it proved, was the resolution.[19]

This may help to explain why Vivaldi remains such a comparatively shadowy figure. The world of the theatre had its seamy side, and there was his relationship with his pupil Anna Girò, and the question of his priesthood. In view of his position in the community, a false move could have brought him down, as it apparently did later at Ferrara. In this context his illness may well have been a godsend, by way of an alibi, since it allowed him to live a very private life. It is doubtful, though, whether one ought to go along with Roland de Candé and envisage a positively dubious background. The way in which Venice was governed actually encouraged secrecy, and Wright got the impression that the populace at large lived in a good deal of fear:

They are very strict in discouraging meetings or cabals of any sort; insomuch that in the public coffee-houses there are no seats, nor dare the masters of them keep any; that company may not with ease to themselves stay long together in such occasional places of meeting; nor is anybody allowed to discourse at all upon the affairs of the government, not even in praise of the administration, any more than against it. Neither are the noblemen themselves indulged in such discourse any more than others; for even they are not to talk over the affairs of state out of the proper place, tho' themselves are actors in them.[20]

This caution was felt necessary by the government particularly as the eighteenth century drew on, and what they regarded as subversive ideas gained currency. And of course in view of the number of foreigners who came to Venice, they were placed in a difficult situation. If they forbade access from outside they would remove one of the props to Venice's continued existence, and probably also would diminish their revenue. So once again the Venetians faced the problem with typical pragmatism. As in modern Peking, they tried to keep all foreign embassies in the same part of the city, in the corner formed by the junction of the Grand Canal and Cannaregio. To this day the Lista di Spagna recalls the site of the Spanish Embassy. In this way the task of keeping an eye on the activities of foreign diplomats was somewhat more easy. Then restrictions were placed on the countries to which Venetians might travel, and those restrictions were renewed or altered from time to time, as on 28 June 1709, when it was decreed that nobles were not to have anything to do with foreigners within the city. Wright had this to say on the matter:

The caution, which I have occasionally hinted before, that they use against being seen with a foreign minister, carried some of them so far, that they forsook a fresco

48

shop (where they sell limonade, and other cooling liquors) they used to frequent, because the resident of our nation was sometimes there; and the poor man was forced to desire he would not come thither, else he should disoblige and lose his noble customers. One of the nobility, an acquaintance of my Lord Parker's, behaved himself very handsomely upon the account of a foreign minister's coming to his house . . . Being told that a curious gentleman, a stranger in Venice, desired a sight of his library, he consented, as not suspecting anything irregular; when to his surprise, upon his coming, he found he was a foreign minister. Tho' struck at first, he recollected himself; entertained the gentleman with all humanity; and as soon as he was gone, went straight to the Inquisitors of State, and acquainted them with the matter, and the circumstances of it; and so avoided the ill consequences, which otherwise might have attended it.[21]

Again, one may rely on Mrs Thrale to give a more rosy account of the matter, and take a rather more complacent view of things:

We have been told much of the suspicious temper of Venetian laws; and have heard often that every discourse is suffered, except such as tends to political conversation, in this city; and that whatever nobleman, native of Venice, is seen speaking familiarly with a foreign minister, runs a risk of punishments too terrible to be thought on.

How far that manner of proceeding may be wise or just, I know not; certain it is that they have preserved their laws inviolate, their city unattempted, and their republic respectable, through all the concussions that have shaken the rest of Europe. Surrounded by envious powers, it becomes them to be vigilant; conscious of the value of their unconquered state, it is no wonder that they love her . . . let us then permit them to be jealous of a constitution which all the other states of Italy look on with envy not unmixed with malice, and propagate strange stories to its disadvantage.

That suspicion should be concealed under the mask of gaiety is neither very new nor very strange ... but here at Venice there are no unpermitted frolics; her rulers love to see her gay and cheerful; they are the fathers of their country, and if they indulge, take care not to spoil her.[22]

It is on this last point especially that Mrs Thrale's view is most to be questioned. Such paternalism had its bad aspects. For one thing, as a way of sublimating any potentially rebellious tendencies or aggressive dissatisfaction, Venice kept up a running rivalry between representatives of two of the six sections or *sestieri* of Venice, the Castellani and the Nicolotti, which persisted until well into the nineteenth century, though by then it had been channelled into such relatively innocuous pursuits as regatta competitions. Under the Republic, however, there were periodic pitched battles on the various *ponti della guerra*, with marble feet set into the ground to mark the touchlines, which are still to be seen. One such is the Ponte della Guerra near the Ca' Rezzonico, and another is near the Palazzo Papafave, at S. Lio. This rivalry was kept alive to such an extent that there is a tradition that the church of S. Trovaso on the Dorsoduro actually has two façades because it stands on neutral ground between the territories of the Castellani and the Nicolotti. If a man and woman from the rival groups wished to marry, then the Castellani entered and left by the south door, and the Nicolotti by the west door.

Almost inevitably this created a kind of insularity amongst the Venetians, with unfortunate consequences for social life. Wright saw further than De Brosses in this matter, for what De Brosses was inclined to ascribe merely to parsimony, Wright saw otherwise:

If some of them live well as to themselves, they very rarely make entertainments for others; and this closeness extends itself, not only to strangers, whom the policy of the place makes them shy of conversing with; but even to one another; so that when they have a mind for a merry

50

meeting, they have it not at their own houses, but at a third place, where they pay their club alike.[23]

Wright also tells the story of a rich old senator who came into the part of Venice where Wright was lodging, in order to visit a French painter. He was halfway up the stairs when he was told that Lord Parker's valet de chambre was there, whereupon he hurried downstairs as if the house had been on fire. Such anecdotes make amusing reading at first, but have some serious implications for social and artistic life in the city. It may be no mere coincidence that many of Venice's greatest artists in the last century of her existence left the city, Vivaldi included.

Of course it was easy to see, as Grosley did, merely practical financial considerations: 'The law which forbids the same people [the nobility] to have any dealings with foreigners, has not yet undergone any weakening. Private interest joins, to maintain it, with reasons of State, particularly since, by the diminution of the riches of Venice, economy is the first concern for the majority of the noble houses.'[24]

Or we can join with Mrs Thrale and see a somewhat bizarre side to things:

A woman of quality near whom I sate at the fine ball Brigadin made two nights ago in honour of this gay season [Ascensiontide], enquired how I passed the morning. I named several churches I had looked into . . . 'You do very right,' says she, 'to look at our churches, as you have none in England, I know – but then you have so many other fine things – such charming steel buttons for example' pressing my hand to shew that she meant no offence: for, added she, *chi pensa d'una maniera, chi pensa d'un altra* (One person is of one mind, you know, another of another).[25]

Venice was capable of being a demanding mother, wife or mistress to her loved ones. Vivaldi does not seem to have been a very easy person to get on with on occasion, and he made enemies. In the climate of the Venice of his day, then,

51

it was better for him to go about his business as quietly as possible, and to keep as much to himself as he could in his position. Yet he was also capable of a seemingly genuine and deeply felt patriotism.

It is this, then, that helps to explain why Vivaldi remains such a comparatively shadowy figure, despite the illness that in any case helped to ensure that he was more of a recluse than most. As Hugh Honour has put it:

> The Serenissima demanded such self-effacing devotion from its citizens that anonymity became a virtue. Anything approaching a cult of personality was discouraged. The Doge was an anonymous figure-head prevented by his coronation oath from meddling in politics. Government was conducted by a committee, or rather a frequently changing series of committees. Generals or Admirals who enjoyed too great a success were liable to find themselves in prison lest they achieve personal power. Every Venetian was expected to put the State before all else.[26]

There was even possibly something in the Venetian character that wanted to be subjected to the State, that was in love with Venice, and was therefore only too happy to suppress the individual in the interests of the State. It became positively virtuous to be anonymous, to the point where one fails to be able to decide which was the more important motivating factor, the all pervading regimentation of the State or the desire for anonymity, and one is faced with something of a chicken and egg situation.

This makes the would-be biographer's task even more difficult. In Vivaldi's case the task is indeed daunting. We do not even have such a document as a will, which in the case of one of his distinguished precursors in Venice, Legrenzi, helps to lift the corner of the veil of anonymity ever so slightly, and therefore shed a beam of common humanity into a rather obscure cavern. Under the terms of his will, Legrenzi left his large breviary and fifty ducats to his friend the priest Bernardino Sartorato, who copied music for him, and the clock that 'came to him from Paris' to another friend

Pompeo Mosca.[27] His largest silver fruit dish, inscribed with his initials, he left to a singer at S. Marco by the name of Giovanni Francesco Pattavino da Kyper; to one of his favourite pupils at the Mendicanti his ring set with seven stones, and his harpsichord to the young Morosina, a singing pupil who lived in the house of the Procurator Valiero. We get the impression that Legrenzi was a gentle soul, who was genuinely mourned by those around him.

With Vivaldi, however, we have the impression of a somewhat irascible personality, though capable at the same time of considerable enthusiasm, especially when things went well. Unfortunately the only direct evidence, from a group of his letters written within four years of his death, must have been written when he was tired and exasperated by the trials of trying to arrange opera performances through intermediaries. There are moments of exhilaration, as in the letter from Verona, dated 3 May 1737: 'Here, praise be to God, my opera is in the stars, there is not a single thing that does not please greatly, whether it be from the musicians or the dancers, each one according to his capabilities.'[28] This was a performance of *Catone in Utica*, to a libretto by Metastasio, given at the Teatro Filarmonico in Verona.

Later that same year, however, he was having grave doubts about the dancer Coluzzi, whom he had engaged for the Ferrara opera, but who had left home and announced that she wished to marry another dancer, Pompeati, whom Vivaldi knew to be of doubtful character, 'a very bad man by character, capable of every mistake and every extravagance'. Moreover, in view of the fact that Pompeati was supposed to dance in Turin at the next Carnival, Vivaldi really doubted whether Coluzzi would be there to dance at all, despite the fact that she was promised the sum of a hundred louis which, as Vivaldi duly pointed out, she had never seen the like of before.[29] As it happened they were all overtaken by events beyond their control when an ecclesiastical interdiction prevented Vivaldi from giving his opera at all. At this juncture it is hard not to feel sympathy for him, despite his difficult character – as indeed one would with any person of talent in such a predicament. As he pointed out in the famous letter of 16 November 1737, he was put in an impossible situation, and he felt that the reasons put forward by the authorities were fabricated: 'For thirty years I have been a master at the Pietà, and without scandal'.[30]

This much was certainly true, and Caffi even went so far as to maintain that Vivaldi 'lived with all the marks of his firmness in the sacerdotal nature with which he was signed, and of whose duties he showed himself even in public a most zealous observer'. If Vivaldi was not regarded with affection by everyone at the Pietà, it was therefore probably because of his temperament rather than his actions or morality. There is a type of grand old man of music – and not only music – who is capable of inspiring intense affection and at the same time intense exasperation, possibly even to the point of hatred, but who is respected and – usually after his death – admired and remembered with affection. It seems that Vivaldi was such a person, and that a certain group of the governing body at the Pietà was always against him. Although he wrote that he had been at the Pietà for thirty years, they were not continuous years of service by any means. Often he was away from Venice for long periods at a time, and for this reason his name does not appear regularly in the registers of the establishment. There were also occasions, however, when he was definitely present in Venice, and desirous of renewing his post at the Pietà, but the governing body was far from unanimous about doing so. Before tracing his career at the institution, however, we must look at the nature of these rather strange Venetian establishments known as the *ospedali*.

3. Maestro at the Pietà

The Pietà was one of the four Venetian institutions originally for children who were either illegitimate, orphaned, or abandoned – Ospedale della Pietà on the Riva degli Schiavoni not far from S. Marco; Ospedale dei Mendicanti up near the Fondamente Nuove; Ospedaletto dei Ss. Giovanni e Paolo near the church of that name, and Ospedale degli Incurabili on the Zattere. At least one of these institutions, the Pietà, dated from the fourteenth century, and the name of *ospedale* came from the fact that they frequently had infirmaries incorporated into them. They were supported out of public funds, private donations and fees, and money they raised for themselves from concerts. On 5 April 1734 they received part of the proceeds of a public lottery, for example. On the other hand they also received legacies, and on 5 July 1704 they had been obliged to pay a *quintello* on all such legacies over 500 ducats in value. At one time it was estimated that some 6,000 children were in the care of these institutions.

Coryate mentioned the Pietà as early as 1608:

> If any of them [the courtesans] happen to have any children (as indeed they have but few, for according to the old proverbe the best carpenters make the fewest chips) they are brought up either at their owne charge, or in a certaine house of the citie appointed for no other use but onely for the bringing up of the courtezans bastards, which I saw eastward above Saint Markes street neare to the sea side. In the south wall of which building that looketh towards the sea, I observed a certaine yron grate inserted into a hollow peece of the wall, betwixt which grate and a plaine stone beneath it, there is a convenient little space to put in an infant.[1]

55

The tradition is that Brother Pieruzzo, moved by the seemingly ever increasing number of abandoned children in Venice, founded the first Pietà in 1346, at S. Francesco della Vigna, to which he added a second home in 1348 at S. Giovanni in Bràgora which was to become the Pietà of Vivaldi's day. However, as the number of children grew, so had Brother Pieruzzo's attempts to cope with them. The Pietà was enlarged in 1388, 1495, 1515, towards the end of the seventeenth century, and again at the beginning of the eighteenth century, and at some point it seems to have become exclusively feminine. Although the church Vivaldi knew was radically altered in 1745, a plaque on the outside wall still warns of the wrath that will descend on anyone who leaves a child to the care of the Pietà when he or she is capable of looking after it:

May the Lord God strike with curses and excommunications those who send, or permit their sons and daughters – whether legitimate or natural – to be sent to this Hospital of the Pietà, having the means and ability to bring them up, for they will be obliged to pay back every expense, and amount spent on them, neither may they be absolved unless they make atonement, as is clearly set out in the bull of our lord Pope Paul III dated ADL 12 November 1548.[2]

By the 1670s, the governors of the Pietà increased their staff by engaging three gentlewomen who were in straitened circumstances, and who agreed to teach the girls without remuneration, only for their keep.[3] On 25 June 1682 they also engaged two brothers, Bonaventura and Giacomo Spada, one to play the organ in the chapel and the other to teach in the orphange. Giacomo was a priest and an organist at S. Marco, and by the terms of his appointment he was first denoted *maestro di musica*, and later *maestro di coro*. Giacomo retired on 5 June 1701 and died in 1704, but we do not know when Bonaventura left. Gasparini then took over from Giacomo.

One of the female teachers was given the title *priora*, and she had to chaperone the girls, who were only to be taught by the masters in her presence (decree of 31 December 1684).[4] On one occasion, when the priora allowed a party from the choir to perform in the Convent of the Celestia without permission, she was dismissed, and the girls were 'gated'.[5] However, the governors found it very difficult to replace her, and so reinstated her.

That the fame of the music teaching began to spread early is confirmed by a request, in 1694, from the Convent of S. Gerolimo in Seraville, in reply to which Adriana *dalla tiorba* was sent.[6] The advent of daughters of the nobility – by 1707 – was rather like the evolution of the British public school insofar as what started out as charitable institutions for the poor became the upholders of an excellence tending to elitism, and so the standards went on improving in response to this success. In fact it looks very much as if Vivaldi's appointment was in direct answer to Gasparini's request to the governors of the Pietà for teachers of violin, viola and oboe.[7]

Music came to be an almost inevitable part of the curriculum, therefore, for both educational and religious reasons, and in Venice, where music was so avidly devoured, the concerts of the *ospedali* soon began to enjoy enormous prestige and popularity. Eminent musicians were on their staffs, and amongst the pupils were musicians of great talent who enjoyed the benefits of excellent training in both singing and instrumental technique, and who occasionally reached the sort of status accorded to stars of stage and screen today.

The idea of women being competent musicians was not rare in Italy, as we see from Evelyn's diary. What was unique to Venice was the fact that it should be organized on such a scale:

Here [Padua] I learned to play on the theorb, taught by Signor Domenico Bassano, who had a daughter married to a doctor of laws, that played and sung to nine several instruments, with that skill and address as few masters in Italy exceeded her; she likewise composed divers excellent pieces: I had never seen any play on the Naples viol before. She presented me afterwards with two recitativos of hers, both words and music.[8]

The musical girls of the *ospedali* were distinguished from the rest of the girls by the designation *di coro*, as opposed to *di commun*, and the State gave one hundred lire each per annum to the Pietà towards their upkeep. Of the *di coro* girls, the distinguished ones were known as *privileggiate di coro*. In his will of 1745 the Procurator Pietro Foscarini left one hundred ducats for the *figlie di coro* of the Pietà to sing a mass and recite the office for the burial of the dead at his funeral, with an additional twelve ducats a year, for the rest of their lives, for six of the best singers and six of the best instrumentalists.[9]

By a decree of 16 December 1729, Maestra Michieletta, a violinist, was granted two baskets of wood per week during the four winter months by the governing body of the hospital. On 13 January 1735 this was altered to include a basket of wood a week for the rest of the year, and this was altered yet again on 4 December 1744 – at the request of Michieletta – to an extra basket of wood for the remaining eight months of the year, thus giving her two baskets all the year round. Venice can be bitterly cold at times, even in summer, and the Pietà's situation on the Riva exposed it to sea breezes, especially if Maestra Michieletta lived on one of the upper floors. Of course if she also cooked for herself, or heated her own water, then she would need a fire all the year round.[10]

The girls seem to have been well looked after, and if they needed a change of air, the doctor of the Pietà was able to recommend a spell in the country. Thus on 6 June 1741 Doctor Domenico Bozzato swore under oath that Apollonia and Alina were both in need of a rest. This Apollonia, incidentally, was described in Von Poellnitz's letters as the finest singer in Italy.[11] The girls seem to have appreciated the attention they received, and responded to it, so that in September 1737 the organists Bianca Maria and Antonia refused to take any payment for a long music copying job they had done.[12]

The *maestre* acted as prefects, and helped the conductor to a certain degree, for example by ensuring that discipline was maintained at rehearsals, and for this they were rewarded at the rate of eighty ducats a year between 1738 and 1754.[13] At the same time they had a certain amount of oversight of the *maestri*, for on 1 March 1740, for example, Giulia and Anna-Maria, both *maestre di coro*, signed the termly accounts to the effect that the *maestri* had carried out their duties in a conscientious manner.[14]

Given the origin of the girls, together with the fact that music dominated their lives to such a point, they were usually known only by their christian names followed by their instruments. So Michieletta, already referred to, is described as *del violin*, and elsewhere one comes across Lucieta *dalla viola*, Cattarina *dal cornetto*, Silvia *dal violino*, and Luciana *organista*. The fact that many of them had no other name in any case was no bar to recognition of their talent. In 1726 the flautist Joachim Quantz put the Pietà first of the four *ospedali*, and mentioned in particular Apollonia the singer already referred to, and Angeletta, both singer and organist, who was one of the stars of the Pietà, and eventually married a banker. Charles de Brosses, in 1739, wrote of:

... Zabetta, of the Incurabili, who is above all astonishing for the range of her voice and the attacks that she has in her throat as if she were playing Somis' violin [G. B. Somis, 1686–1763]. She carries off all the votes; one would be offering oneself to be beaten by the populace in equalling anyone to her, but whilst no one is listening, I will whisper in your ear that Margarita of the Mendicanti is well worth it and pleases me better.

The one of the four *ospedali* I visit most often, and where I enjoy myself most, is the Ospedale della Pietà; it is also the first for the perfection of the symphonies. What strictness of execution! It is only there that one hears the first attack of the bow, so falsely vaunted at the Paris Opéra.[15]

According to De Brosses, Chiaretta of the Pietà would

certainly have been the best violinist in Italy had it not been for Anna-Maria of the Ospedaletto. He had no hesitation in putting Anna-Maria alongside Tartini, for though she did not have the extreme precision of his technique she outshone him, according to De Brosses, in everything else: 'I was rather pleased to hear the latter, who is so whimsical that she scarcely plays once a year.'

When the governing bodies saw the potential profits to be made from encouraging these musical activities – profits which they devoted to the welfare of the institutions themselves – they saw to it that they engaged the best possible staff as *maestri*. The Sunday and feast-day concerts of the *ospedali* were known all over the world, and in their heyday it seemed to visitors that there was virtually a concert every day. We are lucky in that several people have left records of their visits to them. In May 1698, for example, the Russian Petr Andreevic Tolstago wrote from Venice:

In Venice there are convents where the women play the organ and other instruments and sing so wonderfully that nowhere else in the world could one find such sweet and harmonious song. Therefore people come to Venice from all parts with the wish to refresh themselves with these angelic songs, above all those of the Convent of the Incurables.[16]

This was five years before Vivaldi joined the staff of the Pietà. Some years later, in 1720–2, the Englishman Edward Wright made his observations:

Infants are received into these hospitals; into the *Incurabile* (originally destined to another use) not without a sum given with them; into the *Pietà*, and the other two, as I take it, without any.

Those who would choose for a wife one that has not been acquainted with the world, go to these places to look for them; and they generally take all the care they can, they shall be as little acquainted with the world afterwards.[17]

This recalls an earlier passage, a visit to the house of the merchant Natale Bianchi, of whom Wright said: 'This merchant married his wife out of the hospital of the *Incurabile*. She sings admirably well, as the gentleman who introduced us there, told us: but we were not suffered either to hear or see her.' He then went on:

Those put into the Pietà are generally bastards. There are a prodigious number of children taken care of in this hospital: they say they amount sometimes to at least six thousand; and that before the erection of this charity, multitudes used to be found which had been thrown into the canals of the city. Every Sunday and holiday there is a performance of musick in the chapels of these hospitals, vocal and instrumental, performed by the young women of the place; who are set in a gallery above, and (though not professed) are hid from any distinct view of those below, by a lattice of iron-work. The organ-parts, as well as those of other instruments, are all performed by the young women. They have an eunuch for their master, and he composes their musick. Their performance is surprisingly good; and many excellent voices are among them: and there is somewhat still more amusing in that their persons are concealed from view.

Wright's account at once conjures up for us the sort of scene painted by a follower of Longhi in *Il parlatorio*, which hangs in the Ca'Rezzonico in Venice. Despite the lattice of iron-work, the *parlatorio* still manages to be a very lively place, even noisy to judge from the bagpipes being played in the foreground. Not all the concerts were given from behind lattice work, however. In the Galleria Querini Stampalia in Venice there is a painting by Gabriele Bella of a concert given in honour of the Counts of the North (Grand Duke Paul and Grand Duchess Maria Feodorovna of Russia) in the Casino dei Filarmonici, in 1782, in which the women are in three rows, one behind the other, on a balcony, but without any grille. Possibly the best-known version of this is Francesco Guardi's highly evocative painting in the Alte Pinakothek, Munich. Certainly the women's voices were a *spécialité de maison* in Venice.

J. G. Keysler, who made his visit to Venice in 1729, wrote: 'Bologna is the finest voice at present in the Pietà hospital, and Teresia in that of the Mendicanti. The republic allows a salary for a music master to every one of these four hospitals. And the most celebrated musicians do not think the office beneath their acceptance.'[18]

Von Poellnitz, who was there at almost the same time, is more committed in his opinions, and indicates a state of affairs – i.e. the importance attached to the music apparently as an end in itself – that had already caused him to comment, and which became increasingly apparent to visitors as the years went by:

> I am in some doubt whether I should reckon the music of the Venetian churches in the number of its pleasures; but upon the whole, I think I ought, because certainly their churches are frequented more to please the ear, than for real devotion. The church of La Pietà which belongs to the nuns who know no other father but love, is most frequented. These nuns are entered very young, and are taught music, and to play on all sorts of instruments, in which some of them are excellent performers. Apollonia actually passes for the finest singer, and Anna-Maria's for the first violin in Italy. The concourse of people to this church on Sundays and holidays is extraordinary. 'Tis the rendezvous of all the coquettes in Venice, and such as are fond of intrigues have here both their hands and hearts full. Not many days after my arrival in this city I was at this very church, where was a vast audience, and the finest of music.[19]

In August 1739 the Frenchman Charles de Brosses, President of the Parliament of Burgundy, wrote his account in a letter home:

> The transcendant music here is that of the hospitals. There are four of them, all consisting of bastard girls or orphans, and those whom their parents are in no position to bring up. They are brought up at the expense of the State, and they are trained only to excel in music. They

also sing like angels, and play the violin, the flute, the organ, the oboe, the 'cello, the bassoon; in short, there is no instrument so large that it makes them afraid of it. They are cloistered in the manner of nuns. They alone perform, and each concert consists of about forty girls. I swear to you that there is nothing more pleasing than to see a pretty young nun in a white habit, with a spray of pomegranate flowers behind her ear, conducting the orchestra and beating time with all the grace and precision imaginable.[20]

Jean-Jacques Rousseau's account in his *Confessions*, written two years after Vivaldi's death, ended on a somewhat less joyous note, though initially he, too, was carried away with the same kind of enthusiasm:

A [form of] music to my mind far superior to that of the operas, and which has not its like in Italy is that of the *scuole* ... Every Sunday at the Church of each of these schools one has during Vespers motets for full choir and orchestra composed and directed by the greatest masters in Italy, performed in balconies with grilles, entirely by girls of whom the oldest is not twenty. I can imagine nothing so voluptuous, so touching as this music ... The church [the Mendicanti] was always full of those who liked this sort of music; even the actors from the Opera would come and conform themselves to the true taste in singing on these excellent models. What grieved me were those accursed grilles, which only allowed the sound to pass, and hid from me the angels of beauty of which it [the sound] was worthy. I only talked of that. One day when I was talking about it to Monsieur le Blond:

'If you are so curious,' he said to me, 'to see these little girls, it is easy to satisfy you. I am one of the administrators of the house; I want to give you tea there with them.'

I did not let him rest until he had kept his word to me. As we entered the salon which enclosed these such coveted beauties, I felt a shiver of love that I had never felt before.

Monsieur le Blond introduced one after another to me of these famous singers whose voices and names were all that were known to me. 'Come Sophia . . .' she was horrible. 'Come, Cattina . . .' she was blind in one eye. 'Come, Bettina . . .' smallpox had disfigured her. There was hardly one that did not have some notable defect. The executioner laughed at my cruel surprise. Two or three, nevertheless, seemed passable to me; they only sang in the choir. I was grieved. During the tea we provoked them; they amused themselves. Ugliness did not exclude the graces; I discovered some here. I said to myself:

'One does not sing thus in one's soul: they have souls.'

Finally my way of envisaging them changed so happily that I left almost in love with all these ugly little things.[21]

Rousseau's account only concerned the Mendicanti, but in Von Poellnitz's letters, as we have already seen, there is a reference to the Pietà that is quite categorical, and indeed references abound in the literature of the period to the state of affairs in the Venetian *ospedali*: J. Addison's *Remarks on several parts of Italy in the years 1701, 1702, 1703*; Madame du Bocage's *Lettres sur l'Italie*, and the Marquis d'Orbessan's *Mélanges historiques, critiques*. It was all part of the Venetian malaise as painted by Pompeo Molmenti. Out of thirty-five hospices and nunneries in the city, some doubtless kept strictly to their rule, but the only rule that the majority obeyed was that of their whim. As Molmenti wrote:

They went to bed, got up and prayed in their own time and, instead of fasting, ate all kinds of delicacies and exotic dishes. Many of them had taken the veil under constraint and, in the solitude of the cloister, embraced a thousand dreams of love and beauty . . . Even after they had made their vows they retained their worldly habits and dressed elegantly, wearing corsages of smocked silk, curled hair and their throat half bare . . . The silence of the cloister was sometimes interrupted by the sound of trumpets and fifes, sometimes by the joyful shouts of the young patricians who danced with the nuns, who even went so far as to go out at night with their lovers.[22]

One must be careful not to tar the children of the *ospedali* with the same brush, however, for by no means all of them took the veil, and they cannot therefore be reproached for failing to adhere to a rule they were by no means bound to keep. Indeed Francesco Caffi insisted that they received a good general education as well as their specifically musical training, and were often taken in marriage by young men of good family. When Burney was in Venice in 1770 he met Signora Regina Zocchi, who:

> had been brought up as an orphan, but of a good family at the Hospital of Gl'Incurabili and had the advantage of being there under Hasse, but she is now well married and well received everywhere she chuses to go. She is now under thirty with an agreeable figure and a pleasing countenance. She has a powerful voice and sings charmingly with great execution in allegros and expression in slow movements.[23]

As we see from the paintings already referred to, the foundlings did leave their churches, quite lawfully, for important occasions, and in a perfectly sober manner. They were seen, and heads were bound to be turned, whether they encouraged those heads to turn or not. It would be unlike normal young girls, however, if there were not some among them who gave glad eyes in certain directions. On occasion they even left Venice, and Molmenti describes a party given at night by the Contarini family in their villa at Piazzola, near Padua, round about 1720, when some thirty-six girls from the Ospedaletto provided the music.

There was also a certain theatrical flavour about the musicians of the *ospedali* which would have been almost inevitable in any case, when one considers similar bodies today such as the Wienersängerknaben or certain ballet companies, but in eighteenth-century Venice, where everything was larger than life, it was especially pronounced. On feast days the libretto of the oratorio to be performed was handed out at the door of the church as one entered, with the names of the performers. Taddeo Wiel described them as being 'objects of infatuation or cabals, about whom sonnets and songs were published'.[24] Since applause was not permitted in church, the congregation – dare one say audience? – made up for it by coughing, blowing their noses loudly, or scraping their feet on the floor, much as members of an orchestra or choir do today when one of their number or a soloist performs a passage particularly well in rehearsal. Anyone was admitted to the church as long as there was space left, though there were special sections for patricians and distinguished foreign visitors.

It was to such an atmosphere, then, that Vivaldi came. For these performers, and for this public, some of his finest music was written. He made the girls' orchestra into one of the best in the world, but even more important than this, however, it inspired Vivaldi to some of his most daring experiments with form and instrumentation, with far-reaching implications for the development of Western music.

We may begin to trace Vivaldi's career at the Pietà from the autumn of 1703, at a salary of five ducats a month, and with the title of *maestro di violino*. There are further payments recorded in May and June 1704, at the same rate of five ducats a month, but from August onwards he took on the teaching of the viola as well. For this he received an extra forty ducats in addition to the termly instalments of twenty ducats. In the account books of the Pietà in the State Archives of Venice[25] he is referred to as *maestro di violino* and *maestro de' concerti*, though not *maestro di coro*, despite the fact that he deputized for Gasparini when he was *maestro di coro*, and it seemed on two occasions – after the departure of Gasparini and later that of Porta – as if he might be appointed to the post.

On the title page of his Op. I, printed by Giuseppe Sala in Venice, and of which an isolated copy of the first violin part is in the Conservatory in Venice, Vivaldi is described as *D[on] Antonio Vivaldi, Musico di Violino, Professore Veneto*. This collection of twelve trio sonatas was published in 1705, within two years of taking up his appointment at the Pietà. It is interesting to note at this point that Tomaso Albinoni published his Op. I – also a collection of *Sonate a tre* – with the same firm in 1694, and his Op. II, again with Sala, in 1700. The second publication was a group of *Sinfonie e concerti a cinque*. Usually King David playing his harp appeared on the title page of Sala's first editions, since they were sold at the sign of King David near S. Giovanni Grisostomo, unless replaced by the coat-of-arms of a dedicatee. But this did not necessarily hold good for subsequent editions. At any rate, Vivaldi did not choose to take his next work for publication to Sala, and by the time it came to Op. II, a collection of twelve sonatas for violin and continuo, published by Antonio Bortoli in Venice in 1709, Vivaldi was described as *Maestro de' Concerti del Pio Ospedale della Pietà di Venezia*. In this capacity he still continued to teach, but in addition conducted the orchestra on occasion, composed music for the concerts and even took charge of buying instruments.

In the account books of the Pietà for 20 March 1704 he was reimbursed ten ducats for a violin bought from Zanetti;[26] on 2 March 1705, sixteen ducats for another violin, and on 18 December that same year, twenty-four ducats for four violas. On 21 May 1706, two ducats and fourteen *grossi* for a violin bow for Madalena Rassa. On 12 March 1708 there is record of a payment made by Vivaldi for a viola once more, and on 6 April for strings for the viole d'amore, and on 23 April for a violin. On 9 January 1709 he was again paid for strings for the viole. This would seem to suggest that he was building up the stock of instruments over a period of about five years, after which it was more a question of maintaining them.

Outside the Pietà Vivaldi was beginning to be in demand as a recitalist. There is an account, for example, of a soirée given in 1705 by the then French Ambassador, the Abbé de Pomponne, to benefit the nuns of S. Girolamo, whose convent had been burnt.[27] Vivaldi was the soloist, along with the tenor Giovanni Paita, of whom we shall hear more later. The ambassador, Henri-Charles Arnauld de Pomponne

(1669–1756), was the third son of Simon Arnauld, Marquis de Pomponne, and had always been destined for the church. Even so, he was appointed Ambassador to Venice in 1704. In 1708 he became a Councillor of State for the Church, and subsequently a member of the Académie des Inscriptions. He seems to have remained a champion of Vivaldi's music long after his departure from Venice, and may well have been the person most responsible for encouraging Vivaldi to produce the occasional pieces he subsequently wrote for the marriages and births of various members of the French royal family.

Two or three years later, during the Carnival season of 1707–8, Prince Ercolani, the Imperial Ambassador, gave a soirée during the course of which Vivaldi was more or less asked to compete with Giovanni Rueta, also a musician in orders. Rueta was apparently the protégé of the emperor, though his name has not anything like the lustre of Vivaldi's. It was about this time that Alessandro Scarlatti was in Venice, and it would have been interesting to know whether he attended this soirée. As with Vivaldi and Handel, we can only speculate, and musical history has been deprived of one of its more fascinating potential encounters.[28]

The publication of the Op. II was an important step forward in the extension of Vivaldi's fame abroad. Op. I had been dedicated to Annibale Gambara, a Venetian nobleman, though originally from Brescia, which may indicate some connection with the Vivaldi family prior to their move to Venice, and therefore possibly Antonio was recognizing some thanks or obligation in his dedication. When it came to Op. II, however, the intervening four years had seen a great change, and Vivaldi dedicated his work to no less a personage than Frederick IV, King of Denmark and Norway (1699–1732). The king visited Venice for the Carnival of 1708–9, and arrived on 29 December. He announced to the Senate that he wished to be received simply as Count of Olemburg, so that he might be free to enjoy the delights that Venice had to offer during the Carnival, and enjoy the company of the Venetian nobility without the constraints of protocol.

The next morning, which was Sunday, the king was present at a concert of religious music at the Pietà, conducted by Vivaldi, since Gasparini was absent. There is a despatch from the Roman Chancellery in Venice about the visit of the king which Giazotto quotes without giving a reference for it, but which may be translated as follows:

His Majesty made an appearance at the Pietà at eleven o'clock in the morning after hearing the embassy from the lords of Savoy, and the girls sang with the instruments of the maestro [Vivaldi] who occupies the podium in the absence of Gasparini. Great was the applause for the *Credo* and *Agnus Dei* that were performed with the instruments, and then there was a concerto in great taste, as was appropriate.[29]

The king returned to the Pietà for the Feast of the Epiphany, though unfortunately we do not know who conducted on this occasion. Afterwards he attended the ball already referred to given in the Palazzo Foscari, his headquarters during his stay in Venice. When he finally left the city on 6 March he had heard more concerts at the Pietà, and took with him the twelve sonatas Vivaldi had dedicated to him, along with the portraits of twelve pretty Venetian women done in miniature for him by Rosalba Carriera. The Danish musicologist Peter Ryom has listed some forty-five Vivaldi manuscripts in Scandinavia, so it is evident that the association with the Danish–Norwegian court was no transitory matter.

In addition to royal visits to Venice, there were other distinguished foreigners of no less significance, for whom the city was an obligatory stop when entering or leaving Italy. Of particular interest from our point of view are the many musicians who came to the city, and yet despite the testimony of so many visitors to Venice, and the European intellectual and artistic world being so comparatively small, it is amazing that no trace of a meeting between Vivaldi and Handel has survived, for we know that Handel was in Venice in the autumn of 1707, leaving for Rome and Naples in the early spring of 1709, but returning for the Carnival that year, when *Agrippina* had its resounding success. He was again there in 1729, but this time much more briefly, since he was on a 'talent spotting' tour to find opera singers. Of course by the time of Handel's first visit, Vivaldi had not made his debut as an operatic composer, and there is nothing to indicate that Vivaldi was in fact in Venice during Handel's second visit in 1729.

From a musical point of view, however, it would be surprising if Handel were not acquainted with at least some of Vivaldi's music, since the London firm of Walsh and Hare brought out his Op. III, along with various other selections from time to time. And yet there is virtually nothing that one may point to in Handel's music that even faintly hints at Vivaldi – and Handel was never one to forgo the use of anything that appealed to him as interesting or worth incorporating.

And yet from a completely different point of view, there is a considerable amount of similarity between the situations of the two men. Both were life-long bachelors; Vivaldi because of his priestly celibacy, Handel because his friendship for women only seems to have been what we would loosely call platonic (he was also deeply attached to his mother). Both were very private people. We know virtually nothing about their emotional or physical relationships. Both had to contend with illness that might have seriously affected less capable characters (though in Handel's case it was less consistent than Vivaldi's, until later in his career). Both had financial problems, and saw their popularity fluctuate as fashion and taste evolved. Both gave inestimable riches to the world in their music. Both had a prodigious capacity for hard work, and both were capable of fits of temper. Both were in some way exiles – but there the similarities end, for Handel changed the country of his birth at the outset of his career, and managed to become something of a national institution in the country of his adoption, whereas Vivaldi left his homeland at the end of his career, and never re-established himself.

By way of paradox, it was the outcast Vivaldi who handed

so much on to the subsequent development of music, whereas Handel was the final flowering of his particular branch of the musical art.

Then there is the case of Tomaso Albinoni (1671–1750), almost an exact contemporary of Vivaldi and, like Vivaldi, a native of Venice. Albinoni is also an elusive personality, in fact almost as elusive as Vivaldi himself. Michael Talbot, author of a dissertation on Albinoni's instrumental music, suggests that the two Venetians probably did not even know each other, certainly not well, since otherwise Albinoni would have taken up more of Vivaldi's musical innovations. Yet Anna Girò apparently made her Venetian debut in Tomaso's opera *Laodice*, and it would be surprising if Albinoni's name were not known to Vivaldi. As far as Albinoni was concerned with Anna Girò, however, one engagement might have been enough for him, and he may not have wanted to use her again in any case. It is interesting, however, to note en passant that Albinoni, in common with Vivaldi, boasted of the speed with which he composed operas. They at least had that much in common!

Of course Albinoni was not associated with S. Marco, nor any of the *ospedali*. In fact he does not seem to have had any contact with the specifically ecclesiastical musical establishment of Venice, let alone write any music for it that is extant. Being of independent means – the family fortune came from paper mills – he was not, therefore, obliged to look for work in the musical profession. He did not, however, aspire to the noble status of the Marcello brothers.

Albinoni published with both Sala and Roger & Le Cène. As we have seen, his Op. 1 was the by now almost traditional (for Venetian composers) *Sonate a tre* with Sala in 1694, but he had published in Amsterdam also by 1698. His music was also known to J. S. Bach, who used three of his themes as subjects for fugues. It is perhaps unfortunate that the work that made the name of Albinoni heard so much by the public at large a few years ago – an Adagio in G minor for Organ and Strings – is not in fact by him, but mostly by his biographer Remo Giazotto (the bass is Albinoni's). Nevertheless there is today a genuine interest in him, and we are now beginning to have a clearer picture of his *oeuvre*. The Bach accolade is important for his status, but all in all, Albinoni is a lesser light than Vivaldi. For one thing, Vivaldi was much more adventurous, much more inventive, and much more dynamic. If one compares music that both Vivaldi and Albinoni wrote for the same ensemble, namely the Dresden orchestra, then Albinoni hardly used the famous woodwind, whereas Vivaldi was delighted to have its accomplished players and – to him – fascinating tonal potentialities to work with. As Michael Talbot has said: 'It is ironic that Vivaldi should have been accused of writing the same concerto so many times over: of all Albinoni's Italian contemporaries, Vivaldi is the most inventive, the most ready to experiment.'[30] Talbot sees a contrast between the dynamic impulse of Vivaldi and the dreamy melancholy typical of the Venetian music of the period, thinking particularly of Albinoni's slow movements, and those of Galuppi too, but Vivaldi could also write beautifully melancholy slow movements. Such passages as the slow movement of Spring from the *Four seasons* Op. VIII, no. 1 (RV 269), or that of the violin concerto Op. XI, no. 2, *Il favorito* (RV 277), seem full of the poignancy of an era – a civilization even – that is drawing to its close. But then Vivaldi has moments of supreme joy and exhilaration, when he seems to lift the spirit of the listener out of time and place. It is this in particular that accounts for his popularity today, though there is still a great deal to be done to convince people at large, and some musicians in particular, that he is a far greater composer than has yet been recognized.

Vivaldi is also supremely a Venetian composer, not only by his flair, his audacity and his flamboyancy, but because much of his music is an implicit poem to Venice. There are times when he seems to capture the very essence of the city in his music, with its gently lapping water that may suddenly dazzle and sparkle as the sun breaks across the surface; the infinite variety of architectural prospects, or the rich experience of the life of its citizens. It all seems to be there in Vivaldi's music.

So Vivaldi continued to build up his reputation in Venice,

initially through the concerts at the Pietà, of which Remo Giazotto has found traces of twenty-seven for 1709, attended at one time or another by the French Ambassador, the Abbé de Pomponne; the Imperial Ambassador, Prince Ercolani; and the envoys from Poland, Muscovy, Spain, and the Apostolic Nuncio.

He was also playing his violin in the theatre. His father had done the same thing, after all, and there was no earthly reason why the son should not have done likewise. We know, for example, that Antonio had played on occasion at the Grimani theatre of S. Giovanni Grisostomo. There were several ways in which the theatre began to take hold on his imagination, though this very practical one of being present in the pit on numerous occasions was one of the most compelling of all. Remo Giazotto finds it strange that we have no evidence of operatic activity by Vivaldi before he made his debut as a composer in 1713,[31] though since there would seem, from a reference in one of Vivaldi's letters, to have been almost twice as many operas written by him than we so far have record of, others may yet come to light and explain this early period.

On the other hand, the idea of actually writing for the stage may not have occurred to him until he had spent some considerable time witnessing performances, as a result of which he felt he could probably do just as well, if not better, than the men whose works he was playing or listening to. He would not, after all, be the first person to have extended his talent in this way. At all events, there were plenty of people around him to give support to the venture. There was his friendship with the then fashionable tenor Paita, as well as the impresario Santurini, who was a neighbour, and whose wife was Gasparini's daughter Lucrezia, a marriage which took place in 1698 at Vivaldi's parish church of S. Martino. However, these considerations will be treated in more detail in the next chapter. Suffice it to say here that once Vivaldi began to consolidate his Venetian reputation as a teacher, composer and virtuoso violinist, then his career began to develop very quickly, and with so many foreign visitors to Venice, and his contacts with the foreign ambassadors accredited to the Republic, it is indeed small wonder that his fame rapidly began to spread abroad also. It is possible that as a result he began to travel, for after the Carnival season ending in May 1709 there is little evidence that he was in Venice until a mention in the Notatorio on 27 September 1711,[32] when he was to be paid sixty ducats a year as *maestro di violino*.

Roland de Candé has made a conjecture about a visit to Florence,[33] for in 1711 Count Scipione Maffei, who was to provide the libretto for Vivaldi's opera *La fida ninfa*, published a description in Apostolo Zeno's newly founded *Giornale de' Letterati*, of the first pianoforti being made by Cristofori in Florence. As M. de Candé himself observes, if Vivaldi went to hear these new instruments, they certainly did not inspire him to write for them. Without any documentary evidence one cannot judge, though there is the added fact that Vivaldi dedicated his Op. III (published in 1711) to Ferdinand III, Grand Duke of Tuscany, of which Florence is the capital.

Vivaldi's Op. III is the famous *L'estro armonico*, which was extremely important in his development of the concerto, and will be looked at later from this point of view. It was also important because it was printed by the distinguished publisher Estienne Roger in Amsterdam, and in the preface to the work Vivaldi declared that he had at last found the printer of his dreams. So much so, in fact, that he had both Op. I and II reprinted in Amsterdam, and he announced that his Op. IV, *La stravaganza*, would soon be published by the same firm, though in fact the public had to wait some time for its appearance. One can see at a glance the difference between the two styles of printing. In the old Venetian editions the staves were still assembled from individual stamps, and each note with its tail had an individual block. This was not too bad for polyphonic music, but for the groups of semiquavers and demisemiquavers often found in Vivaldi's music, sight reading must have been a positive nightmare. Roger's, on the other hand, are clear, elegant, and easy to read. Moreover he introduced the system of numbering works for ease of reference and ordering, whereas before references had been used only when storing the blocks.

As to how Vivaldi made contact with Roger in Amsterdam we do not know. There was the precedent of Albinoni, dating from 1698, which he must have known about, but until more evidence comes to light we cannot suppose that he actually went to Amsterdam in 1710, though we know that he went there much later in his career. All one can say so far is that there would have been time to do so. Naturally Vivaldi would have wanted to be back in Venice for the publication of his Op. III to see how it was received, and we know that he was certainly back by 27 September 1711 from the Pietà accounts. Another, ostensibly less significant, event was the marriage of Vivaldi's friend Orlandini, who was a composer of sorts, to the sister of the Mauri brothers who ran the S. Giovanni Grisostomo theatre. As a favour, girls from the Pietà were allowed to sing at the wedding, which took place early in 1712.

From this year 1712 date two concerti of which manuscripts are in Turin and Dresden. One was written for the feast of the Tongue of St Anthony of Padua (RV 212), and the other (RV 286) for the feast of St Laurence in Padua. The idea that Padua was the last stop on the return visit from a long journey is attractive, but does not accord with the fact that Vivaldi was back in Venice by the autumn of the previous year; in any case, Padua is near enough to Venice for a journey to be made there almost at any time without Vivaldi having disrupted his more regular occupations in Venice. He might even have accepted a post there in one of the major churches. Even if it did involve a certain amount of leave from the Pietà, the other members of the staff were often doing the same thing, so that in this Vivaldi was no exception.

In addition to the titles which at one time or another Vivaldi held – *maestro di violino, maestro de' concerti* and *maestro di viola* – there were posts for teachers of the organ, sight reading and singing, oboe, 'cello, flute, horn, and – for a period of six months – even timpani. At the top of the hierarchy at the Pietà was the *maestro di coro*, who at this point in Vivaldi's career was Francesco Gasparini (1668–1727), certainly until 1713. Gasparini was born in Camaiore,

Lucca, near Pisa. He had been a pupil of Corelli and Pasquini in Rome before coming to Venice and rising eventually to the post of *maestro di coro* at the Pietà in 1701. Subsequently he returned to Rome, where he became *maestro di cappella* of S. Lorenzo in Lucina in 1717 and then in 1725 of the Lateran. Both Benedetto Marcello and Joachim Quantz were pupils of his. He wrote some sixty operas and intermezzi, mostly for theatres in Venice and Rome, but his fame spread abroad, and some of the operas were among the first Italian works to be given in London. He also composed an enormous amount of church music, as one might expect in view of his succession of ecclesiastical appointments. Certainly that of *maestro di coro* at the Pietà was no sinecure. He had to compose an oratorio or concerto for each feast day, as well as pieces for instruments or voices as occasion demanded. In addition he had to teach music theory and instrumental technique. We see what was expected of such a person in a decree of the Pietà dated 5 August 1735, reinstating Vivaldi in his functions – though in fact designated only as *maestro de' concerti*, and not *maestro di coro* – which sets out all his various duties.

Perhaps it is not surprising that Gasparini constantly turned his eyes towards Rome, as a means of release from the time-consuming young women of the Pietà. In fact it looks as if he asked for leave and simply failed to return.[34] At all events, by 1713 he was absenting himself, and there is record of a special payment to Vivaldi of fifty ducats on 17 March of that year for not only having conducted the orchestra, but for having composed music of his own for the occasion in the absence of Gasparini, *maestro di coro*. Not that Vivaldi was exclusively devoted to the Pietà himself, however, for he had by now made his debut as a composer of opera, and for the rest of his life the two aspects of his vocal writing were to continue side by side. To avoid unnecessary confusion, however, the two activities will be kept apart as far as possible, and this is a convenient point at which to look at the rise of opera, and its organization in Italy by the time Vivaldi became involved in it, and in Venice in particular.

4. The Venetian Opera

If it is no surprise that Italy gave birth to opera, then it is certainly no surprise that the first public opera house in the world was opened in Venice. As we have seen earlier in this book, there were very special factors in the Venetian way of life that encouraged and even demanded this sort of entertainment. Indeed, one feels that it was something of a chicken and egg situation, and it is hard to decide where the real stimulus came from. Girolamo Parabosco, writing in the middle of the sixteenth century, had this to say: 'Those Venetians are the sort of people who climb walls, break down doors and swim across canals in their haste to reach the places where any tragedy or comedy is being performed.'[1]

At all events, the first public opera house in the world was opened in Venice in 1637 with *Andromeda*, music by Manelli to a libretto by Ferrari who, according to Canon Cristoforo Ivanovich of S. Marco, was also a musician and an excellent performer on the theorbo.[2] The birth of opera as we know it is of course usually taken as being the first performance of Monteverdi's *Orfeo* on 24 January 1607 in Mantua, and in Venice itself his *Proserpina rapita* was subsequently given in 1630 in the Palazzo Dandolo (now the Hotel Danieli) – in fact some regard this as the first opera to be given in Venice, though not, of course, the first public opera. The Vendramin family had their own private house at S. Luca (also known as S. Salvatore) as early as the 1620s. It was the Tron family, however, who opened the first public opera house in part of their palace in the area near the church of S. Cassiano, from which the theatre then took its name. This was actually the second theatre on the site, replacing an earlier wooden one.

By the end of the seventeenth century there were some eighteen theatres, and Misson, writing on 14 February 1688, said that there were seven theatres for opera alone in Venice at that time.[3] The situation was somewhat fluid, however, and tended to change fairly quickly. In the next century the number seems to have dropped to fourteen, with seven theatres giving opera all the time, and three more only occasionally.[4] It is difficult to be sure whether some may in fact be rightly regarded as theatres in the true sense, since they were private and sometimes only had one 'performance'.

After the founding of the S. Cassiano by the Tron family, a fashion was set for noble families to own theatres, largely because they owned the land on which they were built, and had the necessary finances. In 1639 the theatre of Ss. Giovanni e Paolo was founded, on the site of what was believed to be Marco Polo's first home in Venice, by the Grimani family.[5] Monteverdi's *Adone* was put on for the opening, and in 1642 his *Incoronazione di Poppea* was given there. By the turn of the century, however, it tended to specialize in comedy, though Albinoni's opera *Zenobia* and Lotti's *Polidoro* were given there in 1694 and 1714 respectively.

The same year, 1639, saw the opening of the S. Moisè theatre, with Monteverdi's *Arianna*. The theatre belonged to the Giustiniani family, and three of Vivaldi's operas were to receive their first performances there – *La costanza trionfante*, *Tieteberga* and *Armida*. Generally, however, it tended to specialize in what we would today call light opera.

In 1645 John Evelyn attended the opera, and we have some idea from him of the magnificence of Venetian opera at that time:

This night, having with my Lord Bruce taken our places before, we went to the Opera, where comedies and other plays are represented in recitative music, by the most excellent musicians, vocal and instrumental, with variety of scenes painted and contrived with no less art of perspective, and machines for flying in the air, and other wonderful notions; taken together, it is one of the most magnificent and expensive diversions the wit of man can invent. The history was, Hercules in Lydia; the scenes changed thirteen times. The famous voices, Anna Rencia, a Roman, and reputed the best treble of women; but there was an

78

eunuch who, in my opinion, surpassed her; also a Genoese that sung an incomparable bass.[6]

Ten years after this, in 1655, the Grimani family, who already owned the Ss. Giovanni e Paolo theatre, opened a second one at S. Samuele. It was a very popular theatre, and came to be the home of many of Goldoni's works. Nevertheless, certain operas received their first performances there, notably Albinoni's *Scipione in Spagna*, Vivaldi's *Griselda* (on which he worked with Goldoni) and *Aristide*, and Gluck's *Demetrio*. A third Grimani theatre was the S. Giovanni Grisostomo, founded in 1674 on the ruins on Marco Polo's home, and opened in 1678, the year of Vivaldi's birth, with the opera *Vespasiano*, music by Pallavicino, to a libretto by Corradi. It held some 2,700 people and was the home of serious opera, giving works by Scarlatti, Caldara, Handel, Lotti, Gasparini, Vinci, Porpora, Leo, Jommelli and Gluck. For a short time – from 1735 until 1741 – Goldoni directed it, and it survived to become the Malibran theatre in 1835.

The Vendramin family owned the S. Salvatore theatre (sometimes known as S. Luca), which was opened in 1661 and specialized in comedy, though also gave operas from time to time.

As far as Vivaldi was concerned, however, it was the S. Angelo theatre, built in 1676 and opened in 1677, that was to be the home of most of his Venetian premières. On the Grand Canal, it belonged technically to the Cappello and Marcello families. As we shall see, however, the whole business of its ownership and management was somewhat irregular, to say the least, and was the cause of a seemingly interminable lawsuit. It was, therefore, neither the oldest, nor the largest, nor yet the most famous of Venetian theatres. Some twenty of Vivaldi's operas are known to have been created there, however, alongside works by Gasparini, Albinoni – for example *Diomede* in the autumn of 1700 – Leo, Galuppi and Porpora.

It has been estimated that, in addition to the theatres already mentioned, there were probably another ten by the end of the seventeenth century, starting with the Novissimo in 1641 (lasting only six years); Ss. Apostoli in 1649 (private, and short lived); S. Apollinare in 1651; Ai Saloni in 1670; Cannaregio in 1679–80; Alle Zattere in 1679 (though only one opera appears to have been given there, and it was in any case in a private house); Altieri in 1690 (again, a private theatre of the Altieri family); S. Marina in 1698 (only one opera); S. Fantino in 1699 (only two operas), and another theatre at S. Moisè, in Calle Lungo (again, private, and only one opera given).[7]

In the next century many of these theatres had disappeared, and others taken their places. In particular one might mention another at S. Fantino (owned by the Michiel family); S. Benedetto (owned by the Grimani family), 1755; La Fenice, 1792; S. Margherita; S. Girolamo (private, owned by the Labia family), and Il Teatro Pepoli in the Palazzo Cavalli at S. Vitale.[8]

Today all that survives to recall many of these theatres are the black and white Venetian street signs such as Campiello del Teatro at S. Angelo on the Grand Canal; Calle del Teatro at S. Moisè; Salizzada del Teatro at S. Benedetto; Ramo del Teatro at S. Samuele; Calle and Ponte del Teatro at S. Luca, and similar names.[9]

Some 150 operas were performed in Venice between 1680 and 1700, and according to Pincherle 432 between 1700 and 1743 – the span of Vivaldi's creative activity. Carlo Francesco Pollaroli, to cite one example, wrote no fewer than seventy operas between 1685 and 1722, making an average of two a year. This, however, was in addition to his involvements as organist and second *maestro di cappella* in S. Marco, and teaching duties at the Ospedale degli Incurabili. Vivaldi himself wrote an average of two a year between 1713 and 1739, and according to a letter discovered in Ferrara, may have composed twice as many operas as was previously imagined.

To those of us who have been brought up in the post-Wagnerian age, it seems inconceivable that opera could ever have been written in any other way than that dictated by the composer's own artistic and creative vision. In eighteenth-century Venice, however, things were very different. In the first place, the actual conditions in the opera houses were very different from the wrapt and hushed concentration of today's theatres. The noise in Venetian theatres was considerable. People laughed and talked, whistled or applauded as the fancy took them, and made animal noises at the entries and exits of the performers. However, as recently as 1976, animal noises have been heard from a cruelly chauvinistic audience at the Paris Opéra. The boxes often had shutters which could be closed to allow their occupants to enjoy their conversations more easily; to eat – on 21 December 1711 the government renewed a decree forbidding the taking of meals at the theatre – or indulge the Venetian passion for gambling. Some theatres even had gambling salons, known as *ridotti*, attached to them, and one can see from Longhi and Guardi's paintings what these establishments looked like. John Evelyn saw one as early as 1645:

This [the opera] held us by the eyes and ears till two in the morning, when we went to the Chetto de san Felice, to see the noblemen and their ladies at bassett, a game at cards which is much used; but they play not in public, and all that have inclination to it are in masquerade, without speaking one word, and so they come in, play, lose or gain, and go away as they please. This time of licence is only in Carnival and this Ascension-Week; neither are their theatres open for that other magnificence, or for ordinary comedians, save on these solemnities, they being a frugal and wise people, and exact observers of all sumptuary laws.[10]

As for the audience in the stalls, or groundlings, as they were referred to in *Hamlet*, Charles de Brosses said quite categorically that they were little better than rabble. The people in the upper boxes spat on their heads or showered them with a variety of missiles, including on occasion copies of poems to the respective glories of the stars, which the rabble would then jostle for. Misson, for example, particularly mentioned this in 1688.[11]

The organization and financing of the theatres was not

made easy by the fact that the stars received enormous fees, operas were rarely performed more than once or twice – when Handel's opera *Agrippina* had a run of seventeen nights at the S. Giovanni Gristostomo theatre in Venice, this was regarded as prodigious – the price of the seats was low, and the people who had the lease of the boxes did everything possible to avoid paying for them. In any case, the cost was in the region of little more than £25 per annum. The public felt no urge to pay more for their entertainment, and indeed, as long as the managers could provide the spectacles, there was little obvious need to change things. In England it was hardly any better, and when the Covent Garden management tried to abolish the habit of charging only half price after the third act, the audience advanced on the stage with bludgeons and rapiers, whilst the orchestra cowered to avoid a shower of missiles, and the singers stood amazed – all of which took place during a performance of Arne's *Artaxerxes* in 1763.

Ivanovich was alarmed in those days that costs of producing opera in Venice had risen sharply since opera first began in 1637, when people paid four lire for the *bollettino*, which served as a 'passport' to the theatre, and which he described as an 'honest contribution'. Despite fluctuations in the fortunes of the theatres, this remained unaltered until 1674, and would have gone on even longer, had it not been for the fact that Francesco Santurini, at the S. Moisè theatre that year, started charging a quarter of a ducat at the door, and with the profits was able to launch the S. Angelo in 1677. As Ivanovich remarked: 'examples of novelty embrace each other willingly when they redound in benefice!'[12]

The singers themselves hardly improved matters, and a volume could be written about their extravagant behaviour. In the first place, they demanded absurdly high fees, not only for the actual hope of obtaining the money, but for the prestige involved. Goldoni later satirized this practice in *L'impresario delle Smirne* in 1761. The castrato Carluccio negotiated at first for a fee of 300 zecchini, but had in the end to agree to take fifty: 'However, for the sake of my reputation, I demand a *scrittura simulata* [a fake contract] stipulating 500, as well as the guarantee of a banker.' Keysler, writing some thirty years earlier – i.e. whilst Vivaldi was at the height of his powers – had equally biting comments to make: 'Some of these singers, however, seem to despise all economy: And as they get large sums without much trouble, so they lavishly spend them by keeping elegant tables, wearing rich dresses, and other extravagances; but throw away still more by gaming.'[13]

Then there was their behaviour once they were on stage. The castrato Luigi Marchesi, no matter what opera he was engaged for, always required that his entrance be made at the top of a hill, wearing a plumed helmet, and armed with sword, shield and lance. He was then greeted with a fanfare, whereupon he sang one of his favourite arias, usually 'Mia speranza io pur vorrei', which Sarti had composed especially for him. Another castrato, Giuseppino, liked to sing complete with accessories judged – by himself – to increase his popularity. Thus Romulus returning victorious from battle was to appear covered with chains.[14]

Nor were the female performers any better. On a famous – or infamous – occasion the two prima donnas Faustina and Cuzzoni actually came to blows on the stage in front of the audience in London in 1727. The stars, of either sex, would beat time with whatever props they had to hand, be they sceptres or fans, they smiled up at friends or possible patrons in the boxes, took snuff, abused the prompter, unbuttoned or unlaced their clothing so as to be able to sing more comfortably, and paid little attention at all to the dramatic requirements of the role. The whole interest lay in the vocal production and the splendour of the stage set.

Giacomo Torelli (1608–78) had perfected machinery which made scene changes of the most complicated and exotic sort relatively simple, and at least three Venetian theatres – S. Cassiano, Ss. Giovanni e Paolo and S. Salvatore – possessed such equipment. Ferdinando Bibiena (1657–1742) was the founder of a whole school of scenic designers. Needless to say, there are numerous extant satires on this lavish form of entertainment. One of the strangest has already been mentioned, namely Zaccaria Seriman's *I viaggi d'Enrico Wanton alle terre incognite australi ed ai regni delle scimmie e dei cinocefali*, published in Venice in 1749. Apart from its satire of Venetian customs, it is also interesting for Fossati's illustrations, which reveal what the theatres looked like whilst an opera was in progress.

Reaction to Venetian opera was mixed. Misson, for example, writing in 1695, had this to say:

It is undeniable matter of fact, that the ornaments of those here [Venetian operas] fall extreamly [*sic*] short of these [Parisian operas]: the habits are poor, no dances, and commonly no machines, nor any illuminations, only some candles here and there, which deserve not to be mentioned. 'Tis dangerous not to magnifie the Italian musick, or to say, at least, anything against it. Neither will I insist on this subject, but confess, in the general, that they have most excellent ayres, and that there are some good voices amongst them. Thus, for example, the Vicentin songster of the Hospitalettes is a little charming creature.[15]

One can only assume that as far as the staging of the operas that Misson saw is concerned, he must have attended a succession of bad nights, since many other accounts contradict him. Of course, being French, he was predisposed to be critical of anything that was different, and the whole concept of the castrato he found impossible to accept:

There is also one thing which charms them, which I believe would not please you; I mean those unhappy men who basely suffer themselves to be maimed, that they may have the finer voices. The silly figure, which in my opinion, such a mutilated fellow makes, who one time acts the bully, and sometimes the passionate lover, with his effeminate voice, and wrinkled face, is not to be endured. It is impossible that fellows of this make can have spirits necessary for the beauty of action; and indeed there is nothing more cold and feeble than the manner after which they act their parts.

Joseph Addison, who visited Italy in 1701–3, was much of the same mind, though by and large the English came to accept the castrati more easily:

Operas are another great entertainment of this season [Carnival]. The poetry of them is generally as exquisitely ill, as the musick is good. The arguments are often taken from some celebrated action of the ancient Greeks or Romans, which sometimes looks ridiculous enough, for who can endure to hear one of the rough old Romans squeaking through the mouth of an eunuch, especially when they may chuse a subject out of courts where eunuchs are really actors, or represent by them any of the soft Asiatic monarchs?[16]

There was a cold logic in Addison's suggestion, but then if castrati were to be restricted to playing actual eunuchs, then either there would be very few roles for them to play – which he would probably not have regretted – or else the theatre would be swamped by such plots. But this would be to ignore completely the fact that the then current convention totally accepted travesty parts, as it was to do so in London, when Italian opera came into fashion. What some people found just as strange was something to which Addison referred earlier, namely the extraordinary plots of these operas. At times things were so bad that even with the best will in the world, the opera-goer was left mystified. The libretto of *Veremonda* by Bisaccioni, set to music by Cavalli, had an *argomento* on the last page which was described as: 'A summary of the opera for those who cannot understand it after having heard and read the same!'

It was not always the librettist's fault, nor the composer's, either. Pier Jacopo Martello, or Martelli, wrote a book entitled *Della tragedia antica e moderna*, published in 1715, in which he gave some consolatory advice to the composer and librettist:

Be resigned to the exchanging of good arias for bad ones if some singer wants to add one to your recitative which had brought him or her applause in Milan, Venice, Genoa, or elsewhere. Though it may express the opposite sentiment to what is required, do not let this grieve you. Let them insert it, else you will have them all after you, sopranos and altos bearing down on you with their complaints.

The librettist has to find out the impresario's intentions, that is, how many changes of scenery he has ordered from the painter; whether he has ordered any machines from the stage engineer, and how many costumes his wardrobe contains . . . how small the stage is, and how stingy the manager might be.[17]

Goldoni related in his *Mémoires* how he discovered to his cost, when embarking on his career, that the efforts of both librettist and composer were ruthlessly subjected to the demands of audience and performer. One day he read one of his works at the home of Signora Grossatesta, revealing that it was intended as an operatic libretto:[18]

The singer Caffariello arrives; he sees me, he recognizes me, he greets me with the tone of Alexander, and takes his seat alongside the mistress of the house, a few minutes later the Count Prata is announced, who is one of the directors of performances [at Milan] and the person who is most informed about the dramatic side of things . . . Everyone takes their places; I begin the reading; I announce the title *Amalasunta*. Caffariello sings the word Amalasunta; it is long and seems ridiculous to him. Everyone laughs. I do not. I read the list of the dramatis personae; there were nine in my play; and a little voice is heard piping up from an old castrato who sang in the chorus and cried like a cat: 'Too many, too many, there are at least two characters too many' . . . I read the first scene and, whilst I spin out my lines, a puny, impotent old man takes a roll of music out of his pocket, and goes to the harpsichord to run through an aria from his part . . .

The mistress of the house makes endless excuses to me, Signor Prata takes me by the hand and takes me into a dressing room far removed from the drawing room; he begs me to read my drama to him alone so as to pass his judgement upon it and tell me his opinion in sincerity. He listened to me attentively and patiently, and when I had finished my reading here is more or less the result of his attention and his judgement: 'It seems to me,' he said, 'that you have studied fairly well the poetic art of Aristotle and Horace, and you have written your play according to the rules of tragedy. But here one must begin by pleasing the actors and actresses; one must satisfy the composer of the music; one must consult the painter-decorator; there are rules for everything, and it would be a crime of *lèse-playwrighting* if one infringed them. The three principle characters in the play must sing five arias each; two in the first act, two in the second and one in the third. The second actress and the second male lead may only have three arias, and the least characters must be content with one or two at the very most. The author of the words must provide the musician with the different nuances that form the light and shade of the music, and make sure that two pathetic arias do not occur together. With the same precaution the bravura arias must be shared out, the action arias, the demi-character arias and the minuets and rondos. Above all, extreme care must be taken not to give passionate arias, nor bravura arias, nor rondos, to second-rank characters.

After this it comes as little surprise to learn that the discouraged Goldoni then went off and burnt his manuscript. There is another famous passage in his *Mémoires* which we shall look at later, in the course of which this imaginary situation almost actually took place, when Goldoni went as a virtually unknown beginner to discuss possible collaboration with Vivaldi, and indeed we have Vivaldi's own letters to the Marquis Bentivoglio as witness to the difficulties involved in mounting operas in such a climate. On the other hand, without such rules for the creation of the operas themselves, it would have been impossible for composers to provide the seemingly insatiable appetite of the Venetian audience with enough to keep them satisfied. In a less artistic climate the results might have been markedly inferior, but there was in Venetian opera at its best a reflection of the quality and richness that marked the whole of Venetian life in this, the final sunset of its history as an independent state. Doubtless it carried within itself the seeds of its own destruction, much as Italian opera did in England, but for a while it lived only for the present.

When Vivaldi made his debut as an operatic composer he was thirty-five years of age, held in high esteem in his native city as a virtuoso violinist, teacher and *maestro* at the Pietà, and he already enjoyed a reputation on a European scale as a composer of instrumental music. It would be a mistake to suppose, however, that he had had no experience of the theatre at all before this, and in the previous chapter we saw one or two of the ways in which he gained it. The sphere of Venetian music, with its two poles of church and theatre, had infinite lines of latitude and longitude, and whole continents in common, so there was considerable interdependence. For one thing, the church music establishment was permanent, and operated year in and year out. The opera season, however, ran in thrice yearly seasons, during the winter Carnival from 26 December to 30 March, the spring or Ascension season from Whit-Monday to 30 June, and the autumn season from 1 September to 30 November. Companies were assembled for individual seasons, and there were virtually no regular companies as such. In the circumstances many musicians, both singers and instrumentalists, would rely on the church for their basic employment and the theatre for the secondary one. Vivaldi must certainly have known singers who performed both in church and on stage, and played in both church gallery and theatre pit.

Then there was the example of Gasparini, Vivaldi's superior at the Pietà, whose operatic career was well known to Vivaldi. In fact it may well have been Gasparini's presence as a composer of opera that prevented Vivaldi from making his Venetian debut sooner. He had, after all, deputized for Gasparini on several occasions when he was absent, either through ill health or pressing engagements. During the

1704–5 season alone Gasparini put on eight new operas in Venice. In his autobiography, Joachim Quantz described Gasparini – whose pupil he had been in Rome in 1724 – as an aimiable and estimable man. Certainly Gasparini seems to have been a good teacher, and his treatise on through bass or continuo playing, *L'armonico pratico al cimbalo* (1708), had a long period of popularity. Perhaps he mellowed in later life, for during his Venetian period his name was linked with somewhat less worthy matters.

In collaboration with Santurini, impresario at the S. Angelo theatre, Gasparini decided to mount his *Tiberio imperatore d'Oriente* at that theatre and engaged female singers from Ferrara. However, when the singers did not receive the amount agreed for their services – a situation by no means confined to eighteenth-century Venice, unfortunately – they decided to withdraw their services and return to their home town. Santurini and Gasparini got to know of their intentions, and before the singers could leave, they were abducted from their lodgings, taken to the theatre by force and beaten up before they were able to escape. To crown all, one of the singers fell into a canal, and the ensuing court case might have gone badly for Santurini and Gasparini were it not for the fact that they had powerful friends. Santurini was able to call on these friends later, when he was due to surrender the lease of the theatre, but managed to hold on for literally years in the face of the perfectly legal protests of the actual owners.[19]

The life of a singer in Venice could hold its rewards, but it also had its seamier side, as we see from the above. It added a certain spice to life, as Evelyn discovered when he was in Venice:

> The diversions which chiefly took me up was [*sic*] three noble operas, where were excellent music and voice, the most celebrated of which was the famous Anna Rencia, whom we invited to a fish-dinner after four days in Lent, when they had given over at the theatre. Accompanied with an eunuch whom she brought with her, she entertained us with rare music, both of them singing to a

harpsichord. It growing late, a gentleman of Venice came for her, to show her the galleys, now ready to sail for Candia. This entertainment produced a second, given us by the English consul of the merchants, inviting us to his house, where he had the Genoese, the most celebrated base [sic] in Italy, who was once of the late opera-band. This diversion held us so late at night, that, conveying a gentle-woman who had supped with us to her gondola at the usual place of landing, we were shot at by two carbines from another gondola, in which were a noble Venetian and his courtezan unwilling to be disturbed, which made us run in and fetch other weapons, not knowing what the matter was, till we were informed of the danger we might incur by pursuing it farther.[20]

On the other hand, life could be made so difficult for singers, that it was virtually impossible for them to pursue their careers, as Freschot, writing in 1709, related in the story of a male singer who refused to go to sing at Piazzola, Marco Contarini's villa on the mainland.[21] Contarini was a famous philanthropist, founding an orphanage at Piazzola, where the girls sang, made lace, and even had a printing press. He then set up an opera house, to which people came free. He caused water to be taken right up to the upper tier of boxes to keep them cool, and both the libretto and the candle with which to read it were given free. Some people came and spent the night at Piazzola, and for this they paid, so some of the cost of mounting the operas was defrayed in this way. One can understand, therefore, why Contarini was displeased that a singer should actually decline to appear in one of his operas. The form of punishment the nobleman chose to impose was tantamount to banishment from Venice, which, although done with no public authority whatsoever, was highly effective. It virtually meant the ruin of the singer's fortunes, since Venice was, in Freschot's words: 'The Peru from whence musicians bring back great riches, especially when they are as highly thought of as that man was!'

Despite verbal and written pleas from the Venetian

nobility to Contarini and 'all the princes of Italy', he merely laughed and said that he had not the faintest idea what they were referring to. He even declared that he was put out that the man did not perform in Venice, since he enjoyed his voice as much as they did. Freschot went on: 'But the musician, well informed that the threats of persons of his [Contarini's] quality never fail to take their effect; seeing that his enemy gave him no word of pardon and would not forget his resentment, never risked visiting Venice again as long as Contarini was alive.'

According to Freschot, he even entered on the ecclesiastical state and took the tonsure, so as to live more securely within the protection of his new status. So much for the thwarted aims of powerful patrons and the careers of the hapless singers who fail to comply with their wishes.

Vivaldi had plenty of insights into the world of Venetian opera, and contacts too. There was Gasparini himself, as well as Santurini, whom Vivaldi may have met through the former, or simply known as a neighbour, since he lived in the parish of S. Martino also. Then there was Vivaldi's own father, who played the violin in the theatre, and the tenor Paita, with whom he was friendly. Paita, who was ranked quite highly by Caffi, sang in Albinoni's *Ciro* in the Carnival of 1709 at S. Cassiano, and possibly also his *Tradimento tradito* of the same year at the S. Angelo theatre, when he is described as Genoese. He also sang in the autumn of 1724 in *La Mariane*, which was a reprise of *Eccessi della gelosia* given two years earlier, both at the S. Angelo.[22]

Any one of these connections, or a combination of them, could well have led Vivaldi on to try his hand at opera. Then one must not underestimate his creative urge to write operatic music. He had a certain amount of scope for vocal writing at the Pietà, but it was not the same as writing for the stage. He also had the energy required not only to produce the music but, as he soon discovered, to act as impresario as well. Then there was the financial consideration. The Pietà alone was not sufficient to provide Vivaldi with the income he required. When he sold his works he no longer derived any benefice from them, and so despite the risk involved in putting on opera in Venice, there was also money to be made.

Even so, it is strange that his first opera commission came, not from Venice, but from Vicenza. It was there that his first opera, *Ottone in villa* (RV 729), had its first performance on 17 March 1713, at the Teatro delle Grazie. It was an undoubted success, and was revived on several occasions (especially in 1715 and 1729). The libretto was by Domenico Lalli (1677–1714), a curious character, with whom Vivaldi worked on subsequent occasions. Lalli was in fact a pseudonym, and his real name was Sebastiano Biancardi. He had left Naples under a cloud, accused of embezzlement from the Bank of the Annunciation where he was employed. He had arrived in Venice in 1710, and soon became known throughout Italy for his libretti, so much so that Alessandro Scarlatti, back in his native Naples, set his words to music. Possibly because they were almost of an age, Vivaldi seems to have had a certain affection for Lalli/Biancardi, at all events he collaborated with him on six libretti that have come down to us, and it may well have been more than a business arrangement. In Goldoni's account of his visit to Vivaldi in 1735, the composer's first reported reaction to the news that Goldoni had been commissioned to prepare the libretto was to express surprise and concern that Lalli appeared to have been dropped. Goldoni then made matters worse by his explanation that Lalli would continue to receive certain benefices, despite the fact that he was *fort âgé*. This can hardly have been calculated to please Vivaldi, who was already rather ill at ease at the prospect of working with a man who was considerably younger, and not one of his circle, but who, in dismissing Lalli so lightly, as being too old, might well dismiss Vivaldi – by implication – in the same way.

Shortly after the success of his first opera, Vivaldi made application for leave to his employers at the Pietà, which was granted on 30 April 1713: 'to be absent from this city for a month, to follow his virtuous occupations (*l'impiego delle sue vertuose applicazioni*), with an assurance to the Pia Congregazione that on his return he will carry out his usual duties with zeal and application'.[23] It is not clear why

Vivaldi requested this leave, though at one stage certain authorities envisaged a visit to Darmstadt, for which there is unfortunately no evidence. It is true that Vivaldi later had the title of *maestro di cappella* to Philip, Landgrave of Hesse-Darmstadt, but this refers to the period when the landgrave was resident in Mantua, and there was therefore no need for Vivaldi to have ever gone to Darmstadt. Besides which, at this point in his career, when he was launching himself as a composer of opera, it would have been unwise of Vivaldi to go far from Venice. It was his home town, and one of the main musical centres of Italy. After success at Vicenza, it was only natural that he should try for Venice, where he already had several ready-made connections with the opera world.

Vicenza is not far from Venice, and the news of Vivaldi's success doubtless soon reached his native city. Santurini, impresario of the S. Angelo theatre – possibly through the somewhat shadowy figure of Modotto – made Vivaldi an offer to secure the new talent for his theatre (though Santurini already knew Vivaldi), and the composer accepted, thus starting a working relationship with that theatre that was to survive, with various forays into other cities and countries, until Vivaldi's last datable opera *Feraspe* (RV 713) in 1739.

The opera world of Venice was given a rude shock on 7 November 1713, when the satirical poet Bartolomeo Dotti was mysteriously assassinated. Whatever the implications of the Dotti affair for the standard of morals in the theatre world, the fact remains that it was not the most gentlemanly of occupations. Indeed the whole history of the S. Angelo theatre and Santurini's involvement with it – and eventually that of Vivaldi as well – is not a particularly brilliant one.

Its history dated back to two years before Vivaldi's birth, on 2 October 1676, to be precise, when Francesco Santurini was granted the concession on a piece of land, belonging to the Marcello and Cappello families in the S. Angelo district, on which he wanted to build a theatre. Remo Giazotto has discovered the contract amongst the papers of the lawyer Bianconi,[24] and according to the contract the term of tenure was for seven years only, after which the owners would regain possession of their land, as well as the theatre newly built on it, and all the benefits it might bring. After the seven years had expired, however, Santurini turned a deaf ear to the private and legal approaches made to him to fulfil the terms of the contract. Not only did he fail to turn the property over to the Marcello and Cappello families, but he began legal proceedings against several notable members of the Venetian aristocracy, who had 'forgotten' to pay the subscriptions for their boxes. Among the famous names were those of Vendramin, Ottoboni, Grimani and a certain Ferigo Marcello.

Eventually, in 1710, however, the legal owners demanded the sequestration of the property, and among the papers relating to the case is a list of their debtors, including those of Santurini and Giovanni Battista, Vivaldi's father. In spite of this, Santurini was able to continue in possession of the theatre, and it was to these strange conditions that Vivaldi was a party when he made his Venetian debut as an opera composer at the theatre in the autumn season of 1714.

5. Impresario and Composer

Vivaldi's first Venetian opera was *Orlando finto pazzo* (RV 727), to a libretto by Grazio Braccioli, and not surprisingly it was given at the S. Angelo theatre, in the autumn of 1714. The manuscript is at Turin, as is that of his first opera, and the libretto bears a dedication to Karl, Margrave of Baden, Colonel of the Imperial Infantry. During this year Vivaldi also wrote an oratorio for the Pietà, *Moyses Deus Pharaonis* (RV 643), but unfortunately only the libretto has survived.

Alongside his activities as a composer of opera, Vivaldi had already established himself as an impresario as well, since his name appears on the libretto of the opera *Rodomonte sdegnato*, dated 20 January 1714. Since Braccioli wrote the libretto and Michelangelo Gasparini (probably the brother of Francesco) wrote the music, and Rosetti was the publisher, then Vivaldi can only have appeared in the capacity of impresario, and indeed this was the Venetian custom at the time.[1]

The next year saw another opera at the S. Angelo, *Nerone fatto Cesare* (RV 724), this time during Carnival. The libretto was by Matteo Noris, and several composers contributed music, including Vivaldi, who provided twelve of the arias. In this year he also wrote a dedication for the libretto of Predieri's opera *Luca Papirio*, which, as we have just seen, was a task usually performed by the impresario, and indeed we have the testimonies of other sources that this is in fact what Vivaldi continued to do for the rest of his career in Venice. Nor were his activities restricted to that city. We have his own written testimony to his activities in Rome, Verona and Mantua, and that of others for Florence, and there must almost certainly have been other instances of which no record has survived or been discovered to date, without even taking into account his ventures outside of Italy.

For the moment, however, we are concerned with his activities in Venice soon after his debut there. It was about this time that an architect and lover of music from Frankfurt-am-Main in Germany, Johann Friedrich von Uffenbach (b. 1687), arrived in Venice. In fact the exact date was 2 February 1715, at the height of the Carnival. One of his first concerns was to attend the opera, and he settled on the Ss. Giovanni e Paolo theatre, where there was a première of what was possibly Carlo Pollaroli's *Marisia deluso*, since two singers mentioned later by Uffenbach sang in it, namely the castrato Senesino and Diamantina Scarabelli.

The visitor was amazed by what he found inside the theatre. He took a seat in what we would call the stalls, but this in itself was a recent development, since hitherto there had usually been standing room only. It was not the seating – or lack of it – that surprised Uffenbach, however, but the noise, the unruly behaviour of the audience, and the constant barrage from the boxes above. Apples and orange peel, even pips, rained down from above, and a particularly revolting gob landed on his libretto.

On stage, however, he found remarkable decor and lighting, with stage machinery frequently in action. He particularly mentioned a temple of Saturn three storeys high, with staircase, balconies, columns and statues. The columns were made of glass, lit from inside, and when they moved they sparkled and glittered. In another scene there was a crowd of people with camels, trained elephants and horses. In spite of all this, Uffenbach was able to recall that the orchestra was excellent and well balanced.

Uffenbach quickly visited the opera again, this time on 4 February, therefore only his third night in Venice:

I went with some knowledgeable people to the S. Angelo theatre, which is somewhat smaller but also less expensive than the one I described earlier. This theatre, of which the impresario was the famous Vivaldi, who was also the composer of the opera, a very pretty opera and one that was very pleasant to watch [probably a repeat of *Orlando finto pazzo*], had less elaborate machinery than the other theatre; the orchestra was smaller, but no less worthy of being heard.[2]

This time Uffenbach was taking no chance. He had quickly learnt his lesson from his first experience of Venetian opera houses:

> For fear of being maltreated and covered with spittle as on the previous occasion, we took a box, not very expensive, and we had our revenge in behaving in relation to the people below as people had to us, a thing which previously would have seemed impossible to me . . . The singers were incomparable, and in no way were inferior to those of the large opera house, principally some women, among whom was a certain Fabri [Anna Maria Fabbri, playing the part of Origille] who distinguished herself as much by her art of musicianship as by her charm. Moreover, she was very pretty, at least on the stage.

What is perhaps even more important about this evening was the fact that Vivaldi himself conducted the orchestra, and towards the end of the opera played a solo accompaniment of the violin with a cadenza which he improvised, much to Uffenbach's amazement. Not so much at the fact that he played – Albinoni, for example, played on the violin in his opera *Griselda*, when it was given at the Teatro del Cocomero, Florence, in February 1703 – but as to how Vivaldi performed. Uffenbach then went on to describe Vivaldi's playing in such a way that we gain important facts about his technique at this time: 'He went with his fingers to within a hairsbreadth of the bridge, so that there was scarcely room for the passage of the bow, and on the four strings, with fugal treatment, incredibly quickly, surprising everyone. But I cannot say that it charmed me, for it was less pleasant to hear than skilfully performed.'

Uffenbach's description leads one to draw certain conclusions about Vivaldi's technique and the positions he was using at this time. For example, it had been thought that Vivaldi used only the ninth position, or eight with the extension of the fourth finger, and was much influenced by the technique of Locatelli, largely as a result of what Pincherle had to say about fingering and the positions in use in the early part of the eighteenth century.[3] Since Pincherle was himself a violinist, his words deserve respect. However, from the manuscript of the violin concerto for the Feast of the Tongue of St Anthony of Padua (RV 212), which is dated 1712, there are indications that Vivaldi was using the twelfth position at this time, simply from the requirements of the cadenza at the end of the third movement, which is written out in the Dresden manuscript. Locatelli at this time, one might note, was only seventeen. Indeed in his single-volume book on Vivaldi, published in 1955, Pincherle said quite clearly that Vivaldi was evolving towards the thirteenth, fourteenth and fifteenth positions, and that he was therefore scarcely indebted to Locatelli in the matter.[4] Certainly Vivaldi had an international reputation for being something of an innovator in violin technique, as we learn from Burney's *General history of music*:[5]

If acute and rapid tones are evil, Vivaldi has much of the sin to answer for. Geminiani used to claim the invention of the half-shift [second position] on the violin, and he probably first brought it to England; but the Italians ascribed it to Vivaldi; and others to the elder Mateis, who came hither in King William's time.

In some respects this only serves to complicate the chronological issue, since the 'elder Mateis' to whom Burney refers was Nicola Matteis, who arrived in London in 1672, whereas William of Orange, the King William (III) to whom he refers, did not become King of England until 1688. However, it proves that Vivaldi was felt to have been a daring innovator in the field of violin technique, and another reference to him, this time linking his name with that of Veracini, strengthens the view: 'Veracini and Vivaldi had the honour of being thought mad for attempting in their works and performances what many a sober gentleman has since done uncensured; but both these musicians happening to be gifted with more fancy and more hand than their neighbours, were thought insane.'[6]

In fact Vivaldi had a considerable following as a violinist abroad, and relatively quickly. One example, from England, will suffice. His Op. III, *L'estro armonico*, was published by Estienne Roger in Amsterdam in 1711, and on 16 October of that year the London *Post Man* informed the public that the work was now on sale. The concerto for violin RV 335 became so popular in England that it is still known today as 'The Cuckow'. Even when dealing with the category 'Cantata or narrative chamber music', Burney returned to the fact of Vivaldi's pre-eminence as a violin composer:

> Don Antonio Vivaldi merits a place among the candidates for fame in this species of composition: several are inserted in the collection mentioned above; but these, and all that I have seen elsewhere, are very common and quiet, notwithstanding he was so riotous in composing for violins. But he had been too long used to write for the voice, to treat it like an instrument.[7]

Burney's opinion about Vivaldi's vocal writing is open to discussion, as we shall see later, and Tartini's opinion, as it was delivered to Charles de Brosses, was that Vivaldi was a better composer of instrumental music than vocal music. Certainly people such as Uffenbach, who sought Vivaldi out in Venice, were drawn to him because he was first and foremost an instrumental composer, and a violin composer at that. Uffenbach again went to hear a Vivaldi opera on 19 February, this time *Agrippina* – or more accurately *Nerone fatto Cesare* (RV 724). On this occasion he disliked the plot, the set and the costumes. He only singled out one singer, Fabri, who played young Nero. Moreover, Vivaldi played only a little solo aria on the violin, much to his disappointment. However, he returned to the theatre to see the same opera, somewhere between 28 February and 3 March, and this time, although the costumes and decor still displeased him, his enthusiasm for the singing knew no bounds. Because he now wanted to meet Vivaldi, he went to yet another of his operas by 4 March, though he did not say which one. Uffenbach sent his servant to ask for an appointment with Vivaldi, and this is how he recorded the result in his diary:

Wednesday, 6 March 1715. After the meal, Vivaldi, the famous composer and violinist came to my lodging, since I had sent to his house several times to invite him. I spoke to him of some *concerti grossi* that I would have liked to have from him, and ordered them from him. Since he belonged to the circle of the Cantores [meaning church musicians] I had some bottles of wine brought, and he played some very difficult improvisations for me on the violin, quite inimitable. Close to I admired his art even more, and I realized from the evidence that he played extraordinarily difficult and varied things, but in a manner that was neither pleasant nor cantabile.

The last reference to Vivaldi in Uffenbach's diary at this point is very interesting, both for the way in which Vivaldi worked, and also for its glimpse of him as a person:

Saturday, 9 March 1715. In the afternoon Vivaldi came to my lodging and brought, as I had ordered them from him, ten *concerti grossi* which he said he had composed specially for me. I bought some of them. So as to let me hear them better he wanted to teach me to play them immediately, and to this end is to come to my lodging from time to time. So we began the very same day.

Could even a composer as swift as Vivaldi have composed ten *concerti grossi* between 6 and 9 March, and did Uffenbach really believe him? Possibly not, but there is no doubt that Vivaldi worked quickly, and that it was almost a necessity in those days. Albinoni, as we know, boasted of the speed with which he composed operas, and on one of the copies of Vivaldi's *Tito Manlio* is the information *Musica del Vivaldi fatta in 5 giorni* (Music by Vivaldi, composed in five days).

One of the ways in which a certain amount of time might be saved was the practice of writing an accompaniment in unison. One sees this at its 'worst' in such a work as the cantata *La Gloria e Imeneo*, along with other features that we might expect in a work composed entirely for an occasion – one might even call it 'speculative' composition – borrowings, for example. Marcello hit out at this in his *Il teatro alla moda*, and he had reason. Giovanni Porta's *Argippo* (Venice, 1717) bears the indication for almost every aria *primi violini colla parte* (first violins with the voice), and the flutes are often used in the same way. This is carried to the extreme in the second act, scene six '*aria di Mesio*', where instrumental bass and voice are in octaves throughout. Under the first measure the words *tutti con il basso* appear, so that the entire orchestra plays in unison with the voice.[8]

Then there is the point in the manuscript of Vivaldi's A major Violin concerto (RV 340) at which he began in disgust writing out the indications for the figured bass, but then gave up with the remark *per i coglioni*, which might be translated politely as 'for the dimwits'. One suddenly has a glimpse of the overworked professional musician who has little time for those who are not, in his opinion, of sufficient capability for the task in hand. Life, in such a situation, is simply too short.

For the Carnival of 1715–16 Vivaldi composed *La costanza trionfante degli amori e degli odii* (RV 706) an opera which, in one or other of its various manifestations, was to outlive him. The libretto was by Antonio Marchi, and the Venetian première was at the S. Moisè theatre. It was revived in Venice and Munich in 1718 under the name *Artabano rè de' Parti* (RV 701). It is possible that the opera given in Hamburg in 1719 *Die über Liebe und Hass siegende Beständigkeit oder Tigrane* (Ryom Anhang 57), which had music by F. Gasparini, F. Conti, G. M. Orlandini and Vivaldi, contained arias from *La costanza trionfante* and one from *Armida al campo d'Egitto* (RV 699). Kolneder, without any reference, mentions a performance in Mantua in 1720.[9] Certainly Vivaldi's arias were used again for Prague in 1726, when the opera was called *La tirannia gastigata* (Ryom

Anhang 55), and it changed titles yet again in 1731 when it was revived for the S. Angelo theatre, touched up by Galeazzi, as *L'odio vinto dalla costanza* (Ryom Anhang 51), and possibly at the same theatre in 1738. There was yet another reworking of *La costanza trionfante*, this time as *Doriclea* (RV 708), for Prague in 1732. The last record we have of it was at Bologna in 1742, at the Teatro Formagliari.

In the autumn of 1716 (though also placed in the spring of that year by some), Vivaldi produced *Arsilda regina di Ponto* (RV 700) at the S. Angelo theatre, and for the libretto Vivaldi turned to a work of his first collaborator, Domenico Lalli. There is a manuscript score in Turin. Vivaldi used the sinfonia again for *Il Teuzzone* (RV 736) for Mantua in 1719.

In the Carnival season of 1716–17 Vivaldi wrote *L'incoronazione di Dario* (RV 719), again for the S. Angelo theatre. Some regard the score, of which there is a manuscript at Turin, as one of his finest, but the libretto, by Adriano Morselli, as one of his worst. Morselli had been dead for some time when the opera was written, and it has been suggested that such a bad libretto could only have been chosen on the grounds of economy. Charles Burney, writing on 5 April 1725, said: 'Dario – a new opera – was originally written in 1716, for the theatre of St Angelo, at Venice, and set by the musical ecclesiastic, Don Antonio Vivaldi.'[10]

The year 1716 probably saw the publication of Vivaldi's Op. v – a collection of four sonatas for violin and continuo, with two trio sonatas – in Amsterdam, where by now Estienne Roger's daughter Jeanne had become associated with the firm. Op. v constitutes the second part of Op. ii, for the title page says so, and the sonatas are numbered 13 to 18, thus following on from 12, the last number in Op. ii.

It may also have been this year, or possibly the next, that Jeanne Roger published Op. vi, which is a collection of six violin concertos, and Op. vii, which is a series of twelve concertos, ten for violin and two for oboe. Peter Ryom only commits himself to the five-year period 1716–21 for the publication dates of these two collections.[11] After this the name of Jeanne Roger appears no more, nor does that of her father Estienne, and both were to die in 1722. Thereupon

Michel le Cène's name appears as the publisher, since he married another daughter of Estienne Roger, Françoise.

We see, then, how active Vivaldi very soon became, for in addition to his operatic ventures, both as composer and impresario, there was his publication of his instrumental works, and of course his work at the Pietà, which one tends at times to forget when he was so busy in other capacities. Whether he had been neglecting his duties there, or whether he had simply alienated a group of the governors – possibly even through nothing he had done so much as simply because of his reputation – in 1716 his appointment was not confirmed at the first ballot on 29 March, and was only done so at a second ballot held on 24 May, some two months later. In fact a closer look at the voting figures over the years reveals that whatever the world outside thought, there were others at the Pietà who were less convinced. The libretto of *Arsilda* of that year, for example, described Vivaldi as the 'celebro virtuoso di violino', and yet there were five or six of the governors who ignored this when it came to regulating the affairs of the Pietà.[12]

It may well have been for this reason that Vivaldi devoted his next work to the Pietà, or it may simply have been that everyone else in Venice was celebrating, and Vivaldi followed suit. There may also have been a genuine patriotic feeling there in his intentions. At all events, we are lucky that the manuscript has survived in this case, and we know much more about it. The work in question was the oratorio *Juditha triumphans* (RV 644), with words by Jacopo Cassetti. The manuscript is in Turin.

The work is interesting both from a historical and a musical point of view. The frontispiece announces that the work is 'sacrum militare oratorium hisce belli temporibus', and Venice in the shape of Judith, is seen triumphing over the Sultan, represented by Holofernes. The illusion of a restoration of Venice to her old splendour that the recapture of Corfu from the Turkish armies, and Prince Eugen's victory of Peterwaradin on 7 August gave to the Venetians was well reflected by Vivaldi in his work. There were several musical celebrations in Venice at this time, such as the soirée in the garden of the Imperial Ambassador on 27 August, when a *cantata a quattro voci* was performed, but unfortunately this exhilaration was short lived, with the blow of the Peace of Passarowitz on 17 February 1718, when Carlo Ruzzini represented Venice at the conference, and had to concede the Morea (the Peloponnesus), a decision that was confirmed on 21 July that same year. For a spell, however, it seemed in 1716 as if Venice had reversed the decline in her fortunes. Vivaldi revealed himself to be a convinced patriot on this occasion, as he did later in his preface to the opera *Adelaide*.

From a musical point of view the orchestration of *Juditha* poses a problem of nomenclature, since a wind instrument called *salmò* is designated. Pincherle was inclined to the view that what was intended was either a member of the shawm family, a clarinet, or a clarino trumpet, and left the matter there. As he himself admitted, the matter was somewhat 'embarrassing'.[13] However, we can go further than that. For one thing, Vivaldi was never vague about orchestration in such a context, and moreover in the same score of *Judith* he indicated two *clareni* at another point, so there must have been some distinction in his own mind. Since it is unlikely that *clareni* were trumpets, for they are designated *trombe*, the solution that seems to commend itself is that the *salmò* was a shawm, therefore a double reed; and the *claren* a clarinet or single reed. Moreover there are two concertos where Vivaldi specified the *salmò* again, namely RV 558 and 579 (*Concerto funebre*).

At all events, the scoring of *Juditha* was a very rich one, calling for recorders, oboes, *salmoe*, clarinets, bassoons, trumpets, timpani, mandoline, theorboes, viole d'amore, viole da gamba, first and second violins, viola, 'cello, double bass, two harpsichords and organ; in other words virtually everything that the resources of the Pietà could muster, and among the performers were doubtless many of Vivaldi's own pupils from that establishment.

Apart from the instrumental pupils taught by Vivaldi at the Pietà, and such amateurs who came to Venice from abroad – Uffenbach, for example – and Venetians such as

Vettor Delfino, to whom *La stravaganza* was dedicated, we know remarkably little and remarkably few names, but at this time, that is in 1717, a distinguished pupil came especially to Venice, at the expense of his ruler, the Prince Elector of Saxony. His name was Johann Georg Pisendel (1687–1755), and he was already a professional violinist of some standing when he arrived in Venice. There seems to have been some special kind of rapport between the two men at the outset, and Vivaldi's affection for Pisendel is shown in the concertos he dedicated to his pupil, reciprocated by the disciple's ornamentation of one of the master's adagios, the manuscript of which is still in Dresden.

History has left us an entirely different side of Vivaldi's relationship with Pisendel – indeed an entirely different side of Vivaldi himself. The two men were walking in the Piazza S. Marco one day, when Vivaldi suddenly interrupted the conversation and asked Pisendel in a low voice to go home with him at once. Naturally Pisendel was surprised, but once they were indoors, Vivaldi explained that he had noticed four constables who had been observing Pisendel. It is rather difficult for us to imagine that in a Venice which seemed so devoted to licence and pleasure the law could have been enforced with any degree of determination, or indeed that there were any very stringent laws at all. There were, however, and in some cases they were very rigidly observed, as we saw earlier on. There again, there was something in the Venetian character that loved intrigue, as witness the trompe l'oeil carving of the spy, representing Curiosity, by Francesco Pianta (*fi.* 1630–90) in the Scuola di S. Rocco, and the pistols concealed in a book in the Correr Museum.

In Pisendel's case it was simply a matter of mistaken identity, and the matter was soon sorted out. Nevertheless, we must recognize Vivaldi's concern for the well-being of his friend and student.[14]

Edward Wright, the English traveller who visited Venice in 1720–2, and who has left us such vivid accounts of life there, had some words to say about arrest:

In cases of arrests here (as in other cities of Italy) there is a band of men, the *Sbirri*, armed with long guns, commanded by a *Barigello* or captain, who makes detachments of them upon occasion. The persons of these are so odious to the people, not only the private men, but their captain too, that notwithstanding his pompous appearance, with a gold chain which he wears, it is scandalous to be seen speaking to him.

Though the excessive caution and jealousy of the governors here be such, that people sometimes are taken up upon slight information, and sometimes perhaps when they know not wherein they have offended, yet these cases do not often happen; and generally speaking, let their politicks and amours alone, and a man may live at Venice quiet and secure enough.[15]

In this Wright took a rather complacent, possibly somewhat naive view. There were, and still are to be seen, lions' mouths in the streets of Venice, into which secret denunciations might be placed. Although one might take the view that those who had nothing to hide had therefore nothing to fear, it was nevertheless inevitable, human nature being what it is, that mischief makers caused trouble for perfectly innocent citizens. There was a brutal side to the Venetian regime that is all too often and too easily ignored.

If Vivaldi in fact composed it, then it is possible that what is usually regarded as his Op. XIII, six sonatas for *musette* (bagpipe), *vielle* (hurdy gurdy), flute, oboe, or violin and continuo, known as *Il pastor fido*, was composed at this time, since there are several indications in the music itself that it was a relatively early work, despite its high opus number. It was published around 1737 by Boivin in Paris, where the *musette* enjoyed great popularity, particularly as a result of the aristocratic ladies' indulgence in mock rusticity.

In the autumn of 1717 Vivaldi returned to the S. Moisè with *Tieteberga* (RV 737) to a libretto by Antonio Maria Lucchini. At one stage a copy of the libretto was discovered with the date 1707 which would have made it Vivaldi's first surviving opera. However, closer inspection of the text revealed that it was in fact a second edition of the libretto, and the date of 1707 was a misprint for 1717. In the same year some of Vivaldi's music was included in *Il vinto trion-fante del vincitore* (Ryom Anhang 58), libretto by Marchi, given at the S. Angelo theatre, and during the ensuing Carnival, the altered version of *La costanza trionfante* known as *Artabano rè de' Parti* was given at the S. Moisè theatre. Then on 22 June 1718 Vivaldi produced the opera *Scanderbeg* (RV 732), to a libretto by Salvi, for the re-opening of the Teatro della Pergola in Florence. Unfortunately we only have the libretto of the opera, but the fact that Vivaldi was chosen for the occasion is a testimony to his standing at that time.

In the Carnival of 1718–19 *Armida al campo d'Egitto* (RV 699), to a libretto by Giovanni Palazzi, was given at the S. Moisè. Only the manuscript score of the first and third acts survives in Turin, but it was reworked as *Gli inganni per vendetta* (RV 720) for Vicenza in 1720, and was revived subsequently in Venice at the S. Margherita in 1731 (though with music by several composers), and at the S. Angelo in 1738. Vivaldi also used the sinfonia himself for *Ercole sul Termodonte* (RV 710) for Rome in 1723. Away from the theatre, Vivaldi wrote a serenata, *Le gare del dovere* (RV 688), in 1719, but only the libretto has survived, dedicated to Francesco Querini.

With the extension of Vivaldi's fame outside of Venice, it is not surprising that he received tempting offers of posts abroad. Between 1718–19 and 1725 only two of his operas were performed in Venice. Having only been an established opera composer for five years, however, it would possibly have been a mistake to abandon Venice entirely at this point in his career, and indeed the dedication to Francesco Querini just mentioned would indicate that Vivaldi still felt it wise to keep in touch with Venice. For these and other considerations, therefore, it seems highly likely that the three years Vivaldi was in the service of the Landgrave of Hesse-Darmstadt are to be placed next. The evidence for this three-year period comes from Vivaldi's own letter of 16 November 1737. The landgrave was in residence in Mantua from 1714 to 1735 (he had also been there in 1707–8), so that Vivaldi could easily accept the offer of a post from a foreign prince and yet be within easy distance of Venice. Certainly if he was in the landgrave's service at this time, then he returned to Venice on more than one occasion.

Scholars are divided on the exact dating of the three years. Peter Ryom is inclined to date them from 1719 to 1721, whereas R. Strohm suggests 1718–20.[16] We now know that *Il Teuzzone* (RV 736) to a libretto by Apostolo Zeno was given at Mantua in 1719, which would fit in with this three-year period. Be that as it may, a new opera, *La verità in cimento* (RV 739), to a libretto by Giovanni Palazzi and Domenico Lalli, was given at the S. Angelo theatre in Venice in the autumn of 1720. The manuscript score is in Turin. The following Carnival (1721), *Filippo rè di Macedonia* (RV 715) was also given at the S. Angelo. The libretto is by Domenico Lalli, but Vivaldi wrote only the third act of the music, and Benvenuti or Giuseppe Boniventi provided the rest of it. Boniventi was a Venetian-born composer employed as *maestro di cappella* by the Duke of Mantua in 1707, and by the Margrave of Baden-Durlach from 1712 to 1721.

It is more than likely that Vivaldi went back to Venice for performances whenever possible. We have the witness of his own letters for this, and also that of Edward Wright, who saw Vivaldi take part in operatic performances in Venice whilst he was there between 1720 and 1722: 'It is very usual there to see priests playing in the orchestra; the famous Vivaldi (whom they call the Prete Rosso) very well known among us by his concertoes [sic], was a topping man among them.' This not only shows that Vivaldi's fame was well established in England – certainly by the time Wright came to publish his account in 1730 – but also that Vivaldi was in Venice at this time. Walsh had published some of Op. IV (*La stravaganza*) some time after 1720, though only five of the original twelve – i.e. nos. 1, 2, 4, 9 and 11 – of those that had appeared in the Amsterdam edition of *c.* 1712–14, along with another concerto (RV 291), making up the six, that did not appear in the Amsterdam edition. On the continent the first seven of the works given opus numbers by Vivaldi himself had probably been published by 1717, certainly by 1721 at the latest.

Wright's account is all the more precious because he actually saw Vivaldi in action, and therefore is one of the few eye-witnesses, certainly in the English language, to have come down to us. He had seen some opera on the way to Venice, at Reggio, and even though Faustina herself was singing, he said that the audience paid no more attention than they would to a sermon. He shows us the delight the Venetians have in Carnival and the opera: 'The only time for operas at Venice is the Carnaval [*sic*], or perhaps sometimes about the Ascension. Those times of masking are the dear delight of the Venetians; and the approach of the Carnaval seems to be to them, as the approach of the sun to the Polar nations after their half year's night.'[17]

He also gives us an account of the major theatres in Venice:

> There are more theatres in Venice than in any city of Italy that I have heard of: there are seven for operas, besides others for comedies, etc. There were operas in three of them, when we were there. The theatres are the properties of several noblemen. That of S. John Chrysostom [S. Giovanni Grisostomo] belongs to one of the Grimani families: and the same family has likewise two other theatres, S. Samuel, and S. John-and-S. Paul [Ss. Giovanni e Paolo], the greatest in Venice. The theatres take their names from the neighbouring churches, and though they are in general the property of such and such noblemen, yet others have boxes as their inheritance, purchased of the general proprietor of the theatre; and of these they keep the keys themselves. But before you can come at your box, there is somewhat to be paid (about 1s. 6d. English) for entrance into the theatre.[18]

In the margin Wright adds the S. Angelo, S. Moisè, S. Fantin, S. Cassiano and S. Luca theatres, the last for comedies. So far this more or less corroborates the details available from other sources, and from what follows we learn that the general standard of behaviour had not improved very appreciably, though there is the intimation that at least some of the people went to listen to the music – or at least some of it:

There are no open galleries, as in London, but the whole from bottom to top is all divided into boxes, which one with another will contain about six persons each. They have a scandalous custom there, of spitting out of the upper boxes (as well as throwing parings of apples or oranges, etc.) upon the company in the pit, (a practice frequent enough here,) which they do at random, without any regard where it falls; though it sometimes happens upon some of the best quality; who, though they have boxes of their own, will often come into the pit, either for the better seeing of the company, or sometimes to be nearer the stage, for the better hearing some favourite songs.

One wonders whether Wright himself was all that interested in going to the opera simply for the performance, for he seems to have expected that it would have been as much a social event as an artistic one, and that the audience was there to be seen, as well as see.

Indeed as to seeing the company in the Venetian theatres there is not much entertainment in that; for, not a face is to be seen; but the chief amusement is, to find out, through the disguise of the masque, who such and such a one is, which those that are accustomed to the place can very readily do. Those that make use of books [libretti] to go along with the performance, have commonly wax-candles in their hands; which are frequently put out by favours from above.

As with almost all the visitors to Venice, it was the stage machinery that caused Wright to marvel:

They are very dextrous at managing the machinery of their opera. In one of them Nero presents Tiridates King of Armenia with a Roman show, of which himself makes a part. The Emperor with the Empress appear in a triumphal chariot, drawn by an elephant. The head, trunk, and eyes of the great beast move as if alive, and Tiridates believes he is so. When all of a sudden, as soon as the Emperor and Empress are dismounted and have taken their seats, the triumphal chariot is transformed into an amphitheatre, and filled with spectators. The elephant falls all in pieces, and out of his belly come a great number of gladiators, armed with bucklers, which were so many parts of the elephant's sides, so that he seems in a moment to be transformed into a company of armed men, who make a skirmish, all in time to the musick.

Pity the poor composer who had to provide the music for this choreographic skirmish. There was yet more to come in the way of splendour, however:

We saw another piece of machinery. In a vast hall were represented the four elements, emblematically, in pictures; these opening themselves, formed two palaces, those of Love and Hymen, these again were transformed in the palace (or temple) of Mars, all surrounded with weapons of war. This scene was so finely imagined, and the lights so well disposed, that I think it was the most entertaining sight I ever saw upon a stage.[19]

After 1721, however, there is no evidence of any operatic activity by Vivaldi in Venice until the autumn of 1725. In the meantime he put on operas in Mantua, Vicenza, Milan and Rome, so his name was certainly now well known throughout northern Italy, and even in Rome itself. It may, therefore, have been jealousy, or family pride, that inspired the publication of a book in 1720, *Il teatro alla moda*, which is one of the most amusing satires on Venetian opera that has come down to us.

Despite the anonymity of the author, it eventually became known, as these things have a habit of becoming known, that the author was, in fact, Benedetto Marcello, the son of

Agostino Marcello and Paolina Cappello, and therefore directly involved in the affair of the S. Angelo theatre. Apostolo Zeno, for example, writing to Antonio Francesco Marmi from Vienna on 2 April 1721, said: 'The *Teatro alla Moda* by Signor Benedetto Marcello, brother of Alessandro, is a delightful satire!'

G. F. Malipiero came across a copy of the original edition, annotated in such a way that the enigma of the frontispiece was solved once and for all. The key, which Malipiero published in 1930, was borne out by another work, *Li diavoli in maschera*, which bears the slightly later date of 1726.[20]

Marcello's motive in writing his satire against Vivaldi is worth looking at in closer detail, because it has considerable bearing on both his own situation and that of Vivaldi and his associates, as well as on society in Venice as its independence ebbed away. In the first place, Marcello was a *dilettante*, much as Albinoni was, and therefore for him his music had not been made a matter of economic expediency as it was, by implication, for Vivaldi. On the other hand, Marcello did not write from any detached point of view, or from Olympian heights. He fired some very well aimed darts at Vivaldi and his entourage on the frontispiece, and then in the body of the work took to task, with biting irony, the world of Venetian opera. He was in love with the singer Rosanna Scalfi, whom he secretly married in 1728, so he had plenty of inside information with which to arm himself.

The frontispiece announces, then, that it is a:

sure way, and easily understood, of executing Italian operas in music in the modern usage. In which are given useful and necessary advertisements to poets, composers of music, musicians of the one, and the other, sex, impresarios, players, mechanics and scene painters, comics, dressers, valets, extras, prompters, copyists, protectors, and mothers of virtuosi, and other persons belonging to the theatre. Dedicated by the book's author to the composer of it.[21]

There then follows an illustration of a barge being rowed

112

by a man standing up with two oars. On the prow is a bear in wig and coat, carrying a flag over one shoulder, and standing on a heap of flour sacks. The boat's cargo also consists of a barrel of oil and a pile of sticks. Standing on the tiller is an angel with a violin, wearing a priest's hat. Underneath is a legend purporting to give details of publication and place of sale: 'Stampato ne' Borghi di Belisania per Aldiviva licante; all' insegna dell'Orso in Peata. Si vende nella strada del Corallo alla porta del palazzo d'Orlando.' Finally, there is the promise that the work will be reprinted each year with new editions – a promise which, in the event, was not made good.

It is the legend underneath the illustration which, according to the annotations discovered by Malipiero, leaves no room at all for doubt as to whom the author refers. Borghi di Belisania refers to two female singers from Bologna, Signora Caterina Borghi who sang at S. Moisè and Signora Cecilia Belisani, who sang at the S. Angelo theatre. Aldiviva is an anagram of the name Vivaldi, and Licante refers to Caterina Teresa Cantelli, another singer from Bologna, at the S. Moisè theatre. *Orso* (a bear) *in peata* (a kind of boat) refers to both Orsatto or Orsatti the impresario of the S. Moisè theatre – the flour, oil and wood being the fruits of his dishonest dealing, and the flag over his shoulder the flag that appeared on the tickets of the S. Moisè theatre – and the boat to the impresario of the S. Angelo theatre Modotto, who was once the owner of such a boat, and who now rows – contrary to usage – with two oars.

The angel symbolizes both the S. Angelo theatre and Vivaldi himself, who directs the whole procedure from the tiller, beating time with his foot and at the same time playing the violin, which in Italian is a play on words meaning to deceive. Since Modotto has remained a somewhat shadowy figure, it may be that this name was used as an alias by Vivaldi in his business dealings. Anna Maria Strada was certainly a real personage, however, as was Corallo – the stage name of Antonio Laurenti – both singers at the S. Angelo theatre. Giovanni Porta, who was also on the staff of the Pietà, was the composer of the first opera of the season at the S. Giovanni Grisostomo theatre; Palazzi a poet who provided the libretto for the first opera at the S. Angelo; and Orlandini was Giuseppe Maria Orlando, the composer of the third opera, which we know to have been *Paride*, to a libretto by Francesco Muazzo, at the S. Giovanni Grisostomo theatre.[22] He was also an impresario and a friend of Vivaldi.

The temptation to quote from Marcello's satire is enormous, but one must restrict oneself to a few select passages. In the section, for example, for composers we read:

It will be no bad thing that the composer has been for many years a violinist or viola player, and even a copyist for some famous composer, whose originals he has kept ...

Before starting his opera he will visit all the stars, promising them parts that match their genius, in other words arias without bass, forlanes, rigaudons, etc., all with violins, bears and extras in unison.

He will take care not to read the opera in its entirety for fear of becoming confused; he will compose rather line by line ...

He will then take care that the arias, right to the end, are in turn happy and sad, with no reference whatsoever to the words, the nature and circumstances of the scene.

There are similarly biting satirical recommendations to the singers, and those to the male singers are particularly interesting, since there may well be a reference in them to a further member of Vivaldi's circle, the tenor Giovanni Paita described as a singer of rank at the S. Angelo:

If he is on stage with another character, who addresses him in the play, or sings an aria, he will greet the masks in the boxes, smile at the musicians, the extras, etc., so that the public understand quite clearly that it is he, Signor Alipio Forconi, castrato, and not Prince Zoroaster that he is supposed to be representing.

There was a character Prince Zoroaster in the opera

Semiramide, with music by C. F. Pollarolo, which was given at the S. Giovanni Grisostomo theatre in Venice in 1714, and the role was sung by Giovanni Paita. *Forcone* means, amongst other things, a pitchfork, and Paita might suggest some connection with *paglia*, straw. Marcello particularly disliked castrati, and therefore would hardly have been likely to restrain himself, especially since Paita was of Vivaldi's circle. There is the problem that there is a world of difference between tenor and castrato, though if this is yet another reflection on the sound Paita produced – in Marcello's opinion – then the confusion on his part may have been deliberate.

John George Keysler, who visited Venice in 1729–30, felt much the same about castrati, and the problems created by the conventions of Italian opera, and that of Venice in particular:

Care has been taken that none of these famous singers should be disfigured with a beard; however, their smooth faces with their shrill and effeminate voice seem to be something out of character, when they make their appearance on the stage like warlike heroes, animating their troops to second their bravery. But we must observe that operas are not calculated to please the judgment, but to tickle the ear; so that propriety of characters is as little to be expected in these pieces, as sublime and poetical language. The music of the airs is often composed before the words; and the author is sometimes obliged in certain syllables pointed out to him, to introduce a word which has the vowels *e* or *a*; those vowels being the two sounds on which a good voice can best display its strength and variety of modulations.

It is certain that no language is so well adapted to music as the Italian, on account of its using so many vowels in proportion to the number of consonants; for even all the substantives terminate in a vowel in that harmonious language.[23]

Although Caffi strongly denied this,[24] there was a firm

tradition that Marcello's satirical attention was also turned towards another Venetian composer, Antonio Lotti (1666–1740), whose career is interesting for the parallels it presents with that of Vivaldi, especially since it is more than likely that they knew each other. Although Lotti's father, Matteo, was *maestro di cappella* to the Court of Hanover, Antonio was probably born in Venice, and he certainly died there. In fact he only left it once, to go to Dresden for a period of three years from 1717–20. After being a pupil of Legrenzi, he joined the staff of S. Marco at the age of twenty-one (1687), was second organist within five years (1682), and was appointed first organist for life in 1704 at the age of thirty-eight. He was also a *maestro* at the Incurabili, and a founder member of the *Sovvegno di S. Cecilia*.

The application he made to go to Dresden is extant, since he had to have government permission to leave the country, and his wife – the famous singer Santa Stella – went with him. However, on his return from Dresden he gave up writing for the theatre, and devoted himself to church music, and in 1736 became *maestro di cappella* at S. Marco. Amongst his pupils the most famous were Bassani, Gasparini, Pescetti, Galuppi, Alberti, and Benedetto Marcello. Lotti published his Op. I, *Duetti, terzetti e madrigali* in Venice with Bortoli, with whom Vivaldi published, in 1705. The work was dedicated to the Emperor Joseph I, and was well received. However, a letter was sent to the academy in Bologna, signed simply by *Un Accademico Filarmonico*, in which Lotti's work was severely criticized. As a result he never published another work.

It seems amazing that a young man of nineteen, as Benedetto Marcello was in 1705, should have dared attack in this way a man who was not only his teacher, but also remarkably well thought of at that time for both his theatrical and ecclesiastical music. Moreover, Caffi maintained that Marcello did not become a member of the Philharmonic Academy of Bologna until December 1712 – i.e. some seven years after the appearance of the letter. Caffi's reasoning is that, since he was not then a member of the academy, Marcello could not have been the author of the letter. The flaw in this argument is that if the letter were sent anonymously, it is impossible to say categorically who may or may not have been its author. From subsequent developments – e.g. the publication of *Il teatro alla moda* – suffice it to say that Marcello would at least have been capable of writing such a letter. In any case, whether he was the author or not, the end product was the same, namely that Lotti stopped publishing his music.

The dating of *Il teatro alla moda* may possibly have some bearing on the placing of the period of Vivaldi's three-year residence in the service of the Prince of Hesse-Darmstadt. As we have already seen, the prince was resident in Mantua between 1714 and 1735. There are no traces in the Pietà archives of any payment to Vivaldi between 1718 and 2 July 1723, and since Vivaldi was in Rome for the Carnival season of that year, this last date is a *terminus ad quem* for the Mantua period. Then as we have already seen, only two operas, *La verità in cimento* (autumn 1720) and *Filippo rè di Macedonia* (Carnival, 1721) were given in Venice between 1718–19 and 1725, whereas at least six, and possibly seven operas were given at Mantua, Vicenza, Milan and Rome during this same period. Then the title of *Maestro di Capella di Camera* to the Prince of Hesse-Darmstadt was first used by Vivaldi in the libretto of *La verità in cimento* in 1720, and if the date of *Il teatro alla moda* is, as on the annotated copy discovered by Malipiero, December 1720, then this would seem to corroborate the culmination of Vivaldi's career at Mantua, rather than its initiation, for such a work would hardly have improved Vivaldi's chances of being appointed – in fact the very opposite – and the continuing success of the composer after his appointment to Mantua is far more likely to have excited Marcello's wrath than prior to it. His opera *La Candace* (RV 704), given during the Carnival in 1720 at the Teatro Arciducale in Mantua, would therefore be a leaving present before his return to Venice. At the same period another opera, *Gli inganni per vendetta* (RV 720) a reworking of *Armida*, was given at the Teatro delle Grazie in Vicenza, where his first opera may well have been performed. The next year, on

26 August, the opera *Silvia* (RV 734), described as a pastorale, was performed at the Teatro Ducale in Milan, but we know little about it. The score has not survived.

Vivaldi had now set his sights on Rome. It is possible that his opera *Tito Manlio* (RV 738 and Anhang 56) was performed there in 1720 at the Teatro della Pace, but almost certainly without Vivaldi's being present. It had also been given in Mantua in 1719. For the time being the doubt must remain, however. We have Vivaldi's own testimony in the letter of 16 November 1737 to the Marquis Bentivoglio, in which he says that he spent three Carnival seasons at Rome for the opera. Two of these were certainly the seasons of 1723 and 1724, but the third has not been identified. If he went for the 1722 season, then one of the last specific references to him in Venice before he left for Rome is in April 1722, when his music was performed at the dinner party given by Marquis Pietro Martinengo for Princess Sultzbach, future bride of the Prince of Piedmont.[25] According to the record, 'a beautiful serenade was heard and two concerti with violins and oboes, works of Monsignor Vivaldi'. There is no definite indication that Vivaldi himself conducted on this occasion, though for such an important celebration it is quite likely that he did.

Then he wrote another oratorio, *L'adorazione delli tre re magi al Bambino Gesù* (RV 645), which was given at Milan in 1722, but only the libretto has survived. Assuming that this was a Christmas or Epiphany piece from its title, then Vivaldi could easily have produced it on his way from Venice to Rome at the end of 1722 or in the first days of 1723.

6. Rome and beyond

The attraction of Rome as a centre for artists where patronage was apparently to be had in abundance must have persuaded Vivaldi to try his luck there also. The pope was a temporal ruler, as well as spiritual head of the Church, and the splendour and magnificence of a secular monarchy was merged with that appropriate to Christ's Vicar on Earth. The city had, however, shrunk by comparison with its former dimensions, and Evelyn, writing in 1645, said that whereas previously it had been fifty miles in circumference, it was by then less than thirteen.

And yet Rome continued to exercise her fascination. Queen Christina of Sweden, for example, after her abdication, gravitated to Rome, and although she died in straitened circumstances in 1689, had nevertheless no less a person than Alessandro Scarlatti as her *maestro di cappella*. His son Domenico had been to Venice, where he made friends with Handel, and although we do not know that he met Vivaldi, he almost certainly met Gasparini. When Gasparini himself decided to leave Venice for Rome in 1713, it must have seemed to Vivaldi that it was worth his while taking the same road, and the example of Gasparini's successful career, both as a church musician and opera composer, after similar occupations in Venice, might well have led Vivaldi to believe that he could probably do likewise.

Although posterity has put a very different value on the relative worth of Gasparini and Vivaldi, in their own day their standing must have seemed very different. Gasparini had, after all, been *maestro di coro* at the Pietà in Venice, whereas Vivaldi had officially only been a string teacher, even if he was recognized as the person best fitted to stand in for Gasparini in his absences. Although he was known as a composer, Vivaldi was nevertheless regarded as more of a violin virtuoso when he travelled to Rome. Indeed from his own letter we know that it was for his skill as a violinist that the pope of the day was interested in him, not as a potential *maestro di cappella* or prospective candidate for some official musical appointment.

Once again, it may well have been Vivaldi's personality that stood in the way of his advancement. We do not know that he actually sought out any post whilst he was in Rome, whether it be from the pope himself or one of the several cardinals who patronized the arts. Nevertheless, the fact that he went there – according to his own account – for three opera seasons, and that he by no means went unrecognized in the city, would seem to indicate that in spite of his reputation, he did not commend himself automatically to the sort of persons who would have been in a position to offer him employment and who, in respect of other musicians, often offered it without being asked.

Of course there was also the fact that he was a priest, which was his undoing when it came to a confrontation with the papal authorities some fifteen years later in Ferrara, and it is possible that in Rome Vivaldi became aware that it was one thing to be a visiting celebrity from Venice, but quite another matter if he were to be a priest, technically bound to the obedience of his ordinary, and yet exercising the full-time profession of impresario, composer and violinist under the very nose of the church authorities.

But Vivaldi was nothing if not enterprising, and if any of these considerations presented themselves to him, he nonetheless determined to take the risk, and so he embarked on yet another stage in his career. He probably left Venice, then, at the end of 1722 or early 1723 for Rome, and his opera *Ercole sul Termodonte*, to a libretto by Bussani, was given on 23 January at the Teatro Capranica there. Seven arias from it are in the Paris Conservatoire, and there are other manuscripts in Münster, Turin and Lund. In the Vatican Library is the striking caricature by Pier Leone Ghezzi with the legend *Il prete rosso compositore di musica che fece l'opera a Capranica del 1723* (the red priest, composer, who made the opera at Capranica in 1723). In fact this is the only

120

authenticated likeness we have of the composer. The next year, during the carnival, he mounted two operas, again at the Capranica. The first was *Il Giustino* (RV 717) to a libretto by Nicolò Berengani, and the second *La virtù trionfante dell'amore e dell'odio ovvero Il Tigrane* (RV 740),to a libretto by Francesco Silvani. The scores of both operas are in Turin, though in fact Vivaldi wrote only the second act of the second opera. The first act is by Benedetto Micheli, and the third by N. Romaldi.

This visit to Rome was highly successful from both a musical and a social point of view. With regard to the first, when J. J. Quantz arrived in Rome on 11 July 1724, he wrote: 'What came most frequently to my ears was the Lombard style. Vivaldi had just brought it to Rome along with his operas and had, with that style, captivated the Romans to such a degree that it was almost as if they would no longer bear what was not composed in that style.'[1] What Quantz particularly noted was the reversal of the rhythmic figure of a dotted quaver followed by a semiquaver, or what we would call a Scotch snap. Vivaldi had not invented it, but he certainly established it.

Then as far as social recognition was concerned, Vivaldi was fêted by the Venetian Ambassador to Rome, as well as by Prince Colonna, for which occasion Vivaldi wrote and performed special music, and then finally by the pope himself. There is a question as to which pope it was, since Innocent XIII died in March 1724, after a long illness, towards the end of which he received no one. Benedict XIII succeeded him in May, and it may well have been this pope who expressed a desire to hear the famous red priest.

During Vivaldi's sequence of seasons in Rome the Congregation of the Pietà decided, on 2 July 1723, that he was to provide two concertos a month:

> with the obligation to be present in person, when he is in Venice, at least three or four times for each concerto, to instruct the girls in the way to play them well ... in consequence of which the governors wish to give a very strong command to the *maestro di coro* to be present always

when the Reverend Vivaldi comes to instruct the girls, so that they are kept under appropriate discipline.[2]

According to Denis Arnold, on 2 August 1723 he was appointed *maestro de' concerti*, though possibly only on a temporary and/or part-time basis.[3] It now seems, therefore, that Vivaldi was of sufficient stature to be able to bestow his talents on the Pietà when it was convenient for him to do so, and the minute of 2 July quoted above tacitly recognizes the fact. His genius was at a premium, and he was probably induced to exploit it to the full. Vivaldi's name only appears infrequently in the accounts of the Pietà during 1724 and 1725, however, and then they cease completely for ten years.

Again we must turn to Vivaldi's own testimony for information on the matter. In the letter of 16 November 1737 he stated that 'fourteen years ago' he went to a good many European cities. In other words, his disappearance from the account books of the Pietà more or less coincides with the start of a long period of travel abroad. There is a discrepancy of about a year in fact, since if Vivaldi's fourteen years are to be taken literally from November 1737, this would take us back to November 1723, but it is not a crucial factor, and he could well have made a mistake. In any case, Vivaldi was frequently in Venice during these ten years, so he was not looking back on those fourteen years as having been an exile from his native city by any means. It is more than likely that, having had a success in Rome, he resolved to try his luck further afield, whilst still keeping a foothold in Venice, and when writing the letter in 1737 he was looking back to a period of which Rome had seemed, in retrospect, to have been the logical starting point.

Vivaldi may have been contemplating a visit to the French Court, and as a means of facilitating his entrée, he wrote the cantata entitled *La Gloria e Imeneo* (RV 687), probably in 1725, from references in the text,[4] for the marriage of the fifteen-year-old Louis XV to the Polish princess Maria Leczinska on 15 August that year. There is no record of that cantata's ever having been performed, either in Venice or Paris, and in it Vivaldi indulges in a certain amount of self-plagiarism. For example, there are two arias which are found in other operas by Vivaldi, and two distinct borrowings from concertos. It has been suggested that Vivaldi's friendship with the Abbé de Pomponne was responsible for the writing of this work, and if Vivaldi were contemplating a visit to France, then such an offering would have been of great utility. On the other hand, the writing of the mezzo part (the work is scored for soprano and mezzo-soprano) is vocally taxing and would seem to suggest that Vivaldi may have had a castrato in mind. Castrati were accepted, indeed admired in Venice and in Italy generally, but were usually anathema in France, certainly by this time, which might indicate that unless Vivaldi were totally ignorant of this fact, he could never have expected the work to have been performed at the French Court.

There were of course plenty of precedents for Italian artists working in France. When Louis XIV married Maria Theresa, Infanta of Spain, in 1660, Cardinal Mazarin commissioned Gaspare Vigarani (1586–1663) to construct a theatre in the Tuileries, and asked the Signoria of Venice to send Cavalli to compose the opera. In the event Cavalli was permitted to take with him two singers, the soprano Giovanni Calegari and the tenor Giannagostino (or Giovanni) Poncelli. The opera he began work on was *Ercole amante*, but since the opening of the theatre was delayed, his *Xerse*, which had already been given in Venice in 1654, was given on 22 November 1660 in the Grande Galerie of the Louvre, with ballets by Lully. *Ercole amante* was not given until February 1662, after the death of Mazarin, and then with only relative success, and Cavalli returned to Venice.

Then Benedetto Vinaccesi, second organist at S. Marco, and native of Brescia, was commissioned by the French Ambassador in Venice to write a *serenata a quattro voci*, *Sfoghi di giubilo*, for the birth of Louis XIV's great-grandson Louis, Duke of Brittany, in 1704. For his pains Vinaccesi was made a chevalier, though the child only lived a few months.[5] Vinaccesi was also *maestro di coro* at the Ospedaletto, and is generally credited with having introduced the

123

minuet into sonatas for the first time with his Op. I (*Suonate a tre*, Sala 1687).

But if Vivaldi's *La Gloria e Imeneo* has the air of having been put together in something of a hurry, other music that appeared at that time certainly did not. His Op. VIII, *Il cimento dell'armonia e dell'inventione*, had been written by this time, and the twelve concertos that comprise it were published by Michel le Cène in Amsterdam in 1725. They were dedicated to Count Wenceslas Morzin, a Bohemian nobleman, and Vivaldi indicates in the dedication that Morzin had heard at least some of the concertos some time before their publication:

When I consider the many years during which I enjoyed the honourable distinction of acting as Your Highness's maestro in Italy, I blush to think that I have not yet given a proof of my deep veneration. So I decided to have this volume printed, so as to lay it at the feet of Your Highness most humbly. I beseech you not to be surprised if Your Highness should find among these few feeble concertos the Four Seasons which, with your noble goodness, Your Highness has looked on indulgently for so long ... I am therefore certain that, although they are the same concertos, they will seem as new to Your Highness.

In view of the fact that Op. VIII includes as its first four concertos the *Four seasons*, which are probably Vivaldi's best known works of all time, one ought to consider them in detail here, along with the whole question of named works and Vivaldi's programme music. Of the published collections, Op. III has the title *L'estro armonico* (*The harmonic inspiration*); Op. IV *La stravaganza* (*The extraordinary*); Op. VIII *Il cimento dell'armonia e dell'inventione* (*The contest between harmony and invention*); Op. IX *La cetra* (*The lyre*) and Op. XIII *Il pastor fido* (*The faithful shepherd*).

In addition there are several works that have individual titles, but by no means all of them emanate from the composer's hand. Basically one might say that they fall into four main groups. The first, one might take as being works

124

composed for special occasions, or those bearing special dedications. Of these the most notable are the one marked *Per la solennità della S. Lingua di S. Antonio in Padua* 1712 (RV 212) and the two marked *Per la solennità di S. Lorenzo* (RV 286 and 556). Then there are two concertos for violin and double orchestra (RV 581 and 582) marked *Per la S.S. ma Assiontione di M(aria) V(ergine)*, a concerto for violin and orchestra (RV 270) marked *Per il natale* (also called *Il riposo*), and a sonata (RV 130) and a sinfonia (RV 169) both marked *Al Santo Sepolcro*. These are obviously intended for the appropriate feasts of the liturgical year. As far as special dedications are concerned, no fewer than five sonatas and six concertos are dedicated to the violinist Pisendel, which is an eloquent testimony to the regard in which he was held by Vivaldi. There is also a joke dedication to Pisendel, for concerto RV 574, *P[er] S.A.S.I.S.P.G.M.D.G.S.M.B.* which, according to Pincherle, stands for His Serene Highness the Signor Pisendel Giorgio ... Surprisingly it is not a solo violin concerto on this occasion, but is additionally scored for two *trombon da caccia*, two oboes, bassoon and orchestra. Another concerto with wind instruments (RB 577) was intended for the Dresden orchestra, and another (RV 568), according to Rinaldi,[6] was played by the girls of the Pietà, from its inscription. Another joke of a different kind, which may well have been a compliment to specific instrumentalists who are not designated is RV 544, *Il Proteo, o sia il mondo al rovescio* (*Proteus, or the world turned upside down*), a concerto for violin, 'cello, orchestra and basso continuo. It also exists in another version (RV 572) for two flutes, two oboes, violin, 'cello, harpsichord, orchestra and basso continuo. The joke here lies in the fact that in RV 544 the solo violin part is written in tenor and bass clefs, whereas the 'cello part is written in the treble clef. The score also says that the solo violin may play the 'cello solos, and vice versa.

A second group have titles associated with them which are not necessarily significant of anything in themselves, but more for a general atmosphere imparted by the work as a whole, such as the concertos known as *La pastorella* (RV 95), *Madrigalesco* (RV 129), *Alla rustica* (RV 151) and several of the violin concertos – *Il piacere* (RV 180), *Il sospetto* (RV 199), *L'inquietudine* (RV 234), *L'amoroso* (RV 271), *Il favorito* (RV 277), and *Il ritiro* (RV 256, 294 & 294a). Possibly to this group should be added RV 208, *Grosso Mogul* and RV 366, *Il carbonelli*, about which Ryom raises a doubt, however.

A third group have titles that obviously have suggested something quite specific, such as *The cuckow* (RV 335), and two works with the title of *Il gardellino* (*The goldfinch*), RV 90, which is a concerto for flute or violin, oboe or violin, violin, bassoon or 'cello, orchestra and basso continuo, and RV 428, which is a closely related concerto for recorder, orchestra and basso continuo from Op. x (no. 3). Then there is *Concerto funebre* (RV 579) and the various works where the violin is thought of either in terms of horn figures, as in *Il cornetto da posta* (RV 363), or trumpet figures – *violine in tromba* – which occurs in RV 221, 311 and 313, or even the strange string instrument (despite its name) known as *tromba marina* (RV 558). Presumably also the indication *conca* on RV 163 is intended to evoke the sound of a conch shell with its repeated descending octaves with which the concerto opens.

This then leaves us with a group of considerable importance which one can only designate as programme music. There is a *La caccia*, RV 362, which recalls the hunt, and there are no less than three concertos with the title *La notte* (RV 104, for flute or violin, two violins, bassoon and basso continuo; RV 439 for flute and orchestra; and RV 501 for bassoon and orchestra). The first two are closely related. Then there are four *Tempesta di mare* concertos; RV 98 for flute, oboe, violin, bassoon and basso continuo; RV 253 for violin and orchestra; RV 433 for flute and orchestra, and RV 570 for flute, oboe, bassoon and violin, orchestra and basso continuo. In fact all except RV 253 are closely related works. Finally, there is the group known as the *Four seasons*, RV 269, 315, 293 and 297 (the fact that the numbers are not consecutive derives from the fact that Ryom classifies the works according to tonality within any one given section). With the *Four seasons* Vivaldi took programme music almost to its limit, since he prefaced the works with sonnets descriptive of the four seasons of the year, and then marked the appropriate moments corresponding to the words in each concerto.

Thus in Winter, the slow movement is clearly indicated to convey the time spent sitting beside the fire, whilst the rain pours down outside, and the last movement sliding across the ice, and walking gingerly for fear of falling. The ice breaks, all the winds of heaven blow, but Winter is, after all, the season that brings us joy. One sees Vivaldi using all the tricks of the trade, and deploying all his considerable technique for effects that go far beyond the somewhat pejorative concept of programme music and are purely baroque, insofar as they surprise, and even startle us – as they must certainly have startled his contemporaries. As Hawkins wrote in his *General history of music*:[7] 'the peculiar characteristic of Vivaldi's music . . . is, that it is wild and irregular'.

In the autumn of 1725 Vivaldi mounted a new opera at the S. Angelo theatre in Venice, *L'inganno trionfante in amore* (RV 721) to a libretto by M. Morris retouched by G. M. Ruggeri, and in the autumn of 1726, again at the S. Angelo theatre, there was another new opera, *Dorilla in Tempe* (RV 709), to a libretto by Antonio Maria Lucchini. The score in Turin was possibly used in connection with the revival of the opera in 1734, and Vivaldi used the sinfonia again for the opera *Farnace* (RV 711). It was possibly *Dorilla* that Quantz saw at the S. Angelo in 1726.

Vivaldi may also have gone to Mantua for the landgrave's birthday in July, for which he wrote a *serenata a quattro voci*, *Questa Eurilla gentil* (RV 692), which is unfortunately lost. It is less likely that he went as far afield as Prague at this time, however, despite the fact that *La tirannia gastigata*, with some of his arias, was given in the Carnival of 1726 there.

For the Carnival season of 1726–7 Vivaldi produced *La fede tradita e vendicata* (RV 712), to a libretto by Abate Silvani and dedicated to Count von Schulemberg, commander of the Venetian army. With music by Galuppi and Gasparini as well, this was presented as *Ernelinda* in 1750.

The same season saw *Cunegoda* (RV 707), to a libretto by A. Piovene, and *Farnace*, to a libretto by Lucchini, with Anna Girò in the role of Tamiri. Abate Conti wrote to Madame de Caylus about it: 'The libretto is passable if you ignore the faults of an episode in it contrary to all possibility. The music is by Vivaldi. It is very varied in the sublime and the tender; his pupil [Anna Girò] does wonders in it, although her voice is not of the most beautiful.'[8]

According to Goldoni, Anna Girò, or Giraud, was born in Venice, the daughter of a French wigmaker. However, in the first two operas in which she appeared in 1724 and 1725, both at the S. Moisè theatre, the adjective 'Mantovana' is added to her name, leading some to believe that Vivaldi met her in Mantua. She was a pupil of Vivaldi, which has also made some authorities think that she may have been at the Pietà. She appeared in the following operas by him: *Dorilla*, 1726; *Farnace*, 1726; *Orlando*, 1727; *Rosilena*, 1728; *Montezuma*, 1733; *Griselda*, 1735; *Armida*, 1738 (this was a revival, the original dated from 1718); *L'oracolo*, 1738; *Rosmira*, 1738. She also sang in operas by other composers, namely *Laodice* by T. Albinoni, 1724; *Gli sdegni cangiati in amore* by Guis. Maria Buina, 1725; *Agide rè di Sparta* by Gio. Porta, 1725; *Medea e Jasone* by Fr. Brusa, 1726; *Gli odi delusi dal sangue* by G. B. Pescetti and B. Galuppi, 1728; *Dalisa* by Hasse, 1730; *Ezio* by G. B. Lampagnani, 1743; and *Achille in Sciro* by G. B. Runcher, 1747.[9]

Anna Girò therefore began her career not later than 1724, two years before she appeared as the singer of Vivaldi's music, and went on until 1747, more than six years after his death. This tends to suggest that her career may have been more independent from that of Vivaldi's than has hitherto been generally suggested.

In May 1727 *Siroe rè di Persia* (RV 735), to a libretto by Metastasio, was given at the Teatro Pubblico in Reggio. John, Earl of Cork and Orrery, writing from Bologna on 21 October 1754 described the theatre in Reggio, which he had attended on his way there, as: 'remarkable, and singularly beautiful. The architecture is different from all other theatres. The several rows of boxes rise above each other like

Vincenzo Coronelli (d. 1718): *View of the Riva degli Schiavoni with the regatta,*
Venice. This engraving shows Vivaldi's place of work, the Pietà, as the second
identified building from the left before the church was altered in 1745 by Giorgio
Massari. On the far left of the illustration is the immediate vicinity of the Convent
of S. Lorenzo, and on the far right Vivaldi's home parish of S. Martino.

Visitors to Venice were often amazed at the amount of music-making that went on
in the city, not only in churches and on state occasions, but also in private houses at
musical gatherings such as this one, painted by an anonymous eighteenth-century
artist. Vivaldi was often in demand as soloist at such gatherings.

Canaletto (1697-1768): *The basin of S. Marco looking towards the East* (detail). The Pietà may be identified as the building almost in the angle created by the mast and its spar on the boat in the foreground, with a companile to the right of it. This view was evidently painted before the alterations to the church in 1745, and is now generally held to date from the early 1730s.

The splendour and magnificence of the French court was always a great temptation to musicians and artists, and Vivaldi was no exception. He was a friend of the Marquis de Pomponne, sometime French Ambassador to Venice, and it was doubtless Pomponne who encouraged Vivaldi to write some of the occasional works celebrating events in the life of the French royal family. This painting by Giovanni Paolo Panini (*c.* 1692-1765) depicts a concert given in Rome in honour of the birth of the Dauphin.

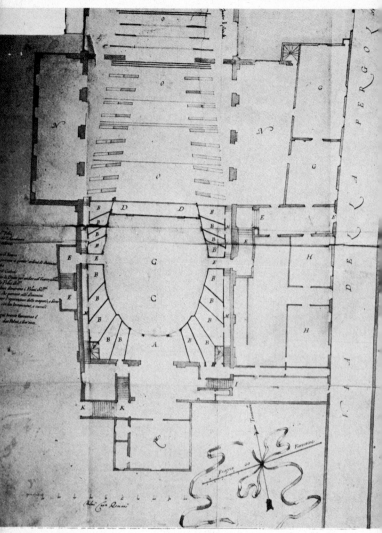

Plan of the Pergola theatre in Florence, whose fortunes Vivaldi helped to restore by writing the opera *Ipermestra* in 1727. One sees quite clearly that the lavish stage sets and large amount of space needed backstage quite overshadowed the size of the horseshoe-shaped auditorium.

steps, and have the most pleasing effect that can be imagined.'[10]

Burney said that Leonardo Vinci first set *Siroe* for Venice, in 1726, so presumably Vivaldi felt that he, too, would like to use it. If Vivaldi went to Reggio he was doubtless back in Venice by the autumn for a new opera *Orlando* (RV 728), to a libretto by G. Braccioli, sometimes known as *Orlando furioso*, and not to be confused with his first opera, *Orlando finto pazzo*. Anna Girò sang the role of Alcina, in what is acknowledged to be one of Vivaldi's best operas. The manuscript is in Turin.

Also from 1727 dates another serenata, this time *a tre*, *L'unione della Pace e di Marte* (RV 694), to a libretto by A. Grossatesta, and on 19 September 1727 there was a concert at the residence of the French Ambassador, by now the Comte de Gergy, in honour of the birth of the French princesses. According to the *Mercure de France*, there was 'a very fine concert of instruments that lasted almost two hours, of which the music, as well as that of the *Te Deum*, was by the famous Vivaldi'. Since the serenata RV 694 is inscribed 'in celebration of the birth of the twin royal princesses, Madame of France and Madame of Navarre', we must assume that this was the same work, and Ryom identifies as RV 622 the *Te Deum* sung on this occasion, though the music is lost. Then on 17 January 1728 the opera *Rosilena ed Oronta* (RV 730), with Anna Girò as Oronta, was given at the S. Angelo theatre. The libretto is by Giovanni Palazzi.

The 1726–7 Carnival season seems to have been something of a *tour de force* for Vivaldi, for the Abate Conti, again writing to Madame de Caylus, on 23 February 1727, said at the end of it: 'Vivaldi has produced three operas in less than three months, two for Venice and the third for Florence; the last has re-established the theatre of that city and brought in much money.'[11]

The opera for Florence was *Ipermestra* (RV 722), to a libretto by A. Salvi, and Vivaldi's opera did indeed save the Teatro della Pergola from financial ruin. Generally, however, this is a particularly difficult period to say with any certainty where Vivaldi was at any given moment. *La cetra*, Op. IX, was published in Amsterdam by Le Cène in 1727, but there is no indication that Vivaldi went to visit his publisher in connection with it.

Vivaldi's fame continued to grow, of that there is no doubt, and on 7 February 1728, for example the *Four Seasons* were played at one of the *concerts spirituels* in Paris with great success.

Some scholars have placed a visit to Vienna during this year, partly on the strength of a reference in the famous letter of 16 November 1737, and partly on the presence in the Nationalbibliothek in Vienna of a collection of 12 concertos entitled *La cetra*.[12] This is not the famous *La cetra*, Op. IX, in fact only one concerto, RV 391, is common to both collections. These are in any case not autograph parts, though the dedication reads: *La Cetra concerti consecrati alla Sacra, Ceserea, Cattolica, Real Maesta di Carlo VI Imperadore* [*sic*] . . . *l'anno 1728*. However, there is no demonstrable necessity for Vivaldi's having gone to Vienna, for a letter of Abate Conti reveals that in the same year Vivaldi met the emperor either in Venice or Trieste (there is a certain amount of ambiguity on this point): 'The emperor stayed two days in Trieste, but he came neither to Bucari nor to Fiume . . . Give my compliments to the count your son; tell him that the emperor has given a great deal of money to Vivaldi with a chain and a medallion of gold, and that he has made him a *chevalier*.' And then: 'The emperor was not too happy with his Trieste . . . the emperor talked to Vivaldi a long time about music, they say that he has said more to him alone in a fortnight than he says to his ministers in two years.'[13]

In view of the considerable number of performances of Vivaldi's operas, or operas in which his music was used, in Prague and Breslau round about this time, it might have been useful for him to make a journey there. After all, his patron the Count of Morzin, who was also Chamberlain and Counsellor to the emperor, may well have encouraged Vivaldi to put on operas in Bohemia. We know of two productions of his works, *La tirannia gastigata* and *Argippo*

(RV 697) that took place in Prague in 1726 and 1730 respectively. Then *Alvilda regina de' Goti* (RV 696) was put on there in 1731. Also for the Breslau opera, arias by Vivaldi were included in *Orlando furioso* (Ryom Anhang 52) in 1724, *Ariodante* (Ryom Anhang 42) in 1727, *Griselda* (Ryom Anghang 48 – but not the *Griselda* he worked with Goldoni on) and *Merope* (Ryom Anhang 49) both in 1728. This list in itself proves nothing, but we now are aware of the fact that there was much more contact with Bohemia than previously had been imagined, and there is nothing that states categorically that Vivaldi never went beyond Vienna. Until more information comes to light, we can simply put all the available evidence down. We do know, for example, that in 1728 Vivaldi wrote another opera, *L'Atenaide* (RV 702), libretto by Zeno, which was given at the Teatro della Pergola in Florence on 20 December, to follow up the success of *Ipermestra*.

It is worth noting that there is no trace of Anna Girò's having sung in Venice between the end of February 1729 and autumn 1733, apart from an appearance in an opera by Hasse, *Dalisa*, given in the spring of 1730. In view of the fact that she was always with Vivaldi, this would strengthen the view that they were travelling during much of this time, for although illness – which has been suggested as one of the explanations for Vivaldi's long absence from historical records – would have confined him to his apartments in Venice, there is no reason why it should have prevented Anna from appearing on stage, apart from loyalty to her friend and tutor. The fact that she was able to sing for Hasse may have been due to exceptional circumstances, such as replacing another singer at the last minute.

Another work of Vivaldi's may be dated to this year 1729. Despite the fact that *La Gloria e Imeneo* may never have been heard at the French Court, Vivaldi was not deterred from trying again with the *Te Deum* already mentioned for the birth of Mesdames de France in 1727, and a work similar to the first cantata, written in 1729, *La Sena festeggiante* (RV 693), to celebrate the birth of the Dauphin Louis, son of Louis XV and Maria Leczinska. This serenata is for

131

soprano, contralto and bass, with two oboes, two recorders, violins and basso continuo, to words by Domenico Lalli. It is altogether more substantial as a composition, and indeed the opening orchestral movement shows Vivaldi at his most accomplished. It is, moreover, in the French style, by way of a tribute to the occasion, as another work – a concerto for string orchestra and basso continuo – (RV 117) with the same first movement, indicates quite clearly, with the marking '*alla Francese*'.

In 1938 Rodolfo Gallo discovered the record of a request on 30 September 1729 from Giovanni Battista Vivaldi – Antonio's father – for a year's leave of absence from Venice to accompany one of his sons to Germany. Since it is unlikely that it would have been either of the other brothers, there is every possibility that Antonio's father had decided to join his son, who now enjoyed imperial favour. Moreover, since his son always travelled with four or five persons, according to the letter of 16 November 1737, there would be adequate provision for a man now well advanced in years. One may safely take Germany as synonymous with Austria, since the Holy Roman Emperor – the German Emperor – had his capital in Vienna. We also know that Vivaldi's opera *L'Argippo* was given in Prague in the autumn of 1730. Whereas it would have been a long journey from Venice to Prague for *La tirannia* four years before, and in any case Vivaldi had only contributed a certain number of arias to it, the journey from Vienna this time was much shorter, and the incentive much greater.

There may also have been visits to Darmstadt in his capacity as *maestro di cappella*, and Dresden, where his pupil Pisendel was solo violinist in the royal band, and where there are more than one hundred Vivaldi manuscripts, or even Amsterdam, to meet and discuss business with his publisher Le Cène. Opus X, XI and XII were published by Le Cène in 1728–9. There is also the possibility that one of the missing opera seasons of the three that Vivaldi himself mentioned as having spent in Rome is to be fitted into this period.

132

In connection with this, Keysler wrote from Venice in May 1730:

Other famous female singers, besides Faustina and Cuzzoni, are Selvai, or Maria Maddalena Frigeri, Anna Ciro [sic], Guistina Turcotti, Ceresina, and Lancetti. A young woman called La Rosa, has been for some years instructed in music here at the expence [sic] of the Elector of Bavaria, and great things are expected from her. Mr Handel, who at present resides at London, the abovementioned M. Hasse, Nicola Porpora, director of the band of music in the hospital of the Incurables at Venice, Giovanni Porta, of the chapel of the hospital della Pietà at Venice, Geminiano Giocamelli, and Luca Antonio Predieri are highly celebrated as excellent composers of music.[14]

Vivaldi, we must assume, was probably not, as far as Keysler was concerned.

In 1730, presumably at a time when he was away from Venice, the legitimate owners of the S. Angelo theatre, Benedetto Marcello and Bernardo Cappello, appointed Fabrizio Brugnolo to administer the theatre, and the new manager recognized the legal rights of the proprietors. This was the end of a campaign that had lasted for years, but had reached its summit ten years previously in the publication of *Il teatro alla moda*. If the theatre had dismissed Vivaldi as impresario, it could not do without his music, however, and the following year (1731) an obscure composer called Galeazzi was called in to adapt *La costanza trionfante degli amori e degli odii*, already produced in 1716, and since reworked by Vivaldi himself as *Artabano rè de' Parti* in 1718, and the new incarnation was known as *L'odio vinto dalla costanza* (Ryom Anhang 51). In the same year *Armida al campo d'Egitto* was revived at the Teatro S. Margherita, with music by several composers, whereas the original, which had been put on at the Teatro S. Moisè in 1718, was entirely by Vivaldi. *Alvilda* was given this year in Prague.

Whether it was illness or travel, or a combination of both, that had apparently clouded the landscape of Vivaldi's creative fervour at this point, and obscured the details of his career, things were soon to change. Towards the end of 1731 (or early 1732) a new opera, *Semiramide* (RV 733), saw the light of day at Verona, and it was repeated at Mantua in January of the next year, 1732. A second followed almost immediately, *La fida ninfa* (RV 714), to a libretto by the Marquis Scipione Maffei, a Veronese patrician. Its première took place on 6 January 1732 in the Teatro Filarmonico in Verona.

The title page of the libretto announces: 'La fida ninfa/ drama per musica/da cantarsi in Verona nel nuovo/teatro dell' accademia/dedicato a S.E. La Signora/Daria Soranza Gradeniga/Podestaressa, e Vicecapitania. In Verona, per Jacopo Vallarsi 1732/Con licenza de' superiori.'[15] The manuscript of the music is in the Biblioteca Nazionale in Turin, Giordano 39bis. The effects are just what we might have expected from a typical opera of the period, as one example taken from the stage directions indicates: 'They leave and the scene changes into a horrid and shadowy mountain with the closed mouth of a huge cave.' Juno then appears on a cloud. After Juno's aria the mouth of the grotto opens to reveal the kingdom of Eolo, 'worked in the bowels of the mountain with rich ornaments of nature and of art'. He himself is seen right at the very back, with a great crowd of winds, some of horrid aspect and some of graceful aspect. There then follows a 'bizarre' symphony, and after a while Eolo comes forward with his suite.

The details of the instrumentation reveal a great deal about the way in which Vivaldi used instrumental tone colour to heighten characterization. The first aria for Oralto, corsair and lord of Naxos, island of the Aegean, for example, has trumpet and drum obbligato, whereas the dance of the sailors who emerge from the ships has two recorders as obbligati. The storm at sea has two horns (*corni da caccia*), but for Juno's aria there are only muted strings. The final chorus re-introduces trumpets and drums, though in both this and the closing *ballo*, with its recorders, the violins merely double the trumpet and recorder parts. One interesting, if problematic, aspect of the instrumentation is the inclusion of an undesignated soloistic fifth string part in one of the orchestral interludes, between the viola and the bass, which might have been for a tenor viol. Elsewhere the string parts are restricted to four.

The very next day – i.e. 7 January 1732 – in Venice, the relics of St Peter Orseolo were translated with great pomp to S. Marco, and a most solemn *Laudate Dominum* by Vivaldi was sung, but there is no record that he was there in person. There is also a possibility that the opera *Sarce* was presented in Ancona in 1733, or this may be a confusion with the opera *Sirce*, which was given there in 1738, since it is only mentioned in Mendel's *Musikalisches Konversationslexicon*.[16] At all events, Vivaldi was certainly back in Venice by the autumn of 1733, for his opera *Montezuma* (RV 723), to a libretto by Alvise Giusti, was produced then at the S. Angelo, or in the Carnival.

It must have been very strange for Vivaldi to be no longer in control of the S. Angelo theatre – or in a position to dictate conditions, and it cannot have been easy from the artistic point of view. Nevertheless he followed it with another opera at the theatre for the Carnival season of 1733–4, and this work, *L'Olimpiade* (RV 725), manuscript in Turin, is generally considered one of his best operas. The libretto – which Burney said Caldara had set in 1733 for the Imperial Court – was by Metastasio, and it was soon put on again at Genoa. However, after *L'Olimpiade* Vivaldi left the S. Angelo for a period of almost five years, apart from a revival of *Dorilla in Tempe* in 1734.

7. Vivaldi and Goldoni

It must have seemed to Vivaldi at this point in his existence that times were changing and old certainties were crumbling. He was well into his late fifties, and new faces were appearing around him. The aspects of his temperament that had probably been responsible for some of his disappointments in earlier life by now must have been even more pronounced. There was the perennial problem of his health which, if it had been exaggerated in the early days, by now may well have become a permanent feature of his day to day existence, and there must also have been the question of finance. From the entry eventually made in the Gradenigo chronicle when news of his death had reached Venice, it is evident that his contemporaries thought that he had made a lot of money and that he had also spent it.[1] Whatever the truth of the matter, finance was soon to become a problem, even if it was not already in 1735.

It was at this point that Vivaldi came into contact with the youthful Goldoni, and we have the picture of a young man in the first flush of creation confronted by that of a man in his late prime, and it is as if, after a dark, rather shadowy period, Vivaldi's life is suddenly brilliantly illuminated. In fact Goldoni left two accounts, and a comparison of the two is interesting, and reveals how it was that, as well as throwing light on this period, Goldoni was also responsible for lending fuel to some of the myths that circulate about Vivaldi to this day.

Carlo Goldoni (1709–93) was chosen by Michele Grimani, proprietor of the S. Samuele theatre, to adapt Apostolo Zeno's *Griselda* to be set to music by Vivaldi for the next Ascension opera season – i.e. the spring of 1735. Albinoni had already set it in 1728. Thus it was that the two came together, in Vivaldi's house, as Goldoni related, some twenty-seven years after it had taken place:

That year, for the Ascension opera, the composer was the priest Vivaldi, known as the red priest because of his hair, and sometimes referred to as Rossi, so that people thought that was his surname.

This most famous violinist, this man famous for his sonatas, especially for those known as the Four Seasons, also composed operas; and although the really knowledgeable people say that he was weak on counterpoint and that he handled his basses badly, he made the parts sound well, and most of the time his operas were successful.

That year the role of the prima donna was to be taken by Signora Annina Girò, or Giraud, the daughter of a wigmaker of French origin, who was commonly called Annina of the red priest, because she was Vivaldi's pupil. She did not have a beautiful voice, nor was she a great musician, but she was pretty and attractive; she acted well (a rare thing in those days) and had protectors: one needs nothing more to deserve the role of prima donna. Vivaldi was very concerned to find a poet who would arrange, or disarrange, the play to his taste, by adapting, more or less, several arias that his pupil had sung on other occasions; since I was the person to whom this task fell, I introduced myself to the composer on the orders of the *cavaliere padrone* [Grimani]. He received me quite coldly. He took me for a beginner and never made a mistake; and not finding me very well up in the business of botching plays, one could see that he very much wanted to send me packing.[2]

Goldoni's *Il Belisario* had been given its first performance at the S. Samuele theatre on 24 November 1734, and its success seemed to have surprised even the author. The following January his *Rosimonda* was put on at the same theatre, and then *Il Belisario* was revived, and lasted until the end of the Carnival. It was this that had induced Grimani, the proprietor of the S. Samuele theatre, to choose Goldoni to collaborate with Vivaldi. As Goldoni continued:

He [Vivaldi] knew the success my *Belisario* had had, he

knew how successful my *intermezzi* had been; but the adaptation of a play was something that he regarded as difficult, and which required a special talent, according to him. I then remembered those rules that had driven me mad in Milan [see pages 86–7] when my *Amalasunta* was read, and I too wanted to leave; but my situation and the fear of making a bad impression on His Excellency Grimani, as well as the hope of being given the direction of the magnificent theatre of S. Giovanni Grisostomo, induced me to feign and almost to ask the red priest to try me out. He looked at me with a compassionate smile and took up a little book:

'Here,' he said, 'is the play that has to be adapted, Apostolo Zeno's *Griselda*. The work is very fine. The part for the prima donna could not be better. But certain changes are necessary . . . If Your Lordship knew the rules . . . Useless. You cannot know them. Here, for example, after this tender scene, there is a cantabile aria. But since Signora Anna does not . . . does not . . . like this sort of aria (in other words she was incapable of singing it), one needs here an action aria . . . that reveals passion, but not pathos, and is not cantabile.'

'I understand,' I replied. 'I will endeavour to satisfy you. Give me the libretto.'

'But I need it for myself,' replied Vivaldi. 'When will you return it?'

'Immediately,' I replied. 'Give me a sheet of paper and a pen . . .'

'What! Your Lordship imagines that an opera aria is like an intermezzo aria!'

I was furious, and replied to him insolently. He gave me the pen and took a letter from his pocket, from which he tore a sheet of white paper.

'Don't get angry,' he said modestly. 'Here, sit down at this table. Here is the paper, the pen and the libretto. Make yourself comfortable.'

Then he went back to his worktable and began to say his breviary. I then read the scene carefully. I analysed the sentiment of the cantabile aria and turned it into another of action, passion and motion. I took my work to him. With his breviary in his right hand and my sheet of paper in his left he began to read gently. When he had finished he threw the breviary into a corner, got up, embraced me, ran to the door and called Signora Annina. Annina arrived, with her sister Paolina. He read them the arietta, shouting: 'He did it here, he did it here, on this very spot!' Again he embraced me and congratulated me, and now I had become his friend, his poet, his *confidant*, and he never abandoned me. I then murdered Zeno's play exactly as he wanted. The opera was put on successfully. As for me, as soon as the Ascension opera season was over, I took myself off to Padua, where Imer and his company were, to finish off the spring season that year in a mediocre way.

Goldoni produced a second version of this incident, a further twenty-six years after the first one, in his *Mémoires* of 1787, written in French. This was therefore some fifty-three years after the event, when his memory was presumably even less reliable, and the temptation to embellish what was already quite a good story even stronger. It would be tedious to give the second version verbatim, but Goldoni's prose is noticeably more epigrammatic in style, the dialogue is much more highly coloured to suit the protagonist, with liberal helpings of Latin quotations from the breviary to give authenticity, and there are appropriate bits of business, such as the sign of the cross, which did not appear in the first version, and Vivaldi's being unable to lay his hands on the libretto, which is buried somewhere amongst the piles of papers on his desk. Moreover Goldoni makes himself more bold in the second version, to the extent of saying that he has heard Anna Girò sing, and that her voice was not very strong, which brings a firm denial from Vivaldi. There is even added movement in the second version, as befits a life-long experience of writing for the theatre, for Vivaldi paces up and down, reciting his office, whilst Goldoni produces the text for the aria.

All in all, the second version presents a portrait of

Vivaldi that is much more of a caricature than the first one, and probably is responsible for perpetuating – if not indeed creating – the idea of Vivaldi as an irascible, eccentric cleric who somehow managed to continue to fulfil his priestly obligations to the minimum as he pursued his career as a musician. From a purely musical point of view, it is interesting that Goldoni also modifies his judgement of Vivaldi as a musician in the second version. By then he was, in Goldoni's words, 'an excellent violinist and a mediocre composer' – which is probably an indication of the average view of Vivaldi in the late 1780s.

As to how Goldoni was seen by others, there is an initial fleeting glimpse of him in Grosley's memoirs, as Grosley was travelling to Venice: 'The lawyer Goldoni, Scarlati [*sic*] the celebrated musician, and a young burgher of Bâle, made up those acquaintances to which we were not disposed.'[3] It is somewhat strange that Goldoni was still referred to as a lawyer, which he had been at the outset of his career, when he had so many successes as a dramatist behind him by that time. However, Grosley made acquaintance all the same, for when he arrived in Venice, on 29 July 1758, the theatres were officially closed. However, Scarlatti and Goldoni, wishing to give him some idea of what Venetian theatre could provide, assembled 'an elite troupe who, in the salon of the theatre of S. Giovanni Grisostomo, gave us one of their best pieces on this sort'. Grosley had really had an extraordinary piece of luck, and yet seems to have taken the whole business quite calmly. However, he recounted with equal detachment, as we shall see later, what happened when Scarlatti tried to conduct Venetians in the Neapolitan manner. A large section of the music was simply omitted.

Vivaldi must have been a veteran of such mishaps, and if Goldoni barely conceals his contempt for what Vivaldi, as a composer, did to the texts, then Vivaldi was surely entitled to some sympathy for what singers, impresarios, stage managers and others did to his music in the interests of self-opinion and spectacle. And yet Vivaldi went on with his operas. True, it was his major source of income, one must assume, and yet there were other possibilities open to him.

140

In the event one is probably quite justified in coming to the conclusion that he actually enjoyed it.

In the Carnival of 1735 Vivaldi gave two new operas at the Teatro Filarmonico at Verona, namely *Tamerlano* (RV 703) for the first, to a libretto by Count Agostino Piovene. The opera was revived at Florence in 1748, and there is a manuscript score at Turin, under the title of *Bajazet*. Despite the fact that it includes music by other composers, Vivaldi is still the most important. The second was *Adelaide* (RV 695), which may have been to a libretto by A. Salvi, though there is some doubt. Certainly on the printed libretto Vivaldi appears as *Maestro di cappella di S.A.S. il Duca di Lorena*. This was Francis of Lorraine, Grand Duke of Tuscany, soon to be husband of Maria Theresa, future Empress of Austria.

Also in 1735 – thus making four operas in one year – was Vivaldi's second collaboration with Goldoni at the S. Samuele theatre, *Aristide* (RV 698). Both librettist and composer used anagrams of their names, namely Calindo Grolo and Lotavio Vandini respectively, on the libretto.

Meanwhile, Vivaldi's name had reappeared in the accounts of the Pietà, and also in the minutes of the governors' meeting.[4] On 5 August 1735 he was designated *maestro de' concerti*:

> . . . a teacher very capable of assuming this function. The same *maestro* will have to provide for our girls concertos and other compositions for all sorts of instruments, and he will have to come with the assiduousness necessary for instructing the girls and making them well able to perform them . . . For his salary the same maestro will receive one hundred ducats annually.

A month later, on 6 September, he was again confirmed in his post, with the desire that he would have no further idea of leaving as had been his wont in years past. He also received on this occasion forty-four lire for *sonate di musica*, though this could mean almost any kind of instrumental music, and he continued to receive money during 1736.

In January 1736 there was another opera for Florence's

Pergola theatre, *Ginevra principessa di Scozia* (RV 716), to a libretto by Antonio Salvi. This opera was to become part of a complicated manoeuvre on Vivaldi's part later that year when negotiations began with an aristocrat from Ferrara, Marquis Guido Bentivoglio, with a view to mounting an opera season in that city. This correspondence constitutes all the letters from Vivaldi that have come down to us, and we are particularly fortunate that the drafts of the replies from the marquis have, for the most part, been retained in the hand of the secretary who drew them up.[5]

Bentivoglio was born in Venice in 1705, and being only the second son, embarked on a career in the church. He went to Rome, where he was under the aegis of his uncle the Cardinal Cornelio, and it is more than likely that it was in Rome that he met Vivaldi, from a reference in one of the letters, and it was there – according to the composer – that he promised Vivaldi that he would help him as a patron. However, on the death of his older brother, Bentivoglio had to abandon his ecclesiastical career and return to Ferrara to take up his duties as the new head of the family. His desire to have opera in Ferrara sprang as much from the fact that it was the traditional role of the aristocracy at that time, as from any very deep musical pretensions on his part. He did in fact play the mandoline, which we again learn from one of the letters, though, in an age when a certain amount of musical accomplishment in a nobleman was accepted as a matter of course, and even regarded as a part of basic education, this in itself is no great matter for comment.

From the somewhat sycophantic way in which Vivaldi enquired whether he still played the mandoline, and from Bentivoglio's rather dismissive reply, one gets the impression that they both knew that it was merely incidental to the main task in hand, namely the mounting of the operas. Certainly it seems unlikely, as some writers have suggested, that Vivaldi wrote the works incorporating mandoline especially for the marquis. It just happens that he is the only person that we actually know of Vivaldi's acquaintance who happened to play the instrument. There may have been many others. In any case, it is more than likely that the works were written for Venice, and the girls of the Pietà in particular.

Bentivoglio sent his own impresario, another cleric, this time Abate Bollani, to see Vivaldi in Venice and discuss the operas with him. A short letter to Vivaldi to this effect from Bentivoglio is dated 28 October 1736. In his reply of 3 November, Vivaldi shows himself keen to co-operate, and already has things in hand:

> I assure Your Excellency that we have succeeded in bringing together such a company as, I hope, will not have been seen on the stage at Ferrara in Carnival time for very many years.
>
> The majority of the virtuosi have appeared several times in the principal theatres, and each one has his individual merit. On my word of honour, Your Excellency must believe that he is well served and content before hearing the company.[6]

So Vivaldi is making sure that the marquis's initial confidence in approaching him is not misplaced, and that Vivaldi will serve him well. The fact that there was an intermediary in the person of Bentivoglio's impresario, Abate Bollani, was an added problem for Vivaldi right from the start, however, as we shall see. The letter continues:

> I have refused to compose the third opera for S. Cassiano for ninety sequins, because they ought to give me my usual fee of one hundred. However, Ferrara will have two operas that will seem to have been composed specially, since they will be entirely adapted and revised in my hand for only six sequins each, which is the fee of a copyist.

Money is a recurrent theme of these letters, and even allowing for the fact that considerable sums were involved, and that Vivaldi was ultimately responsible, at least at the Venetian end of affairs, nevertheless one gets the impression that Vivaldi is rather too concerned, especially over relatively small sums, and he may well have been in some sort of financial difficulties at this time. On occasions he almost becomes frantic, and then reverts to more polite convention:

This is a very humble sacrifice that I have made entirely
out of regard for Your Excellency's most benign media-
tion. I am very sorry that I cannot come personally, since
I am prevented by the above-mentioned opera of S.
Cassiano. At all events, if it is possible, at the end of
Carnival, I will be at the feet of Your Excellency. Signora
Anna Girò sends to Your Excellency her most humble
respects and hopes you will be pleased to endure her
imperfections in Ferrara.

However, as becomes evident from the later letters,
Vivaldi was to some extent playing a game. The purpose of
mentioning 'the third opera for S. Cassiano' seems to have
been entirely so as to let Bentivoglio know what his usual
fee for a newly composed opera was. Obviously for the
paltry sum of six sequins each, Ferrara could not expect to
have new operas. In Vivaldi's next letter, dated 24 November
1736, this much becomes evident, for he mentions the opera
Demetrio, of which we know nothing. Ryom has designated
it Anhang 44, but it seems certain that it was not an original
by Vivaldi, but a reworking of someone else's opera. As he
said in his letter, he had resolved to compose new recitatives
for it, and give 'a great number' of his own arias to the singers. In this way, he went on, the first act was ready and all
the singers knew their parts and were ready to set off from
Venice for Ferrara.

However, at this point a theatrical agent by the name of
Daniele Lanzetti enters into the story, for he wrote to the
marquis on 17 December 1736 about the contract for the
operas. Apparently Bollani was away in Brescia, and Lanzetti had heard that he had been accused of doing nothing
in the matter. He wished to assure the marquis that that was
not so. Meanwhile, Vivaldi had finished his version of
Demetrio, and had by this time prepared the first act of the
second opera, *Alessandro nelle Indie* (Ryom Anhang 40),
which he was sending for copying that same day – 26
December 1736 – as he was writing to the marquis. One

cannot fail to be impressed by Vivaldi's professionalism in this letter, as doubtless he intended the marquis to be impressed also. He meets his deadlines, and usually fulfils his promises:

> I am sending off today the first act, finished and ready for copying. Since I have found myself obliged, so as to improve it, to change some lines, I am taking the liberty of including it in my letter, so that you may examine it with your supreme competence, since if I sent it to the impresario he would be angry.[7]

Vivaldi was obviously not happy with the intermediary of the impresario Bollani, and if Lanzetti was also involved, then that made yet another person with whom Vivaldi had to have dealings. He would obviously have preferred not to have to deal with either of them, chiefly because of his fiercely independent nature but also, as we shall see later, he was not being exactly frank in his dealings. He contents himself in this letter with pouring scorn on impresarios in general: 'It seems that this is the year of the impresarios of little experience. That is what they are all like at S. Casciano [sic], at S. Angelo and those of Brescia. I say nothing of the one from Ferrara ... I beg Your Excellency to have the goodness to let me know if he still enjoys playing the mandoline.'

The second comment, almost thrown in as if Vivaldi might have felt that he ought to be more aware of the social niceties and show that he was still interested in his patron as a person, rather than simply a source of employment, nevertheless draws attention to some of the works Vivaldi wrote for mandoline and lute, and which the marquis might possibly have inspired. There are not many of them. Concerto RV 425 is for one mandoline and strings, and RV 532 is for two mandolines and strings. Vivaldi had included a mandoline as an obbligato solo instrument in the score of *Juditha* for the Pietà, and two of them were to be included again in a work for the girls performed in a concert before Frederick Christian, Elector of Saxony, in 1740. The theorbo lute, which also appears in these last-mentioned works, remained in use as a bass continuo instrument long after the smaller lute had lost ground. Nevertheless Vivaldi also wrote for the lute, two trio sonatas and two concertos (RV 93 and 540), the second of which was also included in the concert given for the Elector of Saxony in 1740, which has led some scholars to speculate that Sylvius Weiss, the famous lutenist, was in the elector's party. Such an occasion, or the regular performances at the Pietà, would therefore seem to make more sense than a potential inspiration from Bentivoglio, for as we learn from his reply to Vivaldi, dated 30 December 1736, he said that he usually played the mandoline once a year, and sometimes not even that.

The whole mention of the mandoline shows that Vivaldi was cleverly trying to get on the right side of Bentivoglio through a little gentle, though possibly rather obvious, flattery, and he may well have remembered hearing Bentivoglio play the instrument when they met in Rome. He was shortly going to need as much good will as he could get from Bentivoglio, as his next letter to the marquis reveals. In fact it must have crossed with that from the marquis, since Vivaldi's is dated 29 December 1736. The cat was now out of the bag in no small way.

Bollani had taken Vivaldi to task, since he was expecting two operas from Vivaldi, *Ginevra* and *L'Olimpiade*. For the 'miserable price' of six sequins each, complained Vivaldi, this was bad enough, but no sooner had Bollani returned to Ferrara than he 'tormented' Vivaldi to let him have *Ginevra*. So, Vivaldi claimed, he set to work with a will, and let some of the singers have their parts, and sent another part to the marquis as proof of what he was doing. Unless the marquis received this part from *Ginevra*, and there is no trace in the archives, we now see that this last manoeuvre was pure politics on Vivaldi's part, but what he overlooked was the fact that the marquis knew that the opera in question was not *Ginevra* that was sent to him by Vivaldi, but *Alessandro*. If it was not a case of oversight on Vivaldi's part, then he must have thought that the marquis would not notice the difference. Of course given the similarity of so many of the plots of operas at this time, and that arias seem to have been highly interchangeable, the marquis could have been forgiven for being taken in. The fact is, however, that he mentioned *Alessandro* specifically by name in his letter of 30 December, but Vivaldi had not received that letter when he embarked on his letter of justification.

Vivaldi then went on to maintain that he had no sooner set to work on *Ginevra* than he was told that what was wanted was *Demetrio*. He then paints a picture of himself going to the theatre to get the parts, and finding that five out of six parts needed changing, and deciding therefore to compose entirely new recitatives. 'See what a kind heart I have, your Excellency' – an interjection that can hardly have helped his case, since what he was recounting seems to have been pure fantasy.

He then went on to maintain that the same thing had happened with *L'Olimpiade*, and that what was now wanted was *Alessandro*. He had had the parts of *L'Olimpiade* copied at his house, under his own eyes, and so all in all he had had the expense of having four operas copied instead of only two. Since Lanzetti seems to have had the job of paying for the copying on behalf of Bollani and Bentivoglio, Lanzetti preferred to use a professional copyist of his own choice, so that in this way he could control the work and the cost. If Vivaldi had the work done at his house, then Lanzetti only had Vivaldi's word for it, and this, as Lanzetti had discovered, was not to be trusted.

Certainly it seems to have mattered little to Vivaldi that two of his own operas were dropped in favour of two re-workings of other compositions; he was apparently only interested in the money. He wrote to Bentivoglio again on 2 January 1737, enclosing the third act of *Alessandro*, the second having already been sent off:

I implore Your Excellency to exert his authority so that the impresario put immediately into the hand of Signora Girò the six sequins and the twenty lire for copying that I ought to have in all justice. I hear that the opera is too long, and it was certain that an opera of four hours was not suitable for Ferrara . . . In composing the recitatives I have done the impossible so as to shorten them, but Lanzetti, on the impresario's orders, prevented me. Your Excellency will see that what I said about la Mancini was true, and will agree that la Moscovita is but a shadow by comparison.[8]

So the poor composer apparently becomes more and more beset by conflicting opinions of those who must be pleased, and at the same time has to deal with the thorny problem of the relative worth of singers and the even more depressing subject of money. At one moment the whole prospect becomes positively gloomy:

> Our theatres continue to go badly. They are trying to get me to compose an opera for S. Cassiano for the 'gift' of one hundred sequins; but my patrons and I do not want to do so because it is a badly run theatre, and the price of the tickets so high that it is impossible to recover the costs, therefore I cannot risk my reputation.

One is reminded of the fact that at one point the government of Venice had to demand deposits from impresarios, so as to ensure that projected operas would actually be put on, since there had been a succession of failures to honour undertakings. What is more important, however, is that in his concern to elicit pity for himself, Vivaldi forgot that he had already told the marquis that he had been asked to compose 'a third opera' for S. Cassiano, whilst here it is only a question of one. Moreover, to paint a slightly better picture of himself, Vivaldi now refers to 'my patrons and I' – thus throwing the responsibility from himself on to some vague unnamed persons.

In the event the plan misfired completely, since Lanzetti suddenly realized what was going on, and wrote two letters to Bentivoglio, dated 9 and 12 January 1737, making it quite plain what had happened, what prices had been agreed between himself, Bollani and Vivaldi, and how Vivaldi had threatened Lanzetti, and 'made him talk with people in his house'. Vivaldi even seems to have tried to play off Lanzetti against Bollani, so that Lanzetti might appear unreliable. In short, the whole affair was somewhat discreditable, and from a reference to Anna Girò in Lanzetti's second letter it would seem that she was certainly an active participant in the affair.

It is a pity that we do not have any more of the correspondence at this point, for somehow the season went ahead, and Vivaldi must have felt that he had had satisfaction, or at any rate affirmed that he had, since from a letter written from Bentivoglio to the composer on 17 March 1737 it would appear that Vivaldi had written to him and thanked him for all that he had done for both Vivaldi and the Girò sisters. The brevity of Bentivoglio's reply would seem to suggest that he was not sorry that the season was ended, and that he wanted to put some distance between himself and the impossible composer:

> I have done little, or nothing, for the Girò ladies. I certainly had – and still have – the desire to do something more than the clearly manifested consideration that I have for their quality. Nonetheless you ought not to thank me for this very slight indication that I have given them here. As for your visit to these parts, I will be happy to see you, but do not put yourself out in any way.[9]

A more polite discouragement would be hard to imagine, and it is not perhaps surprising that this put an end to the first chapter of their professional association. The second chapter was to open very soon, however. In fact within less than two months. Before embarking on it, this is an appropriate point at which to consider some general aspects of Vivaldi's operas, since they bear ultimately on the next chapter.

Venice's continued hostilities with the Turks were reflected in some rather strange ways, in particular they spilled over into the subject matter of the operas seen on its stages. Of course one must not underestimate the threat that the Turks posed not only to Venice herself, but at one point to the whole of western Europe. In July 1683, when Vivaldi was five years old, Vienna itself had been under siege. Had the city fallen, there might have been some very strange consequences for posterity.

Having said as much, however, it would be a mistake to assume that Vivaldi was always concerned to present the Venetian obsession with things Turkish, even when they formed the background to his operas. For example his first recorded Venetian opera, *Orlando finto pazzo*, relates originally to the story of Roland's madness, which was set in the days of Charlemagne, with Saracens and Christians at war for the possession of Europe. The substance of Braccioli's libretto, however, is more like a fairy story, with multiple cases of mistaken identity (and sex), and Ersilia, Queen of the Fairies, presiding over all.

The Crusades and the Turks or Saracens form the background or substance for several operas, however, for example *Armida, Bajazet, Cunegonda, Ginevra principessa di Scozia* (perhaps somewhat surprisingly), *Il Giustino, Orlando furioso, Scanderbeg* and *La verità in cimento*.

Only a short distance away – literally – from the Turkish ambience is that of the Middle East, and it may have been tantamount to the same thing, one suspects, for some of the plots and settings, as for example in *Arsilda regina di Ponto, Artabano rè de' Parti, La Candace, L'incoronazione di Dario, Semiramide, Siroe* and *La virtù trionfante dell'amore e dell'odi ovvero Il Tigrane*.

Not surprisingly for the time, there were several operas set in classical and mythological Greece, such as *Aristide, L'Atenaide, Dorilla in Tempe, Ercole sul Termondonte, La fida ninfa, Filippo rè di Macedonia, Griselda, Ipermestra, L'Olimpiade* – somewhat improbably about the Olympic Games – and *L'oracolo in Messenia*.

Ancient Rome and Italy itself also provided subject matter, though naturally here the issues are more complicated, *Adelaide, Alvilda, Catone in Utica, Nerone fatto Cesare, Ottone in villa*, and *Tito Manlio* are all taken from Roman or early Italian history, and in the case of the first we have an example of an opera that did mean a lot to Vivaldi, as we learn from the dedication, which is to Antonio Grimani, Venetian Governor of Verona:

It was also appropriate that this drama should be dedicated to a Venetian patrician, because the story from which the action comes could only profoundly move a good Italian who was no enemy to his nation, as so many are today, by reminding him how, after the expulsion of the last Italian kings, unhappy Italy fell under the enemy's domination, never again to emerge. In such a deplorable misfortune, the only consolation comes from the illustrious Venetian Republic which, from its birth to our days, is our guarantor of Italian freedom, which may God preserve until the end of time.

In the original story Adelaide was the Queen of Burgundy who was abducted by Berengar II King of Italy, and freed by Otto I King of Germany. However, one can appreciate why Adelaide's devotion to love and duty, and her defence of her liberty appealed, in this context, to the Venetians. One sees this in other operas that do not fall into any of the categories already mentioned, such as *Montezuma*, where the conflict between the hero and the invading foreigner Cortez has captured the imagination of dramatists down to the present day. Then there was *Ernelinda*, set in the exotic climes of Norway, better known by its first title of *La fede tradita e vendicata*. The very title gives away the substance of the plot – faith betrayed and vindicated. In a rather touching note in the libretto, it is explained for the benefit of the audience, that so as to help the singers, the Norwegian names of Umleo, Ataulfo and Scandone had been changed to Grimoaldo, Ricimero and Rodoaldo. Bearing in mind Goldoni's account of the reception of the name Amalasunta by a singer, one can see that this was a matter of no small concern. From the librettist's point of view, this is really tantamount to ensuring that the audience bear in mind the fact that the characters are real, and that they are to be followed through all the vicissitudes of the plot – in other words, because they are human beings. This, in the last resort, was what mattered, and this is what one ought always to bear in mind, because it was something fundamental to appreciation of Venetian opera in Vivaldi's day, and it will enable us to approach it through their eyes. When Abate Conti wrote to Madame de Caylus about the improbable moments in the plot of *Farnace*, he was not doing so as a sophisticated critic today might, but quite genuinely regretting something which, in his eyes, flawed an otherwise valid theatrical experience.

Moreover it did matter what was said and sung on the stage, as the authorities recognized by their censoring of all texts. Often this may well have been a mere formality, but Remo Giazotto has found many of the original records relating to the censorship,[10] proving that it was not merely a matter of form, and occasionally texts were sent back for revision, as apparently with *Arsilda* and *L'incoronazione di Dario*. It even seems as if *Catone in Utica* may have been responsible for contributing to the reasons for the veto that was put on Vivaldi when he was about to produce opera at Ferrara in 1737. The theme of *Catone in Utica* – the hero's last stand for liberty when he was besieged in Utica by Caesar – had not only excited Venetian temperaments. When Addison's tragedy on the same story was put on in England in 1713, at a time when Queen Anne was ill and the question of the succession was still uppermost in people's minds, the play caused considerable emotion. Certainly it was of sufficiently subversive content for the Venetian Council of Ten to suspend a private performance of Metastasio's play which was the basis of the opera, on 26 January 1737, and it may well have been Vivaldi's success in Verona in March that year which led to the subsequent ecclesiastical veto on him in Ferrara. In such a context, the performance at Verona may well have been seen not only as an act of defiance but a positive provocation.

8. A dying close

It always seemed that when Vivaldi used such librettists as Metastasio, Zeno, and Goldoni, then he wrote better operas than at almost any other time. This was certainly true of his next opera, *Catone in Utica* (RV 705), which Burney said had been set by Vinci before Vivaldi used it, and that the libretto, which was by Metastasio, had been written in Rome in 1728. Be that as it may, Vivaldi's version first saw the light of day in 1737, when it was given at the Teatro Filarmonico in Verona in the presence of Charles Albert, Elector of Bavaria, his wife and brother Ferdinand on 26 March, according to De Candé. We know that Vivaldi himself was in Verona later that spring – on 3 May to be precise, for it was from Verona that he wrote to the Marquis Bentivoglio – though we do not know that he was there for the première of his opera. He had a further occasion of providing music for one of the royal brothers during the course of the next year, when Ferdinand came to the Pietà to the '*egloga pescatoria*' *Il Mopso* (RV 691), given by the girls there.

With *Catone in Utica* in Verona, Vivaldi enjoyed a huge success. In fact after only six performances it was evident that not only would the company cover their expenditure, but actually make a profit – possibly even a handsome one. Vivaldi discovered that the Veronesi were not particularly fond of intermezzi, so with highly practical resolution it was decided quite simply to omit them. It seems that Bentivoglio was preparing to go to Bologna at that moment, because Vivaldi would have liked him to see the opera that had brought him such a resounding success in Verona. It was obviously passing through Vivaldi's mind that it would be extremely gratifying to have a similar success in Ferrara, and he may even have been hinting to the marquis that the very opera might be suitable, though he actually wrote:

A similar opera, composed in part to another text, I would think able to command a comparable sum also in Ferrara. However, it is not suitable for Carnival, for the ballets alone, which in summer I can have almost at whatever price I wish, in Carnival would cost me personally 700 louis. I am a frank entrepreneur in such cases, and can pay with my own purse, and am not a borrower.[1]

The sudden insistence on his independence, and his obviously very sensitive position as an impresario, suddenly rise to the surface once more, and one senses that Vivaldi was a man of considerable pride. Also, he was probably keen to demonstrate to the marquis that this time he would be engaged entirely on his own account, in an attempt to dispel whatever unfavourable impression might have been left in the marquis's mind after the dealings he had had with Vivaldi in the previous opera season in Ferrara.

Certainly the marquis's immediate response (dated 5 May) was to express polite and restrained sympathy with Vivaldi in his good fortune that the opera had been so well received and was so financially satisfactory. After that, however, he did all he could to discourage Vivaldi. In the first place, as we have already seen, he said that he regretted that he was unable to go to Verona to see Vivaldi's opera, because he was going to Bologna. Then Bentivoglio tactfully warned Vivaldi that he did not advise him to contemplate putting on the opera in Ferrara for the following autumn season. Moreover Bentivoglio thought – more in hope than in certainty, perhaps – that he would not be in Ferrara in the autumn.

In part Bentivoglio succeeded, for Vivaldi did not put any opera on in Ferrara during the ensuing autumn season. He did so for the subsequent Carnival, however, and one must assume that he persisted with his letters to the marquis, and that in the end he was able to obtain the theatre for the new season. At all events, the sequence of letters begins again in the November of that year, with Vivaldi thanking Bentivoglio, so that the latter may well have found himself drawn into the venture almost in spite of himself. All the same old characteristic Vivaldi touches are there in the letters.

He expresses his fears about the artists engaged, the amount of money involved, and almost inevitably the potential damage to his reputation. As ever, he had his pride, and at this point in his career it seems as if that pride was constantly in danger of being bruised. One cannot help but think of the entry in the *Commemoriali Gradenigo* in the Correr Museum in Venice already referred to:[2] 'Abbate Don Antonio Vivaldi ... made in his time more than 50,000 ducats, but through his inordinate extravagance, died a poor man in Vienna'.

As the Carnival season of 1737 drew nearer, the letters are more abundant. Writing from Venice on 6 November 1737, he informed the marquis that he had signed up the dancer Coluzzi, under obligation to attend all the rehearsals and performances, and with a fee of one hundred louis, the like of which she had certainly never seen before. Even so, Vivaldi was anxious because she had left home, wanted to marry another dancer who was unreliable, and who in any case was supposed to be going to Turin. Then there was a rumour that Coluzzi wanted to dance in Venice that autumn, which would necessitate preparing the ballets in the space of five or six days, which Vivaldi said was impossible, since it would require sixteen or even eighteen days. He therefore asked the marquis to use his influence with the Procuratessa Foscarini and get her to make sure that Coluzzi was in Ferrara by 2 December. This would give them a good three weeks before the opening night on 26 December.

However, in the next letter, dated 13 November, Vivaldi was still worried – since people were expressing surprise that Coluzzi was dancing at the S. Giovanni Grisostomo theatre in Venice – about the opening night. As a true professional, Vivaldi asserted that he would be there, ready on the night, and that he would not default at any price. And then suddenly like a bolt out of the blue, came a totally unexpected disaster: 'After so many exertions and so much hard work the opera at Ferrara is wrecked [literally: on the floor]. Today 16 November 1737 Monsignor the Apostolic Nuncio summoned me and ordered me, in the name of His Eminence Cardinal Ruffo, not to go to Ferrara to mount the opera'.[3] That the church authorities were able to do this at all sprang from the fact that Ferrara was part of Papal territories at this time. In the event the opera did not take place, so they stood by their decision, despite attempts by Vivaldi to have the ban lifted. Even so, it is strange that the authorities should have chosen this moment to impose it, especially in view of the reasons they gave, namely that he was a priest who did not say Mass, and that he had a relationship with Anna Girò. As he pointed out, if they were going to take exception to either or both these factors, they could have done it at any time over the last few years. Quite a different matter was the fact that he felt deeply for Anna and her sister, who had been so devoted to him over so many years, and in a rather arduous capacity, as his house-keepers, nurses and companions.

If the whole thing was simply the result of intrigue inspired by jealousy, then the matter is easily explained, but even if this was not so, the whole incident points to the fact that whereas previously Vivaldi was excused anything, the tide had now turned, and the famous Red Priest was to abide by the rules just like anyone else.

The blow must have been overwhelming not only because it was hard to see why it had happened at all, let alone at that particular juncture, but because of the personal damage it did to Vivaldi and his household. The effect would in any case have been shattering emotionally and psychologically, but it also had severe financial implications for Vivaldi, as he pointed out to Bentivoglio:

I am burdened with the cost of 6,000 ducats in signed engagements for this opera, and at present I have laid out more than one hundred sequins. It is impossible to mount the opera without la Girò, since it is impossible to find another such prima donna. It is equally impossible to mount the opera without me, since I do not want to en-trust such a large sum to others. Moreover, I am bound by my engagements, from whence springs an ocean of troubles.

Obviously here he was concerned to protect the professional standing of his pupil Anna Girò, and her future engagements. At the same time there was his own financial involvement, not only from the point of view of the contracts he would have to annul and the money he had already spent that would be wasted, but also the prospect of losing the hoped-for profit from the whole Ferrara venture. But having said that, he also expresses a genuine concern for the slur that has now been cast on Anna and her sister:

What most pains me is that His Eminence Cardinal Ruffo puts a stain on these poor women that the world never gave them. For the last fourteen years we have travelled together to many cities of Europe, and everywhere their honesty was admired; Ferrara can bear adequate witness to that. They make their devotions every week, as may be confirmed from sworn and authenticated testimonies.

Then he went on to deal with his own position, explaining, as we have already seen, that it was an affliction from birth that prevented him from saying Mass:

That is the reason I do not say Mass. I went to Rome for three Carnival seasons to mount opera and, as Your Excellency knows, I did not say Mass. I have played [the violin] in the theatre, and everyone knows that His Holiness himself wished to hear me, and showered kindness on me. I was called to Vienna and I never said Mass. In Mantua I was for three years in the service of the most pious Prince of Darmstadt, together with these women, who were always treated most warmly by His Serene Highness, and I never said Mass.

Once again, however, the subject turns, almost inevitably, to money: 'My journeys are always very expensive because I always make them with four or five people who help me. All that I can do that is any good I do at home, at the table. For this reason I have the honour to correspond with nine princes of rank, and my letters go all over Europe.'

157

Vivaldi insists on his liability to such an extent that it is obviously extremely important, either in reality, or as the mainstay of his defence:

This is why I have written to Signor Muzzuchi that if he does not give me his house I cannot come to Ferrara. In short, everything arises out of my illness, and these women help me so much because they know all my disabilities. These truths are known to almost the whole of Europe; therefore I have recourse to the kindness of Your Excellency so that he be pleased to inform His Eminence Cardinal Ruffo of it also, for this order means my total ruin. I repeat to Your Excellency that without me they cannot give the opera in Ferrara, and you see for what number of reasons.

By not putting it on either I must take it to another city, which I will never find now, or pay all the engagements, so that if His Eminence does not give way, I would beseech Your Excellency to obtain at least the suspension of the opera from His Eminence the Legate, so that I am dispensed from paying the engagements.

Bentivoglio obviously went to some trouble to try and have the veto lifted, as we learn from his reply to Vivaldi, dated 20 November 1737. The cardinal was adamant, however, in his resolve. We know from an edict that he issued for the Carnival of the next year, dated 8 January 1738, that he was determined to bring the lax clergy to heel, and he may well have issued a similar edict – if not in fact the same one – the year before, as a result of which Vivaldi incurred his displeasure. Bentivoglio told Vivaldi that the cardinal had said to him that he would not have altered his decision if the Holy Father himself had ordered him to do so, and as a result had lost his see – through the cardinal's intervention, one might add, the Bishopric of Ferrara had been elevated into an archbishopric.

The solution that Bentivoglio then put forward was for Vivaldi to allow a man called Picchi to act as impresario, since the cardinal was unable to prevent the opera from taking place itself, since that would mean closing all the theatres, whether musical or not. If Vivaldi himself could not participate directly, at least, in this way, he could do so through Picchi. Vivaldi's reply, dated 23 November 1737, rejected this suggestion out of hand, but what is more interesting in the second part of the letter are the specific replies he makes to his critics. He said that he never stood at the door – presumably of the theatre – a thing that he would be ashamed to do, nor did he play in the orchestra, except on the opening night, since he would not deign to contemplate such a calling. Then he went on to deny that he and Anna Girò lived in the same house, saying that he had his own for which he paid 200 ducats, and that Anna lived in another one, a long way away.

Four days later, Bentivoglio answered this letter with a considerable degree of forbearance, commending the solution with Picchi once again, and expressing regret that Vivaldi would not countenance it. Vivaldi's reply three days later was to declare that the idea was 'ridiculous'. It seems as if Picchi had proposed that Vivaldi hand over the two operas, and all the arrangements already in hand, for a lower sum than Vivaldi was prepared to accept; or quite simply, that he did not want to hand them over at all. At all events, it seems almost certain that the 1737–8 Carnival operas never took place at Ferrara, whether by Vivaldi or anyone else. In a letter to Count Licinio Pepoli in Bologna, dated 20 December 1737, Bentivoglio said that he had had a meeting with another impresario, but that he did not want an indifferent opera season in view of the fact that they had a good drama company already, and that this would therefore be the only diversion that season.

After the debacle of Ferrara, however, Vivaldi had the satisfaction of seeing his talent recognized abroad. The prophet was not without honour after all. The occasion was the centenary of the royal theatre in Amsterdam on 7 January 1738, and Vivaldi was put in charge of the music as a composer of European reputation and renown.

The complete account of the festivities was discovered in 1909 by the Dutch musicologist D. F. Scheurleer in two beautifully bound volumes in the University Library. There were two plays with music: *Caesar and Cato*, a tragedy by Peter Langendijk, and a piece specially written for the occasion by Jan de Marre entitled *Het Eeuwgetyde van den Amsteldamschen Schouwburg* (*The centenary of the Amsterdam theatre*). There were also ten musical items, of which the first was a concerto grosso in three movements by Vivaldi, the orchestration being for solo violin, two oboes, two horns, four-part string ensemble and timpani (RV 562a).

Vivaldi obviously enjoyed a considerable reputation in Holland. He must have been one of the best-selling names on the catalogue of Roger and Le Cène, and it is highly unlikely that he would have been invited such a long distance, and presumably at such a high fee, if the organizers did not think that his presence would add the necessary lustre to such an occasion.

Then we have the reaction of Charles de Brosses, when he arrived in Venice, who was amazed to find that Vivaldi did not enjoy the prestige in his own city that he obviously enjoyed in France. The same would probably have been true of England also, where Vivaldi's music was also very popular.

It is a great pity that we have no record of Vivaldi's own feelings at this point, for we do not even know when he left Venice or when he returned, what itinerary he took, or the people he visited or met en route. We do not even know whether he met his publishers whilst he was in Amsterdam, though this at least we must be able to assume, though Le Cène himself was to die in the same year as Vivaldi, and by the mid-1730s Amsterdam had been losing ground to Paris as a centre of music publishing. If *Il pastro fido* is really Vivaldi's Op. XIII, then the very fact that this was published in Paris by Boivin in 1737 serves to confirm this view.

At all events, the visit to Amsterdam does not seem to have been a very long one, and when it was over, even if he made visits on the return journey, at this period Vivaldi seems to have had no other idea than to return to Venice. After all, he still had his base at the Pietà. His appointment as *maestro de' concerti* which had been achieved somewhat less than unanimously in 1735 – eight votes for, and three abstentions[4] – had been confirmed with no dissenting voice in 1736,[5] and then again in 1736 with eight votes for him and only two against.[6] In March 1738, however, it was a much more closely run thing, with seven for and four against, and on a second ballot the result was the same.[7] We may assume therefore that Vivaldi was not confirmed in his appointment again on this occasion, nor did his name appear on the appointments list in 1739 and 1740.

Perhaps the Ferrara affair had reached the ears of certain governors, who felt that Vivaldi had simply taken things too far. Or it may have been that the cardinal's veto had brought out into the open matters to which the authorities had hitherto been able to turn a blind eye. It may also have been that his repeated absences, or a combination of all of these things, when allied to Vivaldi's personality, had tipped the balance against him. At all events Vivaldi did not totally sever his connections with the Pietà by any means, and continued to be closely involved with it for another two years. What must have affected him, however, was the loss of regular income.

Then, as so often happens in such a situation, Cardinal Ruffo suddenly resigned his see, in June 1738, with a pension of 4,000 ducats. Vivaldi was obviously emboldened to try once again in Ferrara, as we first learn from a letter sent by the Spanish Ambassador in Venice, the Prince of Campoflorido, to Bentivoglio, recommending a protégé of his, the soprano castrato Geremia del Sette. Bentivoglio's reply, dated 5 November 1738, was to tell the ambassador that, since Vivaldi was the composer of the opera, he had better hear the singer. He therefore sent a letter to Vivaldi informing him of this on the very same day – and naturally the composer was delighted, as his reply two days later reveals.

On this occasion Vivaldi was not to be impresario himself, but his old colleague Antonio Mauri. Perhaps he felt it would be tempting fate too much to try yet again to be impresario in Ferrara. At all events, there is a libretto of *Siroe* in the library of the Conservatory in Bologna, which shows that the opera was performed at the Bonacossi theatre in Ferrara during the Carnival of 1739 (meaning the 1738–9 season), and not surprisingly the name part of *Siroe* was played by Geremia del Sette, *virtuoso* of His Excellency the Spanish Ambassador to Venice, and the part of Emira was taken by the Signora Anna Girò. Vivaldi again described himself on the libretto as *maestro di cappella* to the Grand Duke of Tuscany. Also, Olga Rudge pointed out that in the manuscript of *Rosmira fedele* in Turin there is an interpolated aria with the note: Ferrara, 1738, in *Siroe*, scene 13, act 3.[8]

However, all Vivaldi's old fears were realized about the foolishness of allowing his operas to be put on in his absence. *Siroe* – which dated from 1727 – was obviously not a success, and shortly after the opening Vivaldi wrote in desperation to Bentivoglio from Venice on 2 January 1739. He said that his reputation in Ferrara had been 'whipped' to such a point that he could not follow up *Siroe* with *Farnace*, as had been intended, and as had been stipulated in the contract with Mauri. His major fault, it seemed to him, had been that his recitatives were atrocious. With everything in his name, he went on, and the fact that his reputation was held up before the whole of Europe, and in view of the fact that he had composed ninety-four operas, he could not endure such a state of affairs.

This particular letter is perhaps most interesting, however, for the fact that Vivaldi states quite categorically that he had composed ninety-four operas, which is almost twice as many as we have trace of at the present time. Although one can take some of the statistics in the earlier letter as being merely approximate – for example the number of years he has travelled and the period of time since he stopped saying Mass – it is the choice of the exact number that inclines one to believe that it may well be accurate. Even assuming that Vivaldi included all his reworkings as individual operas, this would probably still leave us with more to discover.

He then went on to be more specific, saying that Pietro Antonio Berretta, who was playing the first harpsichord, had never had his confidence from the start, and at the first rehearsals Vivaldi had felt that 'he did not know where his head was when it came to accompanying recitatives'. Berretta was appointed *maestro di cappella* of Ferrara Cathedral that year, and Signor Acciaiolo, a Ferrarese opera singer, had assured Vivaldi that he was a good virtuoso and an honest man, but instead he had turned out to be 'an ignorant temeraire'. The very same recitatives, Vivaldi complained, when performed previously in Ancona, had been highly applauded. In a final outpouring he went on:

> Excellency, I am at the point of desperation. Nor can I endure such an ignorant person to establish his fortune on the destruction of my poor name. I beg you, for mercy's sake, not to abandon me, for I swear to Your Excellency that if I remain unprotected, I will do extreme things to cover my honour, because whoever takes away my honour may take away my life.[9]

In this extraordinary passage Vivaldi seems to be making a last attempt to draw sympathy from Bentivoglio, but the marquis seems to have gone beyond the point where he was either able, or indeed willing, to involve himself further. For one thing there seems to have been some kind of commissioner, possibly representing the ecclesiastical authorities, present in Ferrara, and Bentivoglio said that he could not let himself be mixed up in the matter. His last words – dated 7 January 1739 – are therefore calmly, if not a little coldly, dignified: 'However, I can do nothing in the present situation, nor ought you to build any foundation on the hope of any assistance, which upon careful reflection, I am in no position to give you. I have a very strong desire.'[10]

A few days later Bentivoglio left for Venice, so it is just possible that he saw Vivaldi there, and helped to arrange some sort of indemnity for the composer.

Vivaldi had not been neglecting the Venetian opera world, however, and at this time he had renewed his acquaintance with the S. Angelo theatre, of which Fabrizio Brugnolo was still in charge, and during the Carnival of 1738–9 Vivaldi produced a new opera there, *L'oracolo in Messenia* (RV

726), to a libretto by Apostolo Zeno; a pasticcio *Rosmira fedele* (RV 731), with libretto by Stampiglia, and incorporating arias by Handel, Hasse, Pergolesi and others; and a revival of *Armida*, with Anna Girò singing principal roles in all three.

An event which shook the musical world of Venice that same year was the death of Benedetto Marcello on 24 July.[11] Indeed for some it was Marcello who represented the true spirit of Venetian music, and not Vivaldi. Perhaps Vivaldi did not regret Marcello's passing, for the latter had apparently had little time for the Red Priest. All the same, it was sad that Marcello's career should end in this way. He had gone to Brescia in a somewhat menial official capacity as *camerlengo* or chamberlain, in May of 1738, after spending the years from 1730 to 1737 at Pola in Istria (now Pula in Yugoslavia), then part of the Venetian possessions south of Trieste. The tuberculosis of which he died was probably contracted during his long period of service there.

It was in the summer of this year, in August 1739, that Charles de Brosses made his visit to Venice already referred to, and met Vivaldi. And one sees from his account that any idea of Vivaldi enjoying a golden autumn of his life in his native city was far from the truth. There is the same old Vivaldi there, but times have changed:

Vivaldi has become one of my intimate friends, so as to sell me some very expensive concertos. He has in part succeeded, and I too in that which I desired, namely to hear him and have frequent good musical recreation: he is a *vecchio* with a prodigious fury for composition. I have heard him boast that he has composed a concerto, with all its parts, faster than a copyist could write it out. I have found, to my great astonishment, that he is not as esteemed as he merits in this country, where everything is fashion, where they have long heard his works, and where last year's music is no longer box office. The famous Saxon is fêted today. I heard him in his own home, as well as the celebrated Faustina, his wife, who sings with great taste and charming lightness; but it is no longer a fresh voice. She is the most complaisant and best woman in the world; but she is not the best singer.[12]

The 'Saxon' here is obviously not Handel, as some writers have indicated, when the whole quotation was not given, since Handel never married. In any case, Faustina was married to the composer Johann Adolph Hasse (1706–83), so it must be to him that De Brosses refers.

De Brosses' account is also interesting for the descriptions it gives of the state of music in the *ospedali* at this time, and Venetian musical life in general. We have already seen some of these examples, but there were practices which were quite common in Venice at the time, and indeed had been for some years past, but which appealed as novel to De Brosses: 'They have here a kind of music of which we know nothing in France, and which seems to me more appropriate than any other for small gardens. It consists of large concertos where there is no principal violin.'[13] This sort of concerto (grosso) was certainly not new to Vivaldi or the Venetians at large, and such open-air concerts had been given regularly, as for example the one given on 2 September 1726, described as a *pastorale in musica*, on the Rio S. Severo, in front of the Ottoboni Palace.

The autumn of 1739 saw what may well have been Vivaldi's last opera, *Feraspe* (RV 713), to a libretto by Francesco Silvani, which was performed at the S. Angelo theatre. There was a kind of poetic justice in the fact that he ended where he had begun in Venice – at the S. Angelo – though, if we are to believe De Brosses, Vivaldi was no longer box office there.

There may, however, have been a happy ending to the Ferrara episode after all, for there is a despatch from Madrid sent by Filippo Maria Gaggiolo to Modena, which is dated 7 November 1739, telling of the great success enjoyed in the Spanish capital by an opera *Farnace*, 'sung by the choicest voices in Europe'. Given the fact that it was the Spanish Ambassador to Venice who first wrote to Bentivoglio about his protégé, and almost certainly came into contact with Vivaldi as a result, this may mean that what Vivaldi lost on the Ferrara episode may have been recouped in Madrid. Remo Giazotto mentions a concert at the Spanish Ambassador's given in early 1740, during the course of which Anna Girò sang, accompanied at the harpsichord by ... Vivaldi himself.[14]

This long association with Anna Girò is extremely interesting in a purely professional way when one considers Vivaldi's vocal music. Throughout musical history there have been several notable examples of associations between composers and singers or instrumentalists, and this has almost always encouraged the development of a particular aspect of that composer's talent. It is hard, however, to feel that in the case of Vivaldi and Anna Girò the association was particularly beneficial to Vivaldi's understanding of the voice. Of course she may have had only a limited talent as a singer, and even allowing for the fact that many of the accounts that have come down to us were probably biased against her, it does not seem that she was a very great singer. She managed to make a career for herself, however – and not only in Vivaldi's operas – so she was obviously a competent performer. Further than that, however, it is hard to go, except that even a less than great voice can give much pleasure when it is used intelligently and effectively.

If what Goldoni said is correct, that Vivaldi only gave Anna Girò the sort of arias she preferred, then this is a pity, since had he been prepared to experiment more – as he did with instruments – then his vocal music might have been very different. Of course one must make the distinction between his operatic and secular music, and the more traditional sacred music, and such an ostensibly sacred work as the *Gloria* (RV 589) embraces both.

Considering how much liturgical music Vivaldi wrote, it is strange that only one of his Masses has survived complete, and that is a copy in the University Library in Warsaw (RV 586). Also in this library is a *Credo* (RV 592), otherwise the remaining surviving works are the autograph manuscripts in Turin, which consist of a two-choir *Kyrie* (RV 587), two settings of the *Gloria* (RV 588 and 589) and a *Credo* (RV 591). There is a lost *Gloria* (RV 590) mentioned in the

166

Kreuzherren catalogue, but this is the sum total of settings of sections of the Mass. The *Gloria* in D (RV 589) is probably the most popular of these works, chiefly because it has been available in a performing edition since the 1930s, and has been recorded. In fact it has probably been through this work and the *Four seasons* that modern interest in Vivaldi's music was made possible. Certainly the brilliant opening, with its assertive octave leaps and incisive rhythms for the trumpets, which Vivaldi repeated towards the end of the work, immediately claim the listener's attention. From the traditional sacred music aspect, there are some impressive examples of the composer's technical skill in the fugal passages; then as typical of Vivaldi himself, a pretty tune in 12/8 for oboe and soprano; and in a more secular vein, an effective, if somewhat operatic, aria for contralto interrupted periodically by the chorus – thus creating considerable variety within the work. It may well have been written for the girls at the Pietà, since there are no tenor or bass solos, and it is conceivable that the work could have been performed without male voices. On other occasions male singers were probably brought in from outside.

There are several psalm settings amongst the manuscripts in Turin, most of them the Vesper psalms and antiphons, such as 69, and 109–113; two settings of *Magnificat*; various hymns and sequences, including another well known work, *Stabat Mater* (RV 621) for alto and string orchestra and continuo, and twenty motets and 'introductions' – usually for a *Gloria*, *Miserere* or *Dixit Dominus* – to non-liturgical texts. The fact that all this last group are for soprano or alto inclines one to the belief that they were written for the Pietà, and the preponderance of Marian texts, particularly amongst the hymns and antiphons, tends to strengthen this view, especially since the church of the Pietà is dedicated to the Virgin Mary.

In addition to the sacred vocal works, there are nearly forty cantatas for soprano or alto – not one of them for tenor or bass – most of which are simply for voice and basso continuo, though nine have in addition strings, and occasionally woodwind. Two of this last group bear dedications, the first (RV 685) is in praise of Monsignor da Bagni, Bishop of Mantua, and the second (RV 686) in praise of Philip of Hesse-Darmstadt, Governor of Mantua. As we saw earlier, Vivaldi wrote other works with similar dedications, and on a somewhat larger scale, such as the *serenata a quattro voci* for the birthday of the landgrave in 1726 (RV 692), the two French oriented works, *La Gloria e Imeneo* and *La Sena festeggiante* (RV 687 and 693), and four others, making eight in all of which we have records, though of course more may come to light in time.

One might take as a 'typical' motet *Longe mala umbrae terrores* . . . (RV 629) which exists in an autograph manuscript in Turin. It is conveniently subtitled *Motteto in ogni tempo*, in other words with no particular application to any festival or ceremony of the Church, which is just as well, since not only is the text not liturgical, but it is rather difficult to construe into anything very meaningful apart from a general expression of belief in the efficaciousness of a celestial power in combating unpleasantness. It is virtually a concerto for solo voice accompanied by four-part strings and basso continuo. The first section is a *da capo* aria which opens with repeated figures of three strong chords with the strings in unison, punctuated by rapid semiquaver passages from the upper strings: a typical Vivaldi effect. When the voice enters, the strings are reduced to the three upper parts only most of the time. A recitative then leads into a *largo* in three sections (the last a repeat *dal segno*), and the third 'movement' of this vocal concerto is a brilliant *Alleluia*, demonstrating countless possibilities of runs, trills, syncopation, and the use of sequences to build up climaxes. The central *largo* has some beautiful melodic moments, but one is drawn to the conclusion that there is nothing essentially vocal about those moments. One feels much the same about the *Stabat Mater*, which is possibly more readily accessible, since it has been recorded, and in the last analysis one comes to this conclusion about virtually all of Vivaldi's vocal music. Despite the valiant attempts of many writers to put the composer on the same footing as both an instrumental and a vocal genius, it is hard, in the event, to go along with them.

There is nothing that convinces one that Vivaldi's approach to writing for voices was any different from his approach to writing for instruments. Indeed quite often the vocal music comes across better when played by the instruments without the voice, especially in view of the fact that they so often double each other. One feels that, despite his association with Anna Girò and his long experience of writing opera, Vivaldi was really much more at home when composing for instruments alone. One feels that his knowledge of how instruments could sound was endless, and he was forever exploiting their possibilities to the full, but with the voice he does not even seem to begin to treat it as a medium in its own right. As a result, it is somewhat ungrateful music for a singer to perform, since the phrases are in themselves musically very pleasing. At its most convincing, one gets the impression that Vivaldi's vocal music succeeds in operatic terms, and this is true of the sacred vocal music as well as the secular.

In view of what we have already learnt of contemporary conditions in the churches of Venice, and the all-pervasive influence of operatic music, this should not surprise us, nor should it be in any way regarded as a reflection upon Vivaldi's sincerity in matters of religious conviction, let alone his abilities as a composer. We are only too grateful that he has left to us music that today can speak directly to all sorts and conditions of men.

If the public were growing tired of Vivaldi's operas, as De Brosses' report would suggest, he still held sway at the Pietà, and provided it with music for all occasions. In fact it was soon to see one of the most brilliant foreign visits Venice had known for some time. On 19 December 1739 Prince Frederick Christian, son of Frederick Augustus, King of Poland and Elector of Saxony, arrived in the city. He was returning from Naples, where his sister had married, the year before, Don Carlos, the future Charles III of Spain. Prince Frederick Christian stayed in the Foscari Palace, attended by four sons of aristocratic family. There was a constant round of entertainment – bull fights, jousting, wrestling, aquatic events, masques, operas, serenades and

169

visits to public buildings such as churches, the Arsenale and the glassworks.

Among the many musical events were three soirées given by the girls of the Pietà, the Mendicanti and the Incurabili on 21 and 29 March and 4 April 1740 respectively. The girls of the Pietà performed a cantata *Il coro delle muse*, and all the famous names were there – Albetta, Ambrosina, Apollonia, Bolognese, Chiaretta (who was also an excellent violinist, as we know from De Brosses), Fortunata, Giuletta, Margherita and Teresa. At the end of the first section of the cantata a concerto for viola d'amore and lute, with *ripieno di moltissimi strumenti* was played, the manuscript of which is in the Dresden collection (RV 540). After the second section a concerto with *violini obbligati con eco* (RV 552) was performed, and a sinfonia (RV 149) and another concerto (RV 558) opened and closed the evening's performance.

The orchestration of this last concerto is one of Vivaldi's more exotic, requiring two violins '*in tromba marina*', two recorders, two trumpets, two mandolines, two *salmoe*, two theorboes and 'cello, all in addition to the basic string orchestra and basso continuo. One must assume that Vivaldi, with his delight in orchestral colour, specifically requested the violins to give the effect of the *tromba marina* which, despite its name (meaning marine trumpet), was in fact a stringed instrument, which was bowed above the point of touching or fingering the string. Some examples had two strings, of which one presumably sounded as a drone, whilst the other string passed over a bridge which had one foot shorter than the other, so that it vibrated against a metal or ivory plate on the body of the instrument, which had quite a long sound box.

In his opera *Mitridate Eupatore* (1707), Alessandro Scarlatti used a pair of tromba marinas to echo two muted trumpets, which is interesting in view of Vivaldi's subsequent incorporation of the effect in writing for violins. Nevertheless, the problems of balance posed by writing for such a heterogeneous collection of instruments must have been considerable. In the Pietà accounts are records of the payments made to Vivaldi for these four works, namely fifteen ducats and thirteen lire, on 27 April 1740.[15]

Two days later, on 29 April, however, there is an account of a meeting of the governors of the Pietà, in the course of which they insisted on the necessity of:

> creating a repertoire of concertos for organ and other instruments, to maintain the reputation that the *coro* has established; since it is understood, moreover, that the Reverend Vivaldi is about to leave the Dominante [Venice], and that he possesses an important number of concertos ready made, it would be necessary to acquire these. It is understood that the governors of the *coro* will continue to have the responsibility for buying these concertos, when they think fit, at the cost of one ducat each.[16]

The voting figures on this occasion were unsatisfactory. Only four voted for the motion, and three against, but with three abstentions it was lost. However, on 12 May Vivaldi was paid the much larger sum of seventy ducats and twenty-three lire for twenty concertos, so one must assume that another vote was taken, or some other means was found of putting the purchase through.[17] At all events, one has the impression that Vivaldi was selling off his manuscripts prior to his departure.

There was one more publishing venture, announced by the *Mercure de France* in December 1740, and this was possibly his Op. xiv, a set of six 'cello sonatas, with the firm of Le Clerc le Cadet. In the publication he was still described as *maestro de' concerti* of the Pietà, and in the accounts of the Pietà itself for 12 May 1740, although there is no record that he still held such a title, he is referred to in the same way, when paid 440 lire for expenses.[18] Gone, however, were the days when the ducats were as abundant as the notes he wrote.

In those days a ducat was the cost of a day's lodging at an inn, and in his day, according to the *Commemoriali Gradenigo*, Vivaldi had earned more than 50,000 ducats – or was it a slip of a pen, and the writer really meant 5,000? At all events, it was known that he had died poor in Vienna, 'through his inordinate extravagance'.

Working from this information, Rodolfo Gallo finally established in 1938 that Vivaldi had been buried with what was virtually a pauper's funeral in Vienna on 28 July 1741. Was he contemplating settling in Vienna, or was he bound for Dresden, and visited Vienna en route?

Keysler, writing in 1730, said of Vienna:

> The band of music for the imperial chapel and the palace consists of above a hundred and twenty persons, and stands the emperor, at least, in two hundred thousand guldens a year. Though several of the female vocal performers have a salary of six thousand guldens, yet it is a saying among the Italians, that Vienna is the hospital of the *virtuose* or singers, and that they never go thither till they are worn out.[19]

Did Vivaldi know this, one wonders?

Certainly there had been others in whose footsteps Vivaldi might have followed, such as Antonio Caldara, some eight years his senior, who had been a pupil of Legrenzi, a 'cellist at S. Marco, and then *maestro di cappella* at Mantua and composer to Charles III in Barcelona, before he finally settled in Vienna as second *maestro di cappella* in the Imperial chapel in 1716. For the next twenty years, until his death on 28 December 1736, he was highly thought of by the Habsburgs. Charles VI was apparently very fond of Vivaldi and his music, and we have seen how they met in Italy. Vivaldi may have been hoping for patronage from Charles VI, but, if so, he was thwarted by the death of the emperor on 20 October 1740. Charles VI had always enjoyed excellent health, and his death was totally unexpected. He was taken ill whilst on a hunting holiday at the castle of Halbthurm in Hungary, and the story went that he was poisoned – either by design or accident – by a dish of mushrooms, the famous *plat de champignons* which Voltaire said had altered the history of Europe. Certainly with the death of Charles VI, the male line of the Habsburgs became extinct, and he was succeeded by his daughter Maria Theresa.

Assuming that Vivaldi was on his way to Dresden, then he spent a long time in Vienna, especially considering that his hopes in the emperor's patronage had been dashed almost as soon as he arrived in Vienna. Of course he may have wanted to see what happened in the new reign. There might well have been hope there, for Maria Theresa's husband Francis, who had been successively Duke of Lorraine and Grand Duke of Tuscany, had been the recipient of Vivaldi's dedications, and was to become Holy Roman Emperor in 1745. Already, on 21 November 1740, his wife had made him co-regent. Or Vivaldi may have looked to his connection with Count Morzin. Or the illness which carried him off may already have begun to make itself apparent shortly after his arrival. From the records that we have, it would seem that some trouble in the stomach – a cancer or some internal inflammation – claimed him, and he was buried on 28 July 1741 in the *Bürgerspital*. Only nineteen florins and forty-five kreutzer were spent on the funeral, and he was only entitled to the *Kleingeläut* or pauper's peal of bells, which only cost two florins and thirty-six kreutzer. He had six pall-bearers and six choirboys, too, but one sees how mean all of this was when the same records reveal that a nobleman's funeral might cost at least one hundred florins.[20] Vivaldi, to die in this way, who had known the splendour of Venice in its prime!

9. Venetian Sunset

It has been generally assumed – largely, perhaps, under the influence of Pincherle – that after the departure and death of Vivaldi the standard of the music at the Pietà began a slow decline, and that the appointment of Nicolò Porpora as *maestro di coro* on 26 January 1742[1] did little or nothing to halt this decline. However, Porpora was only at the Pietà for a year, until 15 February 1743, so his presence there can have had little very lasting effect one way or the other. Indeed, there is much to suggest that the standard at the Pietà was maintained for at least another twenty years or so.

In 1750, for example, new teachers were appointed for violin, flute and 'cello, and in 1751 horn and even timpani, though admittedly this last was only a temporary appointment for six months.[2] Even so, the teaching establishment seems to have been kept up to this strength into the mid- to late-1760s. Not all the visitors were perceptive as to the actual musical standards, but we have the testimony of several in this second half of the eighteenth century.

Madame du Bocage, writing on 1 June 1757, still found enough to be charmed with:

> We went after the meal to the hospitals famous for their seraphic concerts, consisting of girls: voices, instruments, all is feminine and divine; their sweet and penetrating harmonies make the vault resound and charm the ears. A veiled grille protects them from curious gazers and imparts to their songs even more resemblance to the melody of the angels.[3]

P. J. Grosley, in his *Nouveaux mémoires* of 1764, though writing of 1758, and therefore only a year after Madame du Bocage, described the situation in a way by now familiar:

174

In these conservatories, administered with fervour by a few old Senators, orphans and foundlings are brought up, provided for and given dowries, out of the very considerable funds belonging to each of these houses, under the direction of the best masters. Music is the chief part of an education that seems most suited to form Laïses and Aspasias than nuns or mothers of families.[4]

When one looks more closely at this account, one sees that it deals only with the general reaction to the system of the *ospedali*, and Grosley gives the impression that things were still not at all bad as far as the general musical standard went, even though the rest left much to be desired. As he continues:

Be that as it may, these conservatories have in turn beautiful vespers with music, followed by a large motet, of which the hirers of chairs sell the words, which are nothing more than a bad rhyming assembly of Latin words, where barbarisms and solecisms are more common than sense and reason; it is ordinarily the work of the sacristan. The most brilliant music decorates this bad base: it is performed, both as to the vocal part and the instrumental, entirely by the girls of the house, whom one sees through the grille decorated with light crêpe, fluttering about and giving themselves up to all the movements required for the execution of the most lively music: the whole is almost always in the Italian style, that is to say with no beating time. One of these motets we heard lacked a large section because Scarlati [*sic*] was beating time in the Neapolitan manner; that is to say, using the *levé* where other Italians use the *frappé*.

The general atmosphere was very similar to that which Grosley found at the convent of S. Lorenzo:

The nuns, all gentlewomen, came and went at two large grilles on either side of the altar, held conversations there and distributed refreshments to the cavalieri and priests

175

who all, fans in their hands, were in a circle at both grilles. The celebrant and his assistants, seated almost all the time, and having as their vista everyone's back, perspired, wiped themselves, and appeared to be awaiting dinner with the greatest impatience. The music and the bustle had begun with the first vespers, which are by no means the less brilliant part of this feast. On Ascension Day we had a similar and even greater spectacle in the larger church of another monastery. There the music was divided into two choirs, which combined for certain pieces. All this music, in spite of the variety and complexity of its parts, is executed without beating time. The composer is only occupied, like a general in the army, in exciting by gesture and voice, those who are going into the attack.[5]

It would be fair to say that by now, however, the secular element had intruded to such a degree that as soon as the musical standard began to fall, then the days of the musical establishments of the *ospedali* were indeed numbered.

When Karl Ditters von Dittersdorf (1739–99) visited the Incurabili in 1764 he heard a very ordinary oratorio performed rather badly, much to his disappointment. The Pietà still attempted to live up to its once justified reputation, certainly when Charles Burney visited Venice in 1770, though he felt that what he heard was little better than mediocrity, despite a certain amount of skill and technique:

I went to the Pietà tonight, but there was little company and the girls performed but indifferently. They played a thousand tricks in their closes especially in the duets, where they in sport tried who could go highest, lowest, quickest etc to the utmost exertion of their powers. This hospital has the reputation of being the best, not for what it does *now*, but for what it *has* done heretofore for I think, in point of singing both the Incurabili Hospital and the Mendicanti are before it.[6]

Just before he left, Burney went to the Mendicanti:

Last night I was prodigiously well entertained by being

176

admitted ... *into* the conservatorio of the Mendicanti, where I *saw* as well as *heard* a charming concert performed in all its parts by females ... I was invited *into* the music school at the Mendicanti for tonight and had an offer of the same interiour [*sic*] entertainment at the other three conservatories, but Satan avaunt, I will positively set off for Bologna to night.[7]

At this time the *maestro di coro* at the Incurabili was no less a person than Baldassare Galuppi (1706–85), which may well have accounted for the excellence of the music, in Burney's opinion. Galuppi had probably only been confirmed in his appointment in December 1768;[8] but he had certainly been composing for the Incurabili for some time before that. Prior to his connection with the Incurabili, Galuppi had had a long period of service with the Mendicanti as *maestro di musica*, from 1740 until some time in 1751, though at the early part of this association he had been absent in London, where some of his operas were performed. He had also had a spell of about two years early in his career – from 1726–8 – as harpsichordist at the Pergola theatre in Florence, during which time Vivaldi's *Ipermestra* was put on, and possibly other of his operas. Since Galuppi's father was also a barber-violinist, and he was born on the island of Burano in the Venetian lagoon, one wonders how much they had in common. Galuppi made his first attempt at composing opera at the tender age of sixteen. In fact the tradition is that it was so bad that it attracted the attention of Benedetto Marcello, who encouraged Galuppi to study seriously with Lotti.

Certainly the connection with Marcello, and the fact that Galuppi was second *maestro* at S. Marco from 1748 onwards, might well explain why we have no record of any friendship between Galuppi and Vivaldi. Vivaldi was never part of the establishment at S. Marco, nor did Galuppi have anything to do with the Pietà. Galuppi was, however, collaborator with Goldoni, so the two men's lives may well have overlapped in some connection. Possibly in the 1770s the Pietà had lost its edge to the Incurabili, as Burney indicated. Certainly with Galuppi there, there would be a good reason.

Perhaps fashion, too, helped to kill off the popularity of the *ospedali*. The author of *De Venise – Remarques sur la musique et la danse ou : lettres de Mr G [oudar] a Milord P [embroke]*, published in 1773, declares:

> For me, when I attend the oratorios of these hospitals, once set up for the subsistence of the poor and today the warehouse of the great singers with drums, side drums and trumpets; music drawn from the noise of battle, which is not at all suited to the sex in general, and even less to the cloistered sex, condemned by their state to silence; instead of being touched by this fashion which inspires veneration for the hymns destined to honour religion: when I am present, I say, at this music, I feel so gay, that I always want to dance the rigaudon or trip a minuet in the middle of a *salve regina*.[9]

The *Psalms* of Marcello, the author declared, were much better, and indeed one must confess that they were probably more suitable for the purpose. The same author – probably Ange de Goudar or his wife Sara – was also responsible for a similar work, *Le brigandage de la musique italienne*, published in 1777. The theme is similar:

> The church, turned into a theatre pit, was full of spectators, for the most part foreigners. The ticket that one took at the door cost only two *soldetti*, which ensured that the place was always full. The violinist, the flautist, the oboist, the timpanist, the organist, the chalumeau player were all of the feminine gender; they prayed to God there with a great deal of gaiety, since it was always to the strain of a rigaudon or a minuet. The actresses of this spiritual spectacle were seen only through a grille. All the same the noble Venetians who were their governors had to keep them locked up, since the organist of these conservatoires who directed the orchestra was found to be pregnant, to the great scandal of those who had not yet been so.[10]

178

This somewhat scurrilous account was now all too common, and provided perfect ammunition for the moral indignation of those who loved to be shocked, or a last breath of the exotic for those who wished to be decadent. And yet Venice, and the *ospedali* in particular, were about to put on one of the most brilliant performances ever when the Grand Duke Paul and Grand Duchess Maria Feodorovna of Russia paid a state visit to the Republic in 1782. Luigi Ballarani, writing to Daniele Dolfin, Venetian Ambassador to France from 1780 to 1786, said in his letter, dated 20 January 1782: 'Tomorrow ... a cantata with the girls of the *ospitali* at the same casino [the Filarmonico, on the corner of the Piazza], the 21st the Arsenale with a banquet and celebration; in the S. Benedetto theatre a grand gala'.[11]

Then again, on 25 January:

The princes ... went on to the S. Samuele theatre to see the ballet *Convitato di Pietra*, excellently done by Vigano [Salvatore Vignano, 1769–1821, the dancer and choreographer] ... In the S. Samuele theatre there were two stages pleasantly hung with tapestry and thrown into one by the Savi Cassieri [Ministry of Finance] ... In the evening I was invited to the Casino Filarmonico, in *baùta calata* [presumably masks were dispensed with by official decree for the occasion], where there was a cantata given by the girls of the *ospitali*, chosen from all four and reduced to eighty. This singular rarity of Venice surprised the princes, and they would have enjoyed themselves enormously if the crowd of people had not created a mortal constriction.

It is this occasion that was depicted by Guardi in the famous painting in Munich, often referred to in the past as a concert given in a convent. If one compares it with Gabriele Bella's version of the same event, however, in the Galleria Querini Stampalia, then it is obvious, even allowing for Bella's somewhat naïve style, that they are of the same room, and that the concert is patently not taking place in a convent.

179

For one thing, there are no grilles in evidence, and even at their most lax, there does not seem to be any record of the grilles having been abandoned in the churches of the *ospedali* and convents.

Unfortunately, however, the whole visit went somewhat sour on the Venetians, as we again learn from a letter of Luigi Ballarini, this time dated 9 February 1782:

> If the magnificence and liberality with which both the public and private persons celebrated the visit of the Counts of the North to Venice was surprising, then just as miserable was the memory of their characters that they left behind them.
>
> At their lodging they only wanted to pay half what their bill came to, and the landlord has already produced a writ against the Minister Maruzzi, who made the contract. The tip at the Arsenale banquet never materialized; not a bean to the girls of the *ospitali*, nor even a penny to the staff of the Casa Filarmonica.

In fact the visit had cost 109,677 lire, of which 5,615 lire were spent on the concert alone.[12]

By this time the *ospedali* had been nationalized (the exact date was 23 March 1776), so the government now had to bear all the cost of their upkeep. Ten years later, the composer A. Gyrowetz came to Venice, and was rather disappointed with what he found: 'The musical conservatory for young women gave a concert from time to time consisting almost entirely of vocal music. It had some talented conductors, but these *maestri* were almost always away, called to other Italian cities to compose operas.'[13]

This followed shortly on the visit made by Mrs Thrale, and as usual, we may rely on her to give her views on the matter:[14]

> A propos to singing; – we were this evening carried to a well-known conservatory called the Mendicanti; who performed an oratorio in the church with great, and I dare say deserved applause. It was difficult for me to persuade myself that all the performers were women, till, watching

carefully, our eyes convinced us, as they were but slightly grated. The sight of girls, however, handling the double bass, and blowing into the bassoon, did not much please *me*; and the deep-toned voice of her who sung the part of Saul, seemed an odd, unnatural thing enough ...

Well! these pretty syrens were delighted to seize upon us, and pressed our visit to their parlour with a sweetness that I know not who would have resisted. We had no such intent; and amply did their performance repay my curiosity, for visiting Venetian beauties, so justly celebrated for their seducing manners and soft address. They accompanied their voices with the forte-piano, and sung a thousand buffo songs, with all that gay voluptuousness for which their country is renowned.

The school, however, is running to ruin apace; and perhaps the conduct of the married women here may contribute to make such conservatorios useless and neglected ... I thought the ardency of their manners an additional proof of their hunger for fresh prey.

Johann Christian Maier's *Beschreibung von Venedig* (*Description of Venice*),[15] in 1789, catalogued all the usual details, but came to the conclusion that: 'even when they performed the most passionate operatic arias, one could, without being a great connoisseur, discover in their most impassioned accents not the natural tone of passion, but an unfortunate imitation!' In the last analysis it was this that killed not only the music of the *ospedali* and of Venice in general, but Venice itself.

Andrea Maier, *veneziano*, writing in 1821, said:

I will end the picture of the state of Italian music in this century with the commemoration of the four seminaries of girls that existed in Venice. The post of *maestro* in the above-mentioned conservatoires was so sought after by the best composers that the names of Caldara, Gasparini, Buranello, Hasse, Traietta, Sarti, Sacchini, Anfossi, Bertoni, etc., are counted among them. One of their obligations was that of composing each year some oratorios, or melodramas in Latin ... which were executed by both the vocalists and instrumentalists of the above-mentioned girls: institutions possibly unique in Europe, and which formed one of the most pleasing entertainments of our city. That revolution which shook almost to its foundations the edifice of civil society, swallowed in its ruins these pious and useful establishments, and also left closed for ever this fountain of delight for the lovers of the musical art.[16]

What musical fashion, with its lethal changes in preference, had begun to undermine, changing social conditions and the financial situation swept away.

The Incurabili had ceased to exist in 1782, then the Mendicanti in 1796, soon to be followed by the Ospedaletto. In 1797 Venice itself fell to Napoleon. The Pietà continued beyond the other three, but Fétis, writing in the *Revue Musicale* in 1831, declared that the Pietà was the only one of the conservatories to have survived until then, despite the fact that it was but a shadow of its former self, and was then under the direction of Perotti. Finally, Francesco Caffi, writing to his friend Cicogna on 5 June 1843, summed up the sad tale: '[The Pietà] still exists but from the musical point of view, more in name than in fact.'[17]

In 1834 the twenty-two-year-old Robert Browning paid his first visit to Italy. It was hearing a toccata of Galuppi's that drew from him his meditation on the life in Venice that had disappeared:

What, they lived once thus at Venice where the merchants were the kings,
Where St Mark's is, where the Doges used to wed the sea with rings?
Dust and ashes, dead and done with, Venice spent what Venice earned!
The soul, doubtless, is immortal – where a soul can be discerned.
As for Venice and its people, merely born to bloom and drop,

Here on earth they bore their fruitage, mirth and folly
    were the crop:
What of soul was left, I wonder, when the kissing had to
    stop?

There was certainly justification, at such a point in time, for Browning's moral censure on the Venetians, though whether the course of history – the course of a civilization's development – could ever have been altered, is very much open to doubt. And indeed, would we have wanted it any other way? We all need a Venice, to greater or lesser degree. Ironically enough Browning fell under its spell sufficiently to buy the Ca' Rezzonico and end his days there. Through that vast, cold building, Venice claimed its due in the end. It can be decidedly cool inside Ca' Rezzonico, even at the height of summer, but in early January the cold is cruelly penetrating, one's breath hangs in the air, and one echoes, with Browning, the last words of his poem: 'I feel chilly and grown old'.

Happily Vivaldi's memory, and above all his music, was not destined to die a lingering death in decaying Venice or remain interred in a pauper's grave in Vienna. In fact it is symbolic that we no longer can point out the site of his grave. His monument knows no time or place. It will last as long as there are human beings to play his music, and remember with thanks the *prete rosso*.

10. The Vivaldi Revival

Although Vivaldi's disappearance from Venetian musical life was sudden and dramatic, elsewhere his reputation was such that his memory was kept alive and his music played for some considerable time after his death. Nor must one forget that the Pietà probably went on using the manuscripts in their possession, certainly as long as there were people there who knew him or knew of him, and even on the Venetian stage his music continued to be heard after his death, as for example in the opera *Ernelinda*, which was given there in 1750. It was in fact a reworking at *La fede tradita e vindicata*, and in its new guise included music by both Galuppi and Gasparini, in addition to Vivaldi's original work.

Abroad his operas lasted even longer. For example, music by Vivaldi was included in an opera by the name of *Siroe rè di Persia* (Ryom Anhang 54) in Brunswick in 1767, along with music by Handel, Hasse, Vinci and Wagenseil. In London his operas had an even longer life. His music had been used as early as 1732–3 for a performance of Ben Jonson's *The alchemist* (Ryom Anhang 39), along with music by Corelli, Geminiani and Handel. Also that year, according to the Grove article on Handel, was the opera *Semiramide* (Ryom Anhang 53), with recitatives by Handel, but the arias probably chiefly by Vivaldi. His arias again figured in *Didone* (Ryom Anhang 67), given in London in April 1737, and *The golden pippin* (Ryom Anhang 47) – an 'English burletta' put together by Thomas Arne, in 1775.

The next year, 1776, saw the start of publication of both Burney's and Hawkins' histories of music, and the interment of Vivaldi's reputation in the encyclopedias and dictionaries from which he gradually disappeared as his music was forgotten, and baroque music generally became neglected. One tends then to imagine that Vivaldi was totally forgotten until some thirty or forty years ago, when the first modern performances were heard, and the first performing editions of his music were published. Certainly as far as the music-loving public at large is concerned, this is largely true.

When one looks a little more closely at the facts, however, then the picture is slightly different. When Arnold Schering published his history of the concerto in 1905, despite the fact that he had little biographical information available and only a fraction of the works now known to us today – largely in the Bach transcriptions and collections such as those in Dresden – he firmly recognized and acknowledged the important, and even fundamental, role played by Vivaldi in the development of the concerto.[1] This showed the direction for scholars to take, and one in particular, Marc Pincherle, made Vivaldi the object of his special attention, and almost single-handed brought about the resurrection of Vivaldi, both as a person and as a first-rank musician.

The second part of this two-fold achievement might never have happened, however, in the way it did, had it not been for one of those extraordinary accidents that happen in the history of scholarship, and which are capable of turning research into detective stories. Such a thing happened in Vivaldi's case, and was largely the work of a music professor from Turin University, Alberto Gentili.

Gentili had always been interested in the history of the court orchestra of Turin, which had flourished in the eighteenth century under the influence of the violinist G. B. Somis (1688–1763) and his followers. When the upheaval of the Napoleonic wars made it too difficult for the orchestra to carry on in Turin, it went with the court to Sardinia. Savoy and Piedmont, of which Turin is the capital, were part of the Kingdom of Sardinia until 1861, when Italy was united under the House of Savoy. Since the music library of the orchestra was much too large to take, it was hidden in a safe place before the court's departure. Unfortunately it was so well hidden that when the orchestra returned, no one could remember where it was, except that it had been placed in a monastery somewhere in Piedmont.

The enigma of the lost library fascinated Gentili for years, and if ever he came across a report of a find of music he would follow it up in case it led him to the famous library. Then in the autumn of 1926 the National Library in Turin, whose director was at that time Luigi Torri, was approached to value a collection of prints and musical manuscripts in the possession of a monastery at Monferrato, almost halfway between Turin and Milan. The monks needed money to carry out repairs to their buildings, and the best method they could envisage for raising the money was to sell a collection of books given them by the Durazzo family of Genoa. There were some ninety-five volumes, of which no fewer than fourteen contained works by Vivaldi.

An ancestor of the Durazzo family, Count Giacomo Durazzo (1717–94) was appointed Genoese Ambassador to Vienna in 1749. He married Aloisa Ernestine Ungnad von Weissenwolff, and mainly through her position in society rapidly made his way into the Imperial service, and in 1752 became an honorary privy councillor. He soon became the superintendent of court spectacles, and then director of the court theatre (June 1754) and administrator of the court orchestra. Perhaps his greatest achievement was the encouragement he gave to Gluck in his collaboration with Calzabigi in the production of *Orfeo*, which had its première on 5 October 1762.

However, Durazzo, it was claimed, was feathering his own nest with the funds at his disposal, and he was forced to give up his posts. He was not disgraced, however, for he then became Austrian Ambassador to Venice in 1765, and in his large palazzo, with its own theatre, he went on patronizing musicians. He also began to collect manuscripts and prints, and in 1784 Count Bartolomeo Benincasa, who was a friend of Durazzo, published his *Descrizione della raccolta di stampe di S. Conte Jacopo Durazzo, esposta in una dissertazione sull'arte dell'intaglio a stampa* (*Description of the collection of prints . . .*), in Parma. As to how the Vivaldi manuscripts came into Durazzo's possession, at least three possibilities would seem to commend themselves. Firstly, he may have bought up whatever manuscripts Vivaldi had in his possession when he arrived in Vienna, and which were on the market after his death, though in view of the fact that Vivaldi was apparently selling them off at a ducat each before he left Venice, these may not have been very numerous. Moreover, Durazzo did not arrive in Vienna until some seven or eight years after Vivaldi's death. Secondly, when Durazzo arrived in Venice in 1765, there may have been Vivaldi manuscripts in circulation which Vivaldi himself had sold during his career, as well as the performing scores of operas which seem, from one of Vivaldi's letters to Benti-voglio, to have been sometimes kept at the theatre. When the operas were no longer performed, these manuscripts may well have come on to the market. Thirdly, there was a large collection of Vivaldi's music at the Pietà. This was doubtless used after Vivaldi's death, but by no means all the staff and governing body felt the same about its worth. So much was made obvious when Vivaldi offered his manu-scripts to the governors before he left Venice, and the motion to go ahead with the purchase was not officially carried.

Durazzo stayed on as ambassador to Venice until his death on 15 October 1794, thus witnessing the national-ization, and much of the gradual disappearance, of the musical establishments of the *ospedali*. In fact had he lived another two or three years he would have witnessed the end of the Venetian Republic also. Be that as it may, he was obviously in a very good position to gather up whatever manuscripts came on to the market. It was a miracle that Durazzo's collection remained intact, since in the upheaval caused by the ensuing Napoleonic wars, incalculable damage was done to libraries and art collections, and treasures were taken from one end of Europe to another. It was a time for unscrupulous dealers and collectors to make large profits and to enrich their collections at the expense of unsuspecting or helpless victims.

When Alberto Gentili was shown the Durazzo collection, a dealer was already involved as agent for the sale, and it was vital on this occasion that he be bypassed in the interests of research and scholarship. As a result Gentili had to indulge in a certain amount of deviousness. The obvious purchaser of the collection ought to have been the Turin

National Library, but it simply did not have the necessary amount of money. Whilst looking for other means of raising the money, Gentili had to hope that news of the find and its availability on the market did not reach the wrong ears. Luckily a banker from Turin, Roberto Foà, said that he would buy the collection and donate it to the library in memory of his son Mauro, who had died in childhood. The business was concluded on 15 February 1927, and on 28 January next year Gentili organized a concert in Turin of transcriptions he had made from the Foà Collection.

Whilst working on these transcriptions, Gentili realized that the Vivaldi scores were all numbered in pairs, consecutively, but some lacked the even pair, and some the odd. This meant that originally the complete collection had been twice as large as what now constituted the Foà bequest, and that it had probably been divided at some point between two heirs. In conjunction with Luigi Torri, director of the National Library, he began to make a systematic search of all possible locations, and the help of a genealogical expert, Marquis Faustino Curlo, was sought, so that all surviving members of the Durazzo family might be traced. Once again, secrecy was of the essence, since once the news of the acquisition of the first half of the collection was announced, and the conditions surrounding its identification, many libraries in monasteries and private hands were being turned upside down in the hopes of bringing the rest to light.

Eventually contact was established with a descendant of the Durazzo family who lived in Genoa, Marquis Giuseppe Maria Durazzo, via Curlo and the marquis's confessor, a Jesuit priest. In fact the marquis turned out to be a nephew of the same Durazzo who had left the first part of the collection to the monks at Monferrato. He had a large and somewhat chaotic library which he had inherited from his father, and it seemed to Gentili that the missing volumes might well be amongst it. However, not only had the marquis forbidden anyone to go near the library, including the servants, but when he heard that the monks had sold their part of the inheritance, he was outraged.

In the circumstances, then, the marquis was hardly likely

to be particularly well disposed when it came to a request to search amongst the books in his library for the missing volumes. Through the offices of the Jesuit confessor permission was, in the end, granted, and of course the missing volumes were identified. It was almost three years, however, before the marquis consented to the sale of the volumes, on 30 January 1930. Gentili was again in luck when he found a second rich donor, this time a textile manufacturer from Turin called Filippo Giordano. By a curious coincidence he too had lost an infant son, Renzo, in whose memory the donation was made.

The last word had not been heard from the marquis, however. One of the conditions under which he had agreed to the sale was that the music should never be published. This effectively meant that it would never be performed either. The fight in both civil and ecclesiastical courts to countermand this condition was long and complicated, in the best Italian manner, but eventually Olga Rudge – whose name will always be remembered as one of the pioneers of the Vivaldi 'revival' – was able to publish a catalogue of the complete collection in 1936, thus making possible a serious study of it. The Accademia Musicale Chigiana in Siena continued the work, and more recent institutions, such as the Fondazione Cini in Venice, have greatly helped to further it.

Unfortunately a certain amount of anarchy has reigned in the business of cataloguing the works as they became known, and no fewer than four systems have been in use hitherto – Rinaldi, Pincherle, Fanna and Ricordi – but since Peter Ryom undertook a thorough revision of the oeuvre, including many works not known to the previous cataloguers, this has made a fifth. In the hopes that his work will now subsume that of the previous systems, it ought to be used as often as possible, and in this way will become the standard system of reference. Hence its use throughout this book.

This, however, is but one step along the road in establishing an *urtext* edition of all the Vivaldi works known to us, for this is fraught with problems, since it is always

189

possible that yet another version of a work will be discovered, after the publication of an 'authentic' version, which may turn out to be the real 'authentic' one. With the operas this aspect of the problem is particularly acute, since in some cases Vivaldi himself left no one 'definitive' version of his operas. To anyone attempting to establish a performing edition of, for example, *Il Teuzzone*, the task is indeed daunting. There are no fewer than ninety-two numbers (recitatives and arias), which imply some three hours or more of opera. This would not only present a problem in our day, but Vivaldi himself found his operas too long on occasion, as we know from his letters to Bentivoglio. Then in the manuscript in Turin, some of the arias are incomplete, or interrupted, so that one has to look for the conclusion amongst fragments that appear to have nothing at all to do with them. In such a situation the libretto is virtually indispensable for picking one's way through this terrible maze.

From what we know of Vivaldi's working methods, however, this ought not to surprise us. One sees it in another manuscript in Turin, Giordano Collection Vol. v, no. 11 (RV 153), which is entitled 'concerto', using the basic string orchestra and basso continuo. It starts out in fact as a concerto for two violins and four-part string ensemble, with the solo violin parts written out on the same stave as the first and second *ripieno* violin parts. Vivaldi then obviously had second thoughts, and where originally he had written *tutti* he replaced the marking with *forte*, and where he had originally written *solo*, he replaced it with *piano*. In this way the concerto becomes a kind of sinfonia.

What is perhaps most striking about these manuscripts is the impression that they give of organic unity. Despite their seeming confusion and changes of mind, one is very much aware of the same hand at work, and more than the same hand, the same teeming brain that was pouring out music almost faster than the fingers could pen it. This is not the product of a hesitant, faltering creative vision, however, but one that had scarcely formulated one musical idea before it saw a variety of potential developments or alternatives that it inspired in him. De Brosses was certainly accurate when he said that Vivaldi had a 'prodigious fury for composition'. One feels that his brain was positively bursting with music.

This must not lead us to imagine that there is anything haphazard or diffuse about his music. On the contrary, it is remarkable for its concision, and the way in which the material is organized. The 'second thoughts' visible in the manuscript are almost always due to the fact that Vivaldi realized that there was an even better, more telling, way to express himself musically, as a writer may choose a better adjective, or a more direct way of expressing his thought.

As an example one could hardly do better than take the first two bars of the sinfonia (RV 153) referred to above, which is in 3/4 time, in the key of G minor. Starting on the off-beat, therefore already giving the music a certain rhythmic tautness with its feeling of syncopation, Vivaldi uses only the notes of the minor triad; G – B flat – G – D – B flat, and then lands on the upper octave G as the first beat of the second bar, during which he descends the whole minor scale to return to his starting point. It is no more difficult, from the point of view of the actual notes involved, than a child's piano exercise. When one looks a little more closely, however, one sees how, with the simplest of basic material, Vivaldi produces the germ of a musical development.

The tautness established by the even, steady quavers of the first bar is emphasized in the second bar, after the octave has been reached, by the downward rush of the semiquavers, and then a re-assertion of the key note with a whole crochet on G, which has the effect of a punctuation mark in the music. Yet much more subtle than this is the fact that by starting on the off-beat, Vivaldi makes G initially the less important note of the chord, since it is the keynote in any case and is repeated twice in the first bar, but the very important B flat (which establishes the minor key, since it is the third) falls on the second beat of the bar, and the D (which is the dominant) falls on the third beat of the bar. With the octave G coming on the first beat of the next bar, Vivaldi therefore establishes the framework or scaffolding of the main notes of the minor scale, thus emphasizing the key or personality of the music, and then with a little subtle rhythmic variation he turns it into a musical theme of almost epigrammatic force worthy of a Bach Invention. This is a very minor example of Vivaldi's skill as a composer, but it nevertheless illustrates one of the basic aspects of his talent.

Since a great deal has been written about the relationship between Bach and Vivaldi, it would be as well to set down the facts first, and then consider the implications later. Bach transcribed several works by other composers, among them ten concertos by Vivaldi. Six are from the latter's Op. III, *L'estro armonico*, which Bach rearranged as harpsichord or organ concertos, namely nos. 3, 8, 9, 10, 11 (with considerable difference from the version Vivaldi prepared for press), and 12. These are RV 310, 522, 230, 580, 565 and 265 – Bach BWV 978, 593, 972, 1065, 596 and 976 respectively.

From Op. IV of Vivaldi, Bach took nos. 1 (first movement) and 6 (with a different finale), which are RV 381 and 316 – BWV 809 and 975 respectively. Then from Vivaldi's Op. VII Bach took nos. 8 (with quite considerable differences) and 11 (first and third movements), which are RV 299 and 208 – BWV 973 and 594 respectively. Finally, there is a manuscript concerto at Lund (RV Anhang 10), which is Bach's BWV 979. There is doubt as to whether it ought to be ascribed to Vivaldi, or rather to Torelli.

In addition, Bach transcribed works by Johann Ernst of Saxe-Weimar, Telemann, Alessandro and Benedetto Marcello, and some whose composers have not been identified.

Assuming, then, that Bach transcribed the Op. III concertos at Weimar (except for no. 10, which is thought to have been written at Leipzig *c.* 1730–3), then at the latest they would be placed prior to 1717. Considering that Vivaldi's Op. III was published *c.* 1710, or even 1711, and that they were certainly composed before that date, then they reached Bach's attention quite speedily. Of course they may easily have been available to him in manuscript before this date, which may well explain the discrepancies when compared with the versions Vivaldi published, and from the way in which Bach selected these works for transcription, it would seem that he chose them from a larger group, and that they therefore had some special appeal for him. He was also attracted by Albinoni's music and used themes of his as material in composition, so Bach presumably saw quite a lot more music than he eventually transcribed.

There were several amateurs of Italian music in Germany at this time. We know, for example, that the Schönborn family of Wiesentheid in Pommersfelden assembled Vivaldi manuscripts, particularly when Rudolf Franz Eberwein was head of the family, and his brother Johann Philipp Franz, Provost of Würzburg Cathedral, was in the habit of ordering music from a Venetian merchant by the name of Ragaznig.[2] In a letter of 27 February 1710 from Rudolf to Johann, he specifically asks him to obtain some more Vivaldi manuscripts. We have already seen that Vivaldi was in the habit of selling his manuscripts, so it is not surprising that so many of them have been discovered in rather odd or remote places.

Not all musicians feel that Bach improved the works he transcribed, but then that is not really the issue at stake. He was not consciously trying to improve them, let alone pass them off as his own work. He was simply retaining them for his own reference in an age when copying or outright purchase were the only means available to him, and he was certainly not interested in what posterity might think of his choice, let alone his contemporaries. Vivaldi's published music was only a small fraction of what he actually wrote, and circulating in northern Italy, in Bohemia and around Dresden, and even as far afield as Sweden, were many manuscripts acquired by those who liked Vivaldi's music, either by themselves directly when they went to Venice, or bought for them through agents. Bach never went to Italy, and so these works were in some way models. He not only transcribed, but he also imitated. In the form in which he left them they may well be inferior to the original versions in some people's opinion, and as much as lovers of Bach would like to detect the hand of his genius in the transcribed versions, it ought surely to be enough that Bach's genius saw the worth of Vivaldi's music, and so left us a point of departure for the re-discovery of that music long after its composer had been forgotten.

At all events, we ought to be grateful that Bach had preserved the Vivaldi works in whatever form, and that the revival of interest in Bach brought eventually in its wake interest in Vivaldi, since scholars were obviously intrigued to know more of the person whom Bach obviously held in such esteem.

The revival of interest in Bach is usually dated from Mendelssohn's performance of the St Matthew Passion in Berlin in 1829, though some would maintain that the work of J. H. Forkel (1749–1818), in a previous generation, must also be taken into account as one of the steps in the process. There is a certain parallel between the reputation enjoyed by both Bach and Vivaldi in their own day, and the judgement of posterity. Bach was perhaps most widely known in his own day as an improviser on the organ, but as far as his compositions were concerned his own sons found him old-fashioned. Vivaldi was known as a virtuoso violinist and composer of operas and concertos, but hardly thought of as a very exceptional composer in his own day, though doubt-less a fairly prolific one. Here, however, the concept is some-thing of an anachronism, since the pre-Romantic period ideas of what constituted an exceptional composer were rather different from ours today. There was no Beethoven, Brahms or Wagner to be used as a yardstick for greatness in some vague, abstract way that nevertheless must hold good for 'all true lovers of music'. The yardstick then was success, and although the public has been notoriously wrong on occasions, it is by no means a bad criterion for a piece of music – not, of course, in a commercial sense, but whether or not the piece of music 'comes off', and in that way succeeds.

Before looking at Vivaldi's music in the most general terms, however, there is one further point of comparison with Bach that ought to be looked at, and that is the way the two composers enlarged the 'cello repertoire. Vivaldi's considerable output for the 'cello deserves more than a passing mention, since until his day, in Venice at least, it had received scant attention. Ryom lists ten sonatas, six of them from the collection published by Le Clerc le Cadet in Paris in 1740, and twenty-seven concertos (though two of them exist in versions for other instruments). There is also a concerto for two 'cellos and orchestra, as well as eight others in which the 'cello appears in a solo capacity.

Unfortunately the dating of Vivaldi's 'cello concertos with any certainty is extremely difficult, because in any consideration of the development of the 'cello repertoire at this time one inevitably has to take into account the figure of Giuseppe Maria Jacchini (*c.* 1670–*c.* 1727). Like Vivaldi, Jacchini was a priest, though he was a native of Bologna, where he was born and where he died, though his professional activities took him away from the city from time to time. He was a member of the famous Accademia Filarmonica in Bologna, and a 'cellist in the Basilica of S. Petronio.

Jacchini is credited with having published the first 'cello concertos with his *Concerti per camera a* 3 *e* 4 *strumenti con violoncello obligato*, Op. IV, in Bologna in 1901, though from the technical point of view they are not especially demanding. Nevertheless Jacchini was evidently something of a curiosity in his own day. Von Uffenbach heard him play in Bologna in 1715, and testified to the fact that he was regarded as a genius, and that his fame had spread through Italy. It is by no means inconceivable that Vivaldi heard him play, too, and was inspired by him, but then on the other hand there were doubtless quite accomplished 'cellists at the Pietà, and Vivaldi may even have taught the instrument himself, though it is hard to go along with De Candé and Giazotto and state that he was actually appointed *maestro* for 'cello at the Pietà. They base their claim on the existence of a record in the Pietà archives of a certain 'Reverendo D. Antonio Vandini' who was appointed on 27 September 1720.[3]

At some point someone corrected Vandini to Vivaldi, and in the *rubricella*, or index, Vivaldi's name is again used. Giazotto maintains that the correction on the page was done in a contemporary (*coeva*) hand. This may well have been the case, but the term contemporary is in itself somewhat relative. Does it mean that the alteration was made within a matter of days, weeks, months, or even years? There would seem to be no definite evidence that it was a scribe's error, and if it was, why was Vandini not altered to Vivaldi throughout the text, since it occurs later, and similarly in a second document, dated 30 January 1722,[4] when Vandini's post was given to Bernardo Aliprandi?

It would appear from the argument put forward by De Candé and Giazotto, that they base their claim entirely on the fact that Vivaldi used the anagram of his name, Lotavio Vandini, on the libretto of *Aristide*. Giazotto maintains that the scribe knew that Vivaldi used this anagram, and wrote Vandini by mistake, but then corrected himself. This is a little far fetched, one feels, but is not in itself improbable. However, the appointment of Vandini to the Pietà took place in 1720, whereas the opera *Aristide* did not appear until 1735. In the circumstances it seems much more likely that Vivaldi was amused to discover that his name made an anagram of a former colleague of his at the Pietà, and therefore used it as a joke on the libretto, and Goldoni did likewise, calling himself Calindo Grolo.

There are further factors against the identification of Vandini as Vivaldi. Firstly, Vandini was a reputed 'cellist in his own right in Venice at that time, and manuscripts of his works reached Berlin. We do not know exactly when he left the Pietà. Certainly his name does not appear on the list of re-appointments for 4 April 1721, but he is referred to again on 30 January 1722, when Aliprandi was appointed in his place, as *già partito* (already left). It would seem a long time to have waited – almost a year in fact – before making a new appointment, so it is possible that he remained on the staff, or someone else was found to do the work. On the other hand, it may only have been a temporary appointment, since the first document says 'at least for a certain period'. Even so, this does not alter the fact that it seems unlikely that Vivaldi was really being referred to all along. One factor which Giazotto and De Candé totally overlook is the placing of the three years when Vivaldi was in Mantua in the service of the Prince of Hesse-Darmstadt. If we are to place them at this time, then Vivaldi was not in Venice.

Basically, of course, whether Vivaldi was appointed to the Pietà as a teacher of 'cello or not would not radically have affected the music he wrote for the instrument. In view of his fascination with exploring the potentials of instruments, there is no reason why Vivaldi should not have simply written the 'cello compositions in response to the inspiration on his doorstep, namely the girls of the Pietà.

When Vivaldi wrote such a work as the two-'cello concerto in G minor (RV 531), he was striking out into virtually virgin territory. Since it was apparently a unique experiment amongst his compositions, unless more come to light, it may have represented for him a blind alley, or it may merely have been part of his over-all exploration of the possibilities of the instrument. In this he may have made his own, first hand, experiments on the instrument, or he may have seen how his colleagues and pupils at the Pietà reacted to his music. Equally well, one cannot exclude entirely the fact that he was inspired by such a virtuoso as Jacchini. Then there was another virtuoso 'cellist in Italy at this time, by the name of Francischello, whom Geminiani heard in Rome in 1713. By 1725 he was in Naples, where Quantz heard him, after which he reappeared in Vienna in 1730. It would have been possible, therefore, for Vivaldi to have heard him in Rome whilst he was there for the opera seasons. However, one might well apply the same observation to Francischello as to Jacchini, namely that there is no demonstrable reason why one or the other should have had any crucial influence on Vivaldi's writing for the 'cello. Certainly to imagine that without such stimulus Vivaldi would not have written the 'cello concertos is seriously to underestimate his originality as a composer, and even to make a wrong assumption about the nature of musical composition.

Vivaldi's legacy to the 'cello repertoire is best put into perspective by bearing in mind the date of Jacchini's concertos – 1705 – and the date of Bach's suites for unaccompanied 'cello – c. 1720 – and then one sees where Vivaldi's contribution stands. Then there are other aspects of the 'cello music that apply to Vivaldi's composition generally, such as his use of, and experiments with, *ritornelli*, and the organization of his material in general.

There is a saying attributed to Luigi Dallapiccola (born

1904) that Vivaldi did not write 500 concertos, but the same concerto 500 times. Or was it 600, even? At all events, a similar verdict is reported from Stravinsky in Robert Craft's *Conversations with Igor Stravinsky*: 'Vivaldi is greatly over-rated – a dull fellow who could compose the same form so many times over.'[5]

It seems hard to accept that a person with any sensibilities in musical matters can make such a sweeping dismissal, especially when an examination of the music itself immediately gives the lie to the opinion. True, Vivaldi did write a considerable amount of perfunctory music, but then so did many of the great composers who followed him. Is there anything more boring than inferior Beethoven? Surely the very fact of Vivaldi's popularity as a composer today demands that one revise such opinions.

There can be no doubt that Vivaldi was a great composer, possibly even a greater composer than some musicians realize or are prepared to admit. He also happens to be a very popular composer with the public at large, and this is not merely a fashion. Vivaldi's popularity has been growing over the last thirty or forty years, and it seems highly unlikely that he will ever fall back into oblivion.

Of course the expert can argue that public popularity does not necessarily in itself confer greatness on a composer. True, but neither are the two things unrelated. The fact that Vivaldi speaks to people today is not simply because his music happens to strike a chord at the present time. For one thing, his rehabilitation has been going on for too long, as has already been pointed out, and shows no signs of being abandoned. His greatness and popularity are merely aspects of the same phenomenon, namely his genius, and his expertise as a composer. To this end we need more and more of his music to be made available both to the public at large and to musical experts, so that it will be apparent just how competent a composer he was.

The basic elements of his technique are simple enough in theory. In fact simplicity is almost always the keynote. His rhythms are never over-complicated, but firm and incisive. Moreover by repetition of rhythmic patterns he takes the listener along with him, and gives him signposts, as it were, along the way. Simplicity is also apparent in the way he concentrates on the main notes of the scale. Tonality is firmly established, and the listener rarely has difficulty – if ever – in knowing where the composer is taking him. When there are abrupt changes of tonality, then they are the more significant as a result. By the same token, sequential passages lead the listener along a familiar path, at the same time serving to build up to the climax of the phrase or passage.

These, it may be argued, are not only the preserve of Vivaldi. So much is true, but there are few composers of the period who make such basic elements into virtues and then build their music out of them. This much is apparent to the listener, even if he does not immediately put his finger on the exact nature of these individual aspects. An examination of the layout of the scores reveals the form, however, and at once Vivaldi's concision becomes apparent. One becomes aware of the way he organizes his material and how, for example, he handles the *ritornello* pattern. Even here, however, it is less the form itself that is important than the manner. Vivaldi created a new style, with its influence far beyond the confines of Italy. It was none the less baroque for that, with its ability to startle, and even today his music can make one draw in one's breath or stop in one's tracks.

There may well have been a falling off towards the end of his career, though for anyone to keep going at the rate that he did for so much of his life, it is perhaps remarkable that so much of his music is of the quality that it is. Some of his effects were, one feels, pointers to the future, such as the three strong chords with which he often liked to start his works, and which find their echo in the symphonies of Mozart. Or again, there are aspects of his Op. XII that look forward to Haydn.

Possibly his greatest contribution to posterity, however, and the most striking evidence of his genius is the way he exploited the possibilities of the instruments tonally. Even today we are just beginning to realize that he knew virtually everything about the way the instruments he used could sound, and a great deal has still to be done to bring this home. His orchestral palette has a richness and exoticism which, when properly displayed, would shock some of his detractors, as if they were seeing a painting for the first time when decades of grime have been removed and a new varnish applied, and yet reputable conductors and orchestras are still playing and recording arrangements of his works.

With the right sort of orchestra and conductor, perhaps we can even begin to listen with the ears of eighteenth-century Venice once again. Not that there is necessarily any great virtue in this, since Vivaldi speaks to us today loud and clear, but they were certainly not indifferent to, or complacent about, his music in his day, and we ought not to be either. From this point of view, those who seek to promote a wider diffusion and recognition of Vivaldi's music would do well to lay more stress on the excellence of his instrumental music, rather than try to put his vocal music on the same level.

Tartini's opinion, as given to De Brosses, is extremely relevant in this connection: 'I was asked to compose for the Venetian theatres, but did not want to, because I know that the throat is not the same thing as a violin finger-board. Vivaldi wanted to compose for both media and was always whistled at in the one and was extremely successful in the other.'[6] This immediately poses the question as to how it was that Vivaldi then went on to compose some fifty operas that are known to us and possibly, by his own reckoning, another forty at least. He must have had some talent as an opera composer, one assumes, to have been able to survive in the climate of the Venetian theatre in the first half of the eighteenth century.

Enough has been shown earlier in this book to demonstrate that the criteria by which the success of opera was judged in Venice then are by no means the same as we apply today. But even allowing for that, there remains the question of Vivaldi's treatment of the voice in its own right, which may legitimately be abstracted from its operatic context, and looked at in conjunction with the rest of his vocal music, both secular and sacred. Since a certain amount of space has already been devoted to the question (see page 169), it would be tedious to repeat those arguments again. In brief the contention is that although Vivaldi brings all his skill to the composition of vocal music, there is nothing intrinsically vocal about it, and one comes to the conclusion that he was not inspired by the human voice to anything like the same degree that he was by instruments.

Even if Anna Girò's voice was not of the very best, one would have expected such a long and close association with a singer to have initiated Vivaldi into the possibilities of exploitation of the voice just as he exploited the possibilities of instruments. Then there was the whole vocal establishment of the Pietà at his disposal. Had he been at all interested, he would surely have experimented with the facilities it afforded him.

Above all else Venice was, after all, the home of massed effects of vocal and instrumental forces in the galleries of churches such as S. Marco, offering considerable possibilities of contrast with antiphonal and homophonic effects, even if the sound was more intimate than has hitherto been imagined. The tradition was already ancient and well established by the time Vivaldi, as a young man, first heard music in S. Marco. Even a church not noted particularly for music, such as the Gesuiti, when it was rebuilt between 1714 and 1729, was automatically given two galleries with organs, one in each transept at the crossing of the church. The church of the Pietà itself was enlarged in 1724, to facilitate more room in the galleries and, by implication, more of the traditional effects of Venetian church music.[7]

And yet if we look at Vivaldi's sacred music, it is usually either very traditional, or else operatic. One is not aware of any very striking originality from Vivaldi in this part of his output, and such originality as is there tends to be common to the rest of his music, and is therefore not especially inspired either by the possibilities of the voices or the lavish effects that galleries and contrasting groups of voices and instruments might have presented him with. If this is so, one is perfectly entitled to ask: how then does one explain the popularity of such works as the *Gloria*, *Magnificat* and *Stabat Mater*?

Basically, one feels, they owe their popularity to their melodic felicitousness, which is certainly an expression of Vivaldi's genius, and their Venetian *éclat*, which is perhaps less intrinsic to him as a composer. The world would be the poorer if it did not possess Vivaldi's sacred vocal music, but it would be considerably more impoverished if it were to lose the best of the violin concertos. Which is another way of saying that the vocal music, and perhaps the sacred vocal music in particular, is not the greatest part of Vivaldi's output. But this need to evaluate relative degrees of greatness is, as has already been intimated, a somewhat contemporary obsession.

One is reminded of some words of that great music teacher Nadia Boulanger, herself responsible almost more than anyone else for bringing the music of another Italian, Monteverdi, back to public recognition after centuries of oblivion:

> Our general knowledge, and especially in regard to the history of music, is limited to a few dates and a few anecdotes, the latter more often destructive of illusion; for we search relentlessly to discover that which may diminish great figures more than we force ourselves to explain their beauty to ourselves – to understand their apparent contradictions.

This was written in 1920, and since then great progress has been made, not only in relation to Vivaldi himself, of course, but in the whole business of music history and musicology. Even so, there is still a tendency at some levels to approach composers and their music in this spirit. As Nadia Boulanger went on:

> As for the works! . . . The label gives us a moderately priced bet with no risk attached to it; and the name of the composer is the point of departure for our judgement. Now, there is no evenness in production, but for discernment one needs independence of thought based on deep knowledge, emotional sincerity and enthusiasm.

A passage earlier in the same article is perhaps even more applicable to the ideal approach to Vivaldi's music.

It is easier to analyse a work in its form, in its progress, than to love it simply with all the lively forces of our heart. It is more easy to detail the peculiarities and the details of it than to extract from it the emotion, the thought. In fact we do not always see in music all that exists in it.[8]

Naturally such an approach is fraught with danger, because it could so easily become a cover for an emotional, and therefore subjective rather than objective, approach to Vivaldi's music – or for that matter any composer's music. Suffice it to say that the whole of Nadia Boulanger's teaching has always been that one only finds true freedom through rigorous discipline, that one only arrives at an emotional understanding of a piece of music when one has explored all its technical aspects.

In our approach to Vivaldi, then, let us consider him and his music with all the detailed knowledge we can assemble, but in the last resort, let us simply delight in what he has given to us. As Camille Mauclair said: 'One does not learn to love, but one learns to understand that which one loves.' As more and more of Vivaldi's music becomes available, we will learn to understand that music more, and through the music the man, for in the last resort without the man there would have been no music.

There were aspects of his character that were less than admirable, as we have already seen. He was at times a difficult person to deal with, but his common humanity shines through time, and the pettiness and failings are forgotten. 'He was a man, take him for all in all' and we may well add with Hamlet, that we 'shall not look upon his like again'.

Catalogue of Works

In compiling the following catalogue, the system adopted is that of P. Ryom (see *Select bibliography*), since he is the first person to have included all the vocal music, as well as instrumental, in a comprehensive system. Since other systems will doubtless continue in use for some time to come, however, it has been decided to include the other numbers as and when appropriate. The Rinaldi numbers are not here, however, since they are generally agreed to be of little value.

The general scheme, then, is to start with all the works given opus numbers by Vivaldi himself, and then by classification according to type of work and key. The first number given – RV – if that of Ryom, then P is for Pincherle, F for Fanna, and R for Ricordi – not, it must be stressed, for Rinaldi. Where there is a blank, then the work was not included in one or all of the systems, apart from that of Ryom himself.

In order to save space, names of cities only have been given when these occur several times, and they represent the following libraries and museums:

BOLOGNA: Civico Museo Bibliografico Musicale
DARMSTADT: Hessische Landes- und Hochschulbibliothek
DRESDEN: Sächsische Landesbibliothek
GRAZ: Diözesanarchiv
LEIPZIG: Musikbibliothek der Stadt Lepizig
LUND: Universitetsbibliotek
MANCHESTER: Henry Watson Music Library, Public Libraries
MILAN: Biblioteca Braidense
NAPLES: Biblioteca del Conservatorio S. Pietro a Maiella
PARIS: Bibliothèque du Conservatoire National de Musique
ROME: Biblioteca del Conservatorio di S. Cecilia
SCHWERIN: Mecklenburgische Landesbibliothek
STOCKHOLM: Kungl. Musikaliska Akademiens Bibliotek
TURIN: Biblioteca Nazionale
UPPSALA: Universitetsbibliotek
WIESENTHEID: Graf von Schönborn'sche Musikbibliothek

Op. I 12 sonatas for 2 violins and basso continuo 1705

published in: Venice by Sala
Amsterdam by Roger – no. 363
Paris by Le Clerc le Cadet

1. RV 73; P S. 1/1; F xiii, 17; R 382 in G minor
2. RV 67; P S. 1/2; F xiii, 18; R 383 in E minor
3. RV 61; P S. 1/3; F xiii, 19; R 384 in C
4. RV 66; P S. 1/4; F xiii, 20; R 385 in E
5. RV 69; P S. 1/5; F xiii, 21; R 386 in F
6. RV 62; P S. 1/6; F xiii, 22; R 387 in D
7. RV 65; P S. 1/7; F xiii, 23; R 388 in E flat
8. RV 64; P S. 1/8; F xiii, 24; R 389 in D minor
9. RV 75; P S. 1/9; F xiii, 25; R 390 in A
10. RV 78; P S. 1/10; F xiii, 26; R 391 in B flat
11. RV 79; P S. 1/11; F xiii, 27; R 392 in B minor
12. RV 63; P S. 1/13; F xiii, 28; R 393 in D minor

Op. II 12 sonatas for violin and basso continuo 1709

published in: Venice by Bortoli
Amsterdam by Roger – no. 2
London by Walsh – no. 450

1. RV 27; P S. 2/1; F xiii, 29; R 394 in G minor
2. RV 31; P S. 2/2; F xiii, 30; R 395 in A
3. RV 14; P S. 2/3; F xiii, 31; R 396 in D minor
4. RV 20; P S. 2/4; F xiii, 32; R 397 in F
5. RV 36; P S. 2/5; F xiii, 33; R 398 in B minor
6. RV 1; P S. 2/6; F xiii, 34; R 399 in C
7. RV 8; P S. 2/7; F xiii, 35; R 400 in C minor
8. RV 23; P S. 2/8; F xiii, 36; R 401 in G
9. RV 16; P S. 2/9; F xiii, 37; R 402 in E minor
10. RV 21; P S. 2/10; F xiii, 38; R 403 in F minor
11. RV 9; P S. 3/1; F xiii, 39; R 404 in D
12. RV 32; P S. 3/2; F xiii, 40; R 405 in A minor

Op. III *L'estro armonico* 12 concertos for various combinations 1711

published in: Amsterdam by Roger – no. 50/51
London by Walsh – no. 451
Paris by Le Clerc le Cadet

L'estro armonico was published in two parts by all three publishers. Although Roger and Le Clerc le Cadet published the works in the same order, Roger presented them as two volumes, and Le Clerc le Cadet as one. Walsh changed the order, and published two editions, the first in two volumes, the second in one. Moreover he put seven concertos in the first part and five in the second.

libro primo
1. RV 549; P 146; F IV, 7; R 406 in D – 4 violins
2. RV 578; P 326; F IV, 8; R 407 in G minor – 2 violins and 'cello
3. RV 310; P 96; F I, 173; R 408 in G – 1 violin (Bach BWV 978)
4. RV 550; P 97; F I, 174; R 409 in E minor – 4 violins
5. RV 519; P 212; F I, 175; R 410 in A – 2 violins
6. RV 356; P 1; F I, 176; R 411 in A minor – 1 violin

libro secondo
7. RV 567; P 249; F IV, 9; R 412 in F – 4 violins and 'cello
8. RV 522; P 2; F I, 177; R 413 in A minor – 2 violins (Bach BWV 593)
9. RV 230; P 147; F I, 178; R 414 in D – 1 violin (Bach BWV 972)
10. RV 580; P 148; F IV, 10; R 415 in B minor – 4 violins and 'cello (Bach BWV 1065)
11. RV 565; P 250; F IV, 11; R 416 in D minor – 2 violins and 'cello (Bach BWV 596)
12. RV 265; P 240; F I, 179; R 417 in E – 1 violin (Bach BWV 976)

Op. IV *La stravaganza* 12 concertos for violin *c.* 1714

published in: Amsterdam by Roger – no. 399/400
London by Walsh – no. 452

La stravaganza was published by Roger in two parts of six concertos each, whereas Walsh took only five of the twelve concertos, to which he added a sixth (RV 291).

libro primo
1. RV 383a; P 327; F I, 180; R 418 in B flat (for related works see RV 381 and 528)
2. RV 279; P 98; F I, 181; R 419 in E minor
3. RV 301; P 99; F I, 182; R 420 in G
4. RV 357; P 3; F I, 183; R 431 in A minor
5. RV 347; P 213; F I, 184; R 422 in A
6. RV 316a; P 328; F I, 185; R 432 in G minor

libro secondo
7. RV 185; P 4; F I, 186; R 424 in C
8. RV 249; P 253; F I, 187; R 425 in D minor
9. RV 284; P 251; F I, 188; R 426 in F
10. RV 196; P 413; D I, 189; R 427 in C minor
11. RV 204; P 149; F I, 190; R 428 in D
12. RV 298; P 100; F I, 191; R 429 in G

Op. V (the second part of Op. II) 4 sonatas for one violin and 2 sonatas for 2 violins and basso continuo 1716

published in: Amsterdam by Roger – no. 418

Since these sonatas followed on from Op. II, they were numbered from 13 to 18 inclusively.
13. RV 18; P S. 3/3; F XIII, 41; R 430 in F
14. RV 30; P S. 3/4; F XIII, 42; R 431 in A
15. RV 33; P S. 3/5; F XIII, 43; R 432 in B flat
16. RV 35; P S. 3/6; F XIII, 44; R 433 in B minor
17. RV 76; P S. 3/7; F XIII, 45; R 434 in B flat
18. RV 72; P S. 3/8; F XIII, 46; R 435 in G minor

Op. VI 6 concertos for violin 1716–21

published in: Amsterdam by Roger – no. 452

1. RV 324; P 329; F I, 192; R 436 in G minor
2. RV 259; P 414/355; F I, 193; R 437 in E flat
3. RV 318; P 330; F I, 194; R 438 in G minor
4. RV 216; P 150; F I, 195; R 439 in D
5. RV 280; P 101; F I, 196; R 440 in E minor
6. RV 239; P 254; F I, 197; R 441 in D minor

Op. VII 2 concertos for oboe and 10 concertos for violin 1716–21

published in: Amsterdam by Roger – no. 470/471

libro primo
1. RV 465; P 331; F VII, 14; R 442 in B flat
2. RV 188; P 5; F I, 198; R 443 in C
3. RV 326; P 332; F I, 199; R 444 in G minor
4. RV 354; P 6; F I, 200; R 445 in A minor
5. RV 285a; P 255; F I, 201; R 446 in F
6. RV 374; P 333; F I, 202; R 447 in B flat

libro secondo
1 (7). RV 464; P 334; F VII, 15; R 448 in B flat
2 (8). RV 299; P 102; F I, 203; R 449 in G (Bach BWV 973)
3 (9). RV 373; P 335; F I, 204; R 450 in B flat
4 (10). RV 294a; P 256; F I, 205; R 451 in F
5 (11). RV 208a; P 151; F I, 206; R 452 in D
6 (12). RV 214; P 152; F I, 207; R 453 in D

Op. VIII *Il cimento dell'armonia e dell'inventione* 12 concertos for violin (two of which also exist for oboe) 1725

published in: Amsterdam by Le Cène – no. 520/521
               Paris by Le Clerc le Cadet

libro primo
1. RV 269; P 241; F I, 22; R 76 in E – Spring
2. RV 315; P 336; F I, 23; R 77 in G minor – Summer
3. RV 293; P 257; F I, 24; R 78 in F – Autumn
4. RV 297; P 442; F I, 25; R 79 in F minor – Winter
5. RV 253; P 415; F I, 26; R 80 in E flat – *La tempesta di mare*
6. RV 180; P 7; F I, 27; R 81 in C – *Il piacere*

libro secondo
7. RV 242; P 258; F I, 28; R 82 in D minor – *Per Pisendel*
8. RV 332; P 337; F I, 16; R 65 in G minor
9. RV 236; P 259; F –; R – in D minor (this concerto also exists as an oboe concerto RV 454; P 259; F VII, 1; R 2)
10. RV 362; P 338; F I, 29; R 83 in B flat – *La caccia*
11. RV 210; P 153; F I, 30; R 84 in D
12. RV 178; P 8; F I, 31; R 85 in C (this concerto also exists as an oboe concerto RV 449)

Op. IX *La cetra* 11 concertos for violin and one concerto for 2 violins 1727

published in: Amsterdam by Le Cène – no. 533/534

libro primo
1. RV 181a; P 9; F I, 47; R 122 in C ·
2. RV 345; P 214; F I, 51; R 126 in A
3. RV 334; P 339; F I, 192; R 127 in G minor (closely related to Op. XI, no. 6 RV 460)
4. RV 263a; P 242; F I, 48; R 123 in E
5. RV 358; P 10; F I, 53; R 128 in A minor
6. RV 348; P 215; F I, 54; R 129 in A (scordatura for the violin)

libro secondo
7. RV 359; P 340; F I, 55; R 130 in B flat
8. RV 238; P 260; F I, 56; R 131 in D minor
9. RV 530; P 341; F I, 57; R 132 in B flat – 2 violins
10. RV 300; P 103; F I, 49; R 124 in G
11. RV 198a; P 416; F I, 58; R 133 in C minor
12. RV 391; P 154; F I, 50; R 125 in B minor (scordatura for the violin)

Op. X 6 concertos for flute *c.* 1728

published in: Amsterdam by Le Cène – no. 544

1. RV 433; P 261; F VI, 12; R 454 in F – *La tempesta di mare* (closely related works are RV 98 and 570)
2. RV 439; P 342; F VI, 13; R 455 in G minor – *La notte* (a closely related work is RV 104)
3. RV 428; P 155; F VI, 14; R 456 in D – *Il gardellino* (a closely related work is RV 90)
4. RV 435; P 104; F VI, 15; R 457 in G
5. RV 434; P 262; F –; R – in F (a closely related work is RV 442)
6. RV 437; P 105; F VI, 16; R 458 in G (a closely related work is RV 101)

Op. XI 5 concertos for violin and one for oboe 1729

published in: Amsterdam by Le Cène – no. 545

1. RV 207; P 156; F I, 89; R 188 in D
2. RV 277; P 106; F I, 208; R 259 in E minor – *Il favorito*
3. RV 336; P 216; F I, 90; R 191 in A
4. RV 308; P 107; F I, 209; R 460 in G
5. RV 202; P 417; F I, 210; R 461 in C minor
6. RV 460; P –; F –; R – (closely related to Op. IX, no. 3 RV 334)

Op. XII 5 concertos for violin, and one without a solo instrument 1729

published in: Amsterdam by Le Cène – no. 546

1. RV 317; P 343; F I, 211; R 462 in G minor
2. RV 244; P 263; F I, 212; R 463 in D minor
3. RV 124; P 157; F XI, 42; R 464 in D
4. RV 173; P 11; F I, 213; R 465 in C
5. RV 379; P 344; F I, 86; R 183 in B flat
6. RV 361; P 345; F I, 214; R 466 in B flat

Op. XIII *Il pastor fido* 6 sonatas for musette, vielle, flute (recorder), oboe or violin and basso continuo 1737 (of doubtful authenticity)

published in: Paris by Mme Boivin

1. RV 54; P S. 3/9; F XVI, 5; R 467 in C
2. RV 56; P S. 3/10; F XVI, 6; R 468 in C
3. RV 57; P S. 4/1; F XVI, 7; R. 469 in G
4. RV 59; P S. 4/2; F XVI, 8; R 470 in A
5. RV 55; P S. 4/3; F XVI, 9; R 471 in C
6. RV 58; P S. 4/3; D XVI, 10; R 472 in G minor

Op. XIV has not been identified, though some writers have attached this number to a collection of 6 sonatas for 'cello and basso continuo, published in Paris by Le Clerc le Cadet in 1740. They are placed at this point since they form the only other published collection of works by Vivaldi, apart from selections of earlier publications made by such publishers as Wright and Walsh, in London, for example.

1. RV 47; P S. 4/5; F XIV, 1; R 473 in B flat
2. RV 41; P S. 4/6; F XIV, 2; R 474 in F
3. RV 43; P S. 4/7; XIV, 3; R 475 in A minor
4. RV 45; P S. 4/8; F XIV, 4; R 476 in B flat
5. RV 40; P S. 4/9; F XIV, 5; R 477 in E minor
6. RV 46; P S. 4/10; F XIV, 6; R 478 in B flat

Sonatas for violin and basso continuo

RV 2; P S. 5/2; F XIII, 11; R 369 in C (Dresden) dedicated to Pisendel and related to RV 4

RV 3; P S. 6/2; F XIII, 8; R 366 in C (Dresden)

RV 4; P –; F –; R – in C (Graz) incomplete, related to RV 2

RV 754; P –; F –; R – in C (Manchester)

RV 5; P S. 5/9; F XIII, 10; R 368 in C minor (Dresden)

RV 6; P S. 5/5; F XIII, 14; R 372 in C minor (Dresden) dedicated to Pisendel

RV 7; P –; F –; R – in C minor (Graz) incomplete
RV 10; P S. 5/10; F xiii, 6; R 364 in D (Dresden)
RV 11; P S. 6/8; F –; R – in D (Graz) incomplete
RV 755; P –; F –; R – in D (Manchester)
RV 12; P S. 6/1; F xiii, 7; R 365 in D minor (Dresden)
RV 13; P –; F xiii, 50; R – in D minor (Stockholm)
RV 15; P S. 5/8; F xiii, 9; R 367 in D minor (Dresden)
RV 756; P –; F –; R – in E flat (Manchester)
RV 17; P –; F –; R – in E minor (Graz) incomplete, though
related to RV 17a in Manchester
RV 19; P S. 6/11; F xiii, 47; R 491 in F (Paris) dedicated to
Pisendel
RV 22; P –; F –; R in G (Bibliothèque du Conservatoire Royal
de Musique, Brussels)
RV 24; P –; F xiii, 49; R 529 in G (Wiesentheid)
RV 25; P S. 5/4; F xiii, 13; R 371 in G (Dresden) dedicated to
Pisendel
RV 26; P S. 5/6; F xiii, 15; R 373 in G minor (Dresden)
RV 28; P S. 6/4; F xiii, 5; R 356 in G minor (Dresden)
RV 757; P –; F –; R – in G minor (Manchester)
RV 29; P S. 5/3; F xiii, 12; R 370 in A (Dresden) dedicated to
Pisendel
RV 758; P –; F –; R – in A (Manchester) related to RV 746
RV 34; P S. 5/7; F xiii, 16; R 374 in B flat (Dresden)
RV 759; P –; F –; R – in B flat (Manchester)
RV 37; P –; F –; R – in B minor (Graz) incomplete
RV 760; P –; F –; R – in B minor (Manchester)

Sonatas for 'cello and basso continuo
RV 38; P S. 5/1; F –; R in D minor – lost, mentioned in Breitkopf
catalogue
RV 39; P S. 6/9; F xiv, 8; R 504 in E flat (Naples)
RV 42; P –; F xiv, 9; R 530 in G minor (Wiesentheid)
RV 44; P S. 6/10; F xiv, 7; R 503 in A minor (Naples)

Sonatas for flute and basso continuo
RV 48; P –; F xv, 3; R 490 in C (Fitzwilliam Museum, Cam-
bridge)
RV 49; P S. 7/9; F xv, 5; R 517 in D minor (Uppsala)
RV 50; P –; F xv, 6; R – in E minor (Stockholm)
RV 51; P –; F –; R – in G minor (Leipzig)

Sonata for recorder (?) and basso continuo
RV 52; P S. 7/10; F xv, 4; R 501 in F (Querini Stampalia, Venice)

Sonata for oboe and basso continuo
RV 53; P S. 6/3; F xv, 2; R 375 in C minor (Dresden)

Other sonatas for 2 violins and basso continuo
RV 60; P –; F xiii, 48; R 528 in C (Wiesentheid)
RV 68; P S. 7/6; F xiii, 3; R 57 in F (Turin)
RV 70; P S. 7/4; F xiii, 4; R 58 in F (Turin)
RV 71; P S. 7/5; F xiii, 1; R 17 in G minor (Turin)
RV 74; P –; F xiii, 51; R – in G minor (Lund)
RV 77; P S. 7/7; F xiii, 2; R – 4 in B flat (Turin)

Sonata for 2 recorders and basso continuo
RV 80; P –; F xv, 7; R – in G (Lund)

Sonata for 2 oboes and basso continuo
RV 81; P –; F xv, 8; R – G minor (Lund)

Sonatas and trios for two instruments and basso continuo
RV 82; P S. 7/3; F xvi, 3; R 63 in C (Turin) trio for violin and lute
RV 83; P S. 7/1; F xvi, 1; R 20 in C minor (Turin) sonata for violin and 'cello
RV 84; P S. 6/5; F xii, 43; R 355 in D (Dresden) for flute and violin
RV 85; P S. 7/2; F xvi, 4; R 75 in G minor (Turin) trio for violin and lute
RV 86; P S. 7/8; F xv, 1; R 18 in A minor (Turin) trio for recorder and bassoon

Concertos for various instruments and basso continuo
RV 87; P 81; F xii, 30; R 155 in C (Turin) for recorder, oboe and 2 violins
RV 88; P 82; F xii, 24; R 143 in C (Turin) for flute, oboe, violin and bassoon
RV 89; P –; F xii, 51; R – in D (Stockholm) for flute and 2 violins
RV 90; P 155; F xii, 9; R 42 in D (Manchester) for 3 violins and 'cello or flute, oboe, violin and bassoon. Closely related to RV 428, and both works are entitled *Il gardellino*
RV 91; P 206; F xii, 27; R 149 in D (Turin) for flute, violin and bassoon
RV 92; P 198; F xii, 7; R 39 in D (Turin) for recorder, violin and bassoon or 'cello
RV 93; P 209; F xii, 15; R 62 in D (Turin) for lute and 2 violins

213

RV 94; P 207; F xII, 25; R 144 in D (Turin) for recorder, oboe, violin and bassoon

RV 95; P 204; F xII, 29; R 154 in D (Turin) for recorder, oboe, violin, or 3 violins, and bassoon – entitled *La pastorella*

RV 751; P –; F –; R – in D for 2 flutes, 2 violins and 2 bassoons – a lost work, mentioned in Sonsfeld catalogue

RV 96; P S. 6/7; F xII, 42; R 354 in D minor (Dresden) for flute, violin and bassoon

RV 97; P 286; F xII, 32; R 248 in F (Turin) for viola, 2 horns, 2 oboes and bassoon

RV 98; P –; F –; R – in F (Turin) for flute, oboe, violin and bassoon. This work is related to RV 433 and RV 570, all entitled *La tempesta di mare*

RV 99; P 323; F xII, 26; R 147 in F (Turin) for flute, oboe, violin and bassoon. This work is related to RV 571

RV 100; P 322; F xII, 21; R 106 in F (Turin) for flute, violin and bassoon

RV 101; P –; F xII, 13; R 52 in G (Turin) for recorder, oboe, violin and bassoon. This work is related to RV 437

RV 102; P –; F xII, 52; R – in G (Lund) for flute and 2 violins

RV 103; P 402; F xII, 4; R 23 in G minor (Turin) for recorder, oboe and bassoon

RV 104; P –; F xII, 5; R 33 in G minor (Turin) for flute and 2 violins, or 3 violins, and bassoon. This work is related to RV 439, both entitled *La notte*

RV 105; P 403; F xII, 20; R 103 in G minor (Turin) for recorder, oboe, violin and bassoon

RV 106; P 404; F xII, 8; R 41 in G minor (Turin) for flute, violin and bassoon or 2 violins and 'cello

RV 107; P S. 6/6 & 360; F xII, 6; R 40 in G minor (Turin) for flute, oboe, violin and bassoon

RV 108; P 77; F xII, 11; R 44 in A minor (Turin) for recorder and 2 violins

Concertos, sinfonias and sonatas for string orchestra and basso continuo
RV 109; P 67; F xI, 23; R 185 in C (Turin) concerto
RV 110; P 61; F xI, 25; R 200 in C (Turin) concerto
RV 111; P 95; F –; R – in C (Gesellschaft der Musikfreunde, Vienna) concerto. This work is related to the sinfonia for the opera RV 717 *Il Giustino*
RV 111a; P Sinf. 15; F –; R – in C (Staatsbibliothek, Berlin)

sinfonia with a different second movement from the above, but still related to RV 717

RV 112; P Sinf. 23; F xi, 47; R 507 in C (Österreichische Nationalbibliothek, Vienna) sinfonia

RV 113; P 94; F xi, 48; R 509 in C (Österreichische National-bibliothek, Vienna) concerto

RV 114; P 27; F xi, 44; R 493 in C (Paris) concerto

RV 115; P 63; F xi, 38; R 309 in C (Turin), concerto *ripieno*

RV 116; P Sinf. 2; F xi, 46; R 506 in C (Archives Départe-mentales, Agen, France) sinfonia

RV 117; P 64; F xi, 37; R 308 in C (Turin) concerto. This work is related to the serenata *La Sena festeggiante* RV 693

RV 118; P 438; F xi, 9; R 32 in C minor (Turin) concerto

RV 119; P 422; F xi, 20; R 177 in C minor (Turin) concerto

RV 120; P 427; F xi, 8; R 30 in C minor (Turin) concerto

RV 121; P 175; F xi, 30; R 246 in D (Turin) concerto

RV 122; P Sinf. 7; F xii, 45; R 362 in D (Dresden) sinfonia

RV 123; P 191; F xi, 16; R 114 in D (Turin) concerto

RV 125; P Sinf. 14; F –; R – in D (Staatsbibliothek, Berlin) sinfonia – incomplete

RV 126; P 197; F xi, 15; R 113 in D (Turin) concerto

RV 127; P 280; F xi, 19; R 176 in D minor (Turin) concerto

RV 128; P 294; F xi, 31; R 251 in D minor (Turin) concerto

RV 129; P 86; F xi, 10; R 36 in D minor (Turin) concerto *madrigalesco*

RV 130; P 441; F xvi, 2; R 21 in E flat (Turin) sonata *al Santo Sepolcro*

RV 131; P Sinf. 19; F xi, 18; R 161 in E (Turin) sinfonia

RV 132; P Sinf. 13; F xi, 50; R 515 in E (Staatsbibliothek, Berlin) sinfonia

RV 133; P 113; F xi, 43; R 492 in E minor (Paris) concerto

RV 134; P 127; F xi, 13; R 56 in E minor (Turin) sinfonia/concerto

RV 135; P Sinf. 5; F xii, 46; R 363 in F (Dresden) sinfonia

RV 136; P 279; F xi, 14; R 59 in F (Turin) concerto

RV 137; P Sinf. 17; F xi, 51; R 516 in F (Staatsbibliothek, Berlin) sinfonia

RV 138; P 313; F xi, 34; R 288 in F (Turin) concerto

RV 139; P –; F –; R 265 in F (Turin) concerto. There is a related work RV 543

RV 140; P Sinf. 4; F xi, 29; R 242 in F (Turin) concerto/sinfonia

RV 141; P 291; F xi, 28; R 241 in F (Turin) concerto

RV 142; P 292; F xi, 2; R 6 in F (Turin) concerto

RV 143; P 443; F xi, 35; R 289 in F minor (Turin) concerto
RV 144; P 145; F xi, 49; R 512 in G (Österreichische National-
bibliothek, Vienna) *introdutione*
RV 145; P 123; F xi, 32; R 252 in G (Turin) concerto
RV 146; P Sinf. 8; F xi, 41; R 361 in G (Breitkopf catalogue
under Roellig. Also exists for 3 violins and basso continuo)
concerto or sinfonia
RV 147; P Sinf. 6; F –; R – in G (Lund) sinfonia
RV 148; P Sinf. 12; F xii, 49; R 360 in G (Dresden) sinfonia.
Ryom has subsequently placed this in his appendix as Anh. 68
RV 149; P Sinf. 3; F xi, 40; R 321 in G (Dresden) sinfonia
RV 150; P 114; F xi, 36; R 290 in G (Turin) concerto
RV 151; P 143; F xi, 11; R 49 in G (Turin) concerto *alla rustica*.
There are 2 oboes added in the third movement
RV 152; P 371; F xi, 27; R 226 in G minor (Turin) concerto
ripieno
RV 153; P 394; F xi, 33; R 287 in G minor (Turin) concerto
RV 154; P 362; F xi, 39; R 310 in G minor (Turin) concerto
RV 155; P 407; F xi, 6; R 11 in G minor (Turin) concerto
RV 156; P 392; F xi, 17; R 115 in G minor (Turin) concerto
RV 157; P 361; F xi, 21; R 182 in G minor (Turin) concerto
RV 158; P 235; F xi, 4; R 8 in A (Turin) concerto *ripieno*
RV 159; P 231; F xi, 1; R 5 in A (Turin) concerto
RV 160; P 230; F xi, 22; R 184 in A (Turin) concerto
RV 161; P 60; F xi, 26; R 201 in A minor (Turin) concerto
RV 162; P Sinf. 11; F xii, 44; R 359 in B flat (Dresden) sinfonia
RV 163; P 410; F xi, 5; R 9 in B flat (Turin) concerto *conca*
RV 164; P 363; F xi, 12; R 50 in B flat (Turin) concerto
RV 165; P 378; F i, 78; R 172 in B flat (Turin) concerto
RV 166; P 398; F xi, 3; R 7 in B flat (Turin) concerto
RV 167; P 400; F xi, 24; R 190 in B flat (Turin) concerto
RV 168; P Sinf. 22; F xi, 52; R 518 in B minor (?) sinfonia
RV 169; P Sinf. 21; F xi, 7; R 22 in B minor (Turin) sinfonia *al
Santo Sepolcro*

Concertos and sinfonias for violin, orchestra and basso continuo
RV 170; P 20; F i, 172; R 379 in C (Dresden)
RV 171; P 66; F i, 93; R 194 in C (Turin)
RV 172; P 19; F i, 140; R 322 in C (Dresden) dedicated to
Pisendel
RV 172a; P –; F –; R – in C (Dresden) of doubtful authenticity
RV 174; P –; F –; R – in C (Ringmacher catalogue) a lost work

RV 175; P 93; F I, 232; R 508 in C (Österreichische National-
bibliothek, Vienna)

RV 176; P 26; F I, 226; R 495 in C (Paris)

RV 177; P 21; F I, 67; R 160 in C (Turin)

RV 179; P 14; F –; R – in C (Dresden) closely related to RV 581

RV 181; P 9; F –; R – in C (Turin)

RV 182; P 68; F I, 94; R 195 in C (Turin)

RV 183; P 38; F I, 111; R 256 in C (Turin)

RV 184; P 22; F I, 146; R 328 in C (Dresden)

RV 186; P 88; F I, 3; R 13 in C (Turin)

RV 187; P 62; F I, 135; R 311 in C (Turin)

RV 189; P 29; F I, 169; R 376 in C (Österreichische National-
bibliothek, Vienna)

RV 190; P 59; F I, 46; R 120 in C (Turin)

RV 191; P 39; F I, 114; R 259 in C (Turin)

RV 192; P Sinf. 20; F I, 68; R 162 in C (Turin) sinfonia

RV 193; P –; F –; R – in C (Rheda catalogue) a lost work

RV 194; P 40; F I, 73; R 167 in C (Turin)

RV 195; P 12; F I, 217; R 481 in C (Roger no. 417)

RV 197; P 431; F I, 79; R 173 in C minor (Turin)

RV 198; P –; F –; R – in C minor (Dresden)

RV 199; P 419; F I, 2; R 4 in C minor (Turin) *Il sospetto*

RV 200; P –; F –; R – in C minor (Pirnitz catalogue) a lost work

RV 201; P 426; F I, 105; R 230 in C minor (Turin)

RV 761; P –; F –; R – in C minor (Manchester)

RV 203; P 160; F –; R – in D (Österreichische National-
bibliothek, Vienna)

RV 205; P 173; F I, 149; R 331 in D (Dresden) dedicated to
Pisendel

RV 206; P 177; F I, 228; R 497 in D (Schwerin)

RV 208; P –; F I, 138; R 314 in D (Turin) *Grosso Mogul*. Bach
BWV 594

RV 209; P 193; F I, 120; R 286 in D (Turin)

RV 211; P 182; F I, 116; R 261 in D (Turin)

RV 212; P 165; F –; R – in D (Turin) concerto *fatto per la
Solennità della S. Lingua di S. Antonio in Padua* 1712

RV 212a; P –; F I, 136; R 312 in D (Turin)

RV 213; P 163; F I, 162; R 347 in D (Dresden)

RV 215; P 194; F I, 132; R 305 in D (Turin)

RV 217; P 201; F I, 19; R 69 in D (Turin)

RV 218; P 196; F I, 134; R 307 in D (Turin)

RV 219; P 167; F I, 153; R 335 in D (Dresden)

RV 220; P 158; F I, 218; R 482 in D (Roger no. 432/433)
RV 221; P 179; F I, 97; R 203 in D (Turin) *violino in tromba*
RV 222; P 192; F I, 124; R 294 in D (Turin)
RV 223; P 174; F I, 225; R 494 in D (Paris) Ryom gives precedence to the version in E at RV 762
RV 224; P 161; F I, 158; R 343 in D (Dresden)
RV 224a; P –; F –; R in D (Dresden)
RV 225; P 186; F I, 80; R 174 in D (Turin)
RV 226; P 170; F I, 129; R 302 in D (Turin)
RV 227; P 211; F I, 234; R 513 in D (Gesellschaft der Musikfreunde, Vienna)
RV 228; P 162; F I, 160; R 345 in D (Dresden)
RV 229; P 171; F I, 45; R 117 in D (Turin)
RV 231; P 199; F I, 8; R 31 in D (Turin)
RV 232; P 200; F I, 18; R 68 in D (Turin)
RV 233; P 195; F I, 133; R 306 in D (Turin)
RV 234; P 208; F I, 10; R 37 in D (Turin) *L'inquietudine*
RV 752; P –; F –; R – in D (Sonsfeld catalogue) a lost work
RV 235; P 293; F I, 113; R 258 in D minor (Turin)
RV 237; P 277; F I, 143; R 325 in D minor (Dresden) dedicated to Pisendel
RV 240; P 269; F I, 142; R 324 in D minor (Dresden)
RV 241; P 270; F I, 154; R 336 in D minor (Dresden)
RV 243; P 310; F I, 11; R 45 in D minor (Turin) *violino senza cantin*. For a violin without an E string, and with scordatura
RV 245; P 276; F I, 151; R 333 in D minor (Dresden)
RV 246; P 272; F I, 119; R 285 in D minor (Turin)
RV 247; P 312; F I, 126; R 296 in D minor (Turin)
RV 248; P 316; F I, 21; R 74 in D minor (Turin)
RV 250; P 425; F I, 102; R 227 in E flat (Turin)
RV 251; P 428; F I, 109; R 254 in E flat (Turin)
RV 252; P 418; F I, 164; R 349 in E flat (Biblioteca Comunale, Assisi)
RV 254; P 429; F I, 9; R 38 in E flat (Turin)
RV 255; P –; F –; R in E flat (Pirnitz catalogue) a lost work
RV 256; P –; F I, 231; R 502 in E flat (Naples) *Il ritiro*
RV 257; P 439; F I, 92; R 193 in E flat (Turin)
RV 258; P 430; F I, 75; R 169 in E flat (Turin)
RV 260; P 421; F I, 166; R 352 in E flat (Dresden)
RV 261; P 437; F I, 131; R 304 in E flat (Turin)
RV 262; P 420; F I, 156; R 340 in E flat (Dresden)
RV 263; P –; F –; R – in E (Turin)
RV 264; P 245; F I, 72; R 166 in E (Turin)

RV 266; P 247; D I, 84; R 180 in E (Turin)

RV 267; P 243; F I, 145; R 327 in E (Dresden)

RV 268; P 244; F I, 7; R 29 in E (Turin)

RV 270; P 248; F I, 4; R 15 in E (Turin) *Il riposo – Per il Natale*

RV 271; P 246; F I, 127; R 297 in E (Turin) *L'amoroso*

RV 762; P –; F –; R – in E (Manchester) see RV 223

RV 272; P 110; F –; R – in E minor, a work which Ryom now classifies in appendix as Anh. 64 and 64a

RV 273; P 125; F I, 70; R 164 in E minor (Turin)

RV 274; P –; F I, 238; R – in E minor

RV 275; P 109; F I, 220; R 484 in E minor (Roger no. 432/433)

RV 275a; P –; F –; R – in E minor (Darmstadt) a closely related work is RV 430, though their authenticity is doubtful

RV 276; P 108; F I, 216; R 480 in E minor (Roger no. 188)

RV 278; P 144; F I, 37; R 93 in E minor (Turin)

RV 281; P 126; F I, 74; R 168 in E minor (Turin)

RV 282; P 325; F I, 33; R 87 in F (Turin)

RV 283; P 314; F I, 128; R 301 in F (Turin)

RV 285; P 275; F I, 161; R 346 in F (Dresden)

RV 286; P 290; F I, 20; R 70 in F (Turin) *Per la solennità di S. Lorenzo*

RV 287; P 317; F I, 88; R 187 in F (Turin)

RV 288; P 324; F I, 17; R 66 in F (Turin)

RV 289; P 296; F I, 17; R 165 in F (Turin)

RV 290; P –; F –; R – in F (Pirnitz catalogue) a lost work

RV 291; P 252; F I, 215; R 479 in F (published by Walsh as no. 6 of his edition of Op. IV)

RV 292; P 271; F I, 167; R 357 in F (Dresden)

RV 294; P –; F –; R – in F (Manchester) *Il ritiro*

RV 295; P 315; F I, 130; R 303 in F (Turin)

RV 296; P 295; F I, 66; R 158 in F (Turin)

RV 302; P 112; F I, 168; R 358 in G (?)

RV 303; P 121; F I, 103; R 228 in G (Turin)

RV 304; P –; F –; R – in G (Pirnitz catalogue) a lost work

RV 305; P –; F –; R – in G (Ringmacher catalogue) a lost work

RV 306; P 136; F I, 87; R 186 in G (Turin)

RV 307; P 124; F I, 110; R 255 in G (Turin)

RV 309; P –; F –; R – in G (Pirnitz catalogue) *Il mare tempestoso* – a lost work

RV 311; P 117; F I, 96; R 202 in G (Turin) *violino in tromba*

RV 312; P 122; F I, 107; R 247 in G (Turin)

RV 313; P 138; F I, 64; R 156 in G (Turin) *violino in tromba*

RV 314; P 111; F I, 91; R 192 in G (Turin) dedicated to Pisendel

RV 314a; P –; F –; R – in G (Dresden)

RV 316; P –; F –; R – in G minor (Darmstadt) a lost work –
Bach BWV 975

RV 319; P 351; F I, 165; R 351 in G minor (Dresden)

RV 320; P 399; F –; R – in G minor (Turin) incomplete

RV 321; P 395; F I, 122; R 292 in G minor (Turin)

RV 322; P 348; F –; R – in G minor (Österreichische National-
bibliothek, Vienna) incomplete

RV 323; P 352; F I, 147; R 329 in G minor (Dresden)

RV 325; P 372; F I, 108; R 253 in G minor (Turin)

RV 327; P 374; F I, 112; R 257 in G minor (Turin)

RV 328; P 357; F I, 82; R 178 in G minor (Turin)

RV 329; P 354; F I, 152; R 334 in G minor (Dresden)

RV 330; P 408; F I, 36; R 92 in G minor (Turin)

RV 331; P 393; F I, 125; R 295 in G minor (Turin)

RV 333; P 379; F I, 81; R 175 in G minor (Turin)

RV 335; P 219; F I, 223; R 487 in A (Walsh no. 435) related to
RV 518, but of doubtful authenticity

RV 337; P –; F –; R – in A (Pirnitz catalogue) a lost work

RV 338; P 217; F I, 221; R 485 in A (Walsh no. 454) Ryom now
assigns this to appendix Anh. 65. From a manuscript in Schwerin,
Meck is the composer

RV 339; P 232; F I, 227; R 496 in A (Schwerin)

RV 340; P 228; F I, 141; R 323 in A (Dresden) dedicated to
Pisendel

RV 341; P 227; F I, 148; R 330 in A (Dresden)

RV 342; P 221; F I, 224; R 489 in A (Fitzwilliam Museum,
Cambridge)

RV 343; P 229; F I, 39; R 100 in A (Turin) for violin with
scordatura

RV 344; P 223; F I, 155; R 339 in A (Dresden)

RV 346; P 237; F I, 104; R 229 in A (Turin)

RV 349; P 225; F I, 123; R 293 in A (Turin)

RV 350; P 234; F I, 106; R 245 in A (Turin)

RV 351; P –; F –; R – in A (Ringmacher catalogue) a lost work

RV 352; P 236; F I, 5; R 16 in A (Turin)

RV 353; P 239; F I, 137; R 313 in A (Turin)

RV 763; P –; F –; R – in A (Manchester) *L'Ottavina*

RV 768; P –; F –; R – in A (Turin)

RV 355; P 92; F I, 236; R 519 in A minor (Uppsala) of question-
able authenticity

RV 360; P 347; F –; R – in B flat (Österreichische National-
bibliothek, Vienna) incomplete

RV 363; P 350; F i, 163; R 348 in B flat (Dresden) *Il cornetto da posta*

RV 364; P 346; F i, 219; R 483 in B flat (Roger no. 432/433)

RV 364a; P 346; F –; R – in B flat (Mme Boivin & Le Clerc)

RV 365; P 376; F i, 69; R 163 in B flat (Turin)

RV 366; P 358; F i, 150; R 332 in B flat (Dresden) *Il carbonelli?*

RV 367; P 405; F i, 1; R 1 in B flat (Turin)

RV 368; P 396; F i, 121; R 291 in B flat (Turin)

RV 369; P 356; F i, 65; R 157 in B flat (Turin)

RV 370; P 349; F i, 95; R 199 in B flat (Turin)

RV 371; P 375; F i, 117; R 262 in B flat (Turin)

RV 372; P 370; F i, 118; R 284 in B flat (Turin)

RV 375; P 373; F i, 32; R 86 in B flat (Turin)

RV 376; P 377; F i, 76; R 170 in B flat (Turin)

RV 377; P 364; F i, 230; R 499 in B flat (Schwerin)

RV 378; P 380; F –; R – in B flat (Turin) incomplete

RV 380; P 409; F i, 15; R 64 in B flat (Turin)

RV 381; P 327; F i, 235; R 514 in B flat (Deutsche Staatsbibliothek, Berlin) Bach BWV 980. RV 528 is a closely related work

RV 382; P 412; F i, 233; R 511 in B flat (Österreichische Nationalbibliothek, Vienna) of doubtful authenticity

RV 383; P 353; F i, 170; R 377 in B flat (Dresden)

RV 764; P –; F –; R – in B flat (Manchester) related to RV 548

RV 384; P 168; F i, 144; R 326 in B minor (Dresden)

RV 385; P 178; F i, 229; R 498 in B minor (Schwerin) of doubtful authenticity

RV 386; P 183; F i, 1151; R 260 in B minor (Turin)

RV 387; P 202; F i, 83; R 179 in B minor (Turin)

RV 388; P 172; F i, 171; R 378 in B minor (Dresden)

RV 389; P 184; F i, 38; R 96 in B minor (Turin)

RV 390; P 185; F i, 77; R 171 in B minor (Turin)

Concertos for viola d'amore, orchestra and basso continuo

RV 392; P 166; F ii, 5; R 337 in D (Dresden)

RV 393; P 289; F ii, 4; R 198 in D minor (Turin)

RV 394; P 288; F ii, 2; R 196 in D minor (Turin)

RV 395; P 287; F –; R – in D minor (Turin)

RV 395a; P –; F ii, 3; R 197 in D minor (Turin)

RV 396; P 233; F ii, 1; R 189 in A (Turin) related to RV 744

RV 397; P 37; F ii, 6; R 341 in A minor (Turin)

Concertos for 'cello, orchestra and basso continuo
RV 398; P 31; F III, 8; R 218 in C (Turin)
RV 399; P 33; F III, 6; R 211 in C (Turin)
RV 400; P 30; F III, 3; R 204 in C (Turin)
RV 401; P 434; F III, 1; R 19 in C minor (Turin)
RV 402; P –; F III, 27; R 527 in C minor (Wiesentheid)
RV 403; P 181; F III, 16; R 235 in D (Turin)
RV 404; P 176; F III, 20; R 500 in D (Schwerin)
RV 405; P –; F III, 24; R 524 in D minor (Wiesentheid)
RV 406; P 282; F III, 7; R 212 in D minor (Turin) related to RV 481
RV 407; P –; F III, 23; R 523 in D minor (Wiesentheid)
RV 408; P 424; F III, 5; R 206 in E flat (Turin)
RV 409; P 119; F XII, 22; R 137 in E minor (Turin)
RV 410; P 285; F III, 17; R 243 in F (Turin)
RV 411; P 284; F III, 14; R 233 in F (Turin)
RV 412; P 283; F III, 11; R 221 in F (Turin)
RV 413; P 120; F III, 12; R 231 in G (Turin)
RV 414; P 118; F III, 19; R 317 in G (Turin) related to RV 438
RV 415; P –; F III, 22; R 522 in G (Wiesentheid)
RV 416; P –; F III, 26; R 526 in G minor (Wiesentheid)
RV 417; P 369; F III, 15; R 234 in G minor (Turin)
RV 418; P 35; F III, 18; R 244 in A minor (Turin)
RV 419; P 32; F III, 10; R 220 in A minor (Turin)
RV 420; P –; F III, 21; R 521 in A minor (Wiesentheid)
RV 421; P 34; F III, 13; R 232 in A minor (Turin)
RV 422; P 24; F III, 14; R 205 in A minor (Turin)
RV 423; P –; F III, 25; R 525 in B flat (Wiesentheid)
RV 424; P 180; F III, 9; R 219 in B minor (Turin)

Concerto for mandoline, orchestra and basso continuo
RV 425; P 134; F V, 1; R 98 in C (Turin)

Concertos for flute, orchestra and basso continuo
RV 426; P –; F VI, 17; R – in D (Stockholm)
RV 427; P 203; F VI, 3; R 102 in D (Turin)
RV 429; P 205; F VI, 10; R 153 in D (Turin)
RV 430; P –; F –; R – in E minor (Darmstadt) see RV 275a
RV 431; P 139; F –; R – in E minor (Turin) incomplete
RV 432; P 142; F –; R – in E minor (Turin) incomplete
RV 436; P 140; F VI, 8; R 151 in G (Turin)
RV 438; P 118/141; F VI, 6; R 138 in G (Turin)
RV 440; P 80; F VI, 7; R 148 in A minor (Turin)

Concertos for recorder, orchestra and basso continuo
RV 441; P 440; F vi, 11; R 159 in C minor (Turin)
RV 442; P –; F vi, 1; R 46 in F (Turin) related to RV 434

Concertos for flautino, orchestra and basso continuo
RV 443; P 79; F vi, 4; R 105 in C (Turin)
RV 444; P 78; F vi, 5; R 110 in C (Turin)
RV 445; P 83; F vi, 9; R 152 in A minor (Turin)

Concertos for oboe, orchestra and basso continuo
RV 446; P –; F vii, 20; R – in C (Lund)
RV 447; P 41; F vii, 6; R 216 in C (Turin) related to RV 448 and
RV 470
RV 448; P 43; F vii, 7; R 217 in C (Turin) related to RV 447 and
RV 470
RV 450; P 50; F vii, 11; R 283 in C (Turin) related to RV 471
RV 451; P 44; F vii, 4; R 222 in C (Turin)
RV 452; P 91; F vii, 17; R 520 in C (Uppsala)
RV 453; P 187; F vii, 10; R 279 in D (Turin)
RV 455; P 306; F vii, 2; R 14 in F (Turin)
RV 456; P 264; F vii, 16; R 488 in F (Walsh no. 384) of doubtful
authenticity
RV 457; P –; F vii, 12; R 315 in F (Turin) related to RV 485
RV 458; P –; F vii, 18; R – in F (Lund)
RV 459; P –; F –; R – in G minor (Wiesentheid) incomplete?
RV 461; P 42; F vii, 5; R 215 in A minor (Turin)
RV 462; P –; F vii, 19; R – in A minor (Lund)
RV 463; P –; F vii, 13; R 316 in A minor (Turin) related to RV
500

Concertos for bassoon, orchestra and basso continuo
RV 466; P 51; F viii, 28; R 274 in C (Turin)
RV 467; P 48; F viii, 18; R 239 in C (Turin)
RV 468; P 55; F –; R – in C (Turin) incomplete?
RV 469; P 49; F viii, 16; R 237 in C (Turin)
RV 470; P 43; F viii, 33; R 281 in C (Turin) related to RV 447
and RV 448
RV 471; P 50; F viii, 34; R 382 in C (Turin) related to RV 450
RV 472; P 45; F viii, 17; R 238 in C (Turin)
RV 473; P 90; F viii, 9; R 118 in C (Turin)
RV 474; P 69; F viii, 4; R 47 in C (Turin)
RV 475; P 56; F viii, 21; R 267 in C (Turin)
RV 476; P 57; F viii, 31; R 277 in C (Turin)

223

RV 477; P 46; F VIII, 13; R 224 in C (Turin)
RV 478; P 71; F VIII, 3; R 34 in C (Turin)
RV 479; P 52; F VIII, 26; R 272 in C (Turin)
RV 480; P 432; F VIII, 14; R 225 in C minor (Turin)
RV 481; P 282; F VIII, 5; R 67 in D minor (Turin) related to RV 406
RV 482; P 303; F –; R – in D minor (Turin) incomplete?
RV 483; P 433; F VIII, 27; R 273 in E flat (Turin)
RV 484; P 137; F VIII, 6; R 71 in E minor (Turin)
RV 485; P 318; F VIII, 8; R 109 in F (Turin) related to RV 457
RV 486; P 304; F VIII, 22; R 268 in F (Turin)
RV 487; P 298; F VIII, 15; R 236 in F (Turin)
RV 488; P 299; F VIII, 19; R 240 in F (Turin)
RV 489; P 305; F VIII, 20; R 266 in F (Turin)
RV 490; P 307; F VIII, 32; R 278 in F (Turin)
RV 491; P 300; F VIII, 25; R 271 in F (Turin)
RV 492; P 128; F VIII, 29; R 275 in G (Turin)
RV 493; P 131; F VIII, 30; R 276 in G (Turin)
RV 494; P 130; F VIII, 37; R 300 in G (Turin)
RV 495; P 384; F VIII, 23; R 269 in G minor (Turin)
RV 496; P 381; F VIII, 11; R 214 in G minor (Turin) dedicated to the Marquis of Marzin
RV 497; P 72; F VIII, 7; R 72 in A minor (Turin)
RV 498; P 70; F VIII, 2; R 28 in A minor (Turin)
RV 499; P 47; F VIII, 12; R 223 in A minor (Turin)
RV 500; P 89; F VIII, 10; R 119 in A minor (Turin) related to RV 463
RV 501; P 401; F VIII, 1; R 12 in B flat (Turin) *La notte*
RV 502; P 382; F VIII, 24; R 270 in B flat (Turin)
RV 503; P 387; F VIII, 35; R 298 in B flat (Turin)
RV 504; P 386; F VIII, 36; R 299 in B flat (Turin)

Concertos for 2 violins, orchestra and basso continuo
RV 505; P 65; F I, 85; R 181 in C (Turin)
RV 506; P 18; F I, 157; R 342 in C (Dresden)
RV 507; P 23; F I, 43; R 112 in C (Turin)
RV 508; P 17; F I, 44; R 116 in C (Turin)
RV 509; P 436; F I, 12; R 48 in C minor (Turin)
RV 510; P 435; F I, 14; R 60 in C minor (Turin)
RV 511; P 190; F I, 35; R 89 in D (Turin)
RV 512; P 189; F I, 41; R 108 in D (Turin)
RV 513; P 159; F I, 222; R 486 in D (Witvogel no. 48)
RV 514; P 281; F I, 100; R 209 in D minor (Turin)

224

RV 515; P 423; F I, 101; R 210 in E flat (Turin)
RV 765; P –; F –; R – in F (Royal Academy of Music, London)
RV 516; P 132; F I, 6; R 27 in G (Turin)
RV 517; P 366; F I, 98; R 207 in G minor (Turin)
RV 518; P –; F –; R – in A (Uppsala) related to RV 335, but of doubtful authenticity
RV 520; P 220; F –; R – in A (Österreichische National-bibliothek, Vienna) incomplete
RV 521; P 224; F I, 159; R 344 in A (Dresden)
RV 523; P 28; F I, 61; R 140 in A minor (Turin)
RV 524; P 390; F I, 40; R 107 in B flat (Turin)
RV 525; P 389; F I, 63; R 145 in B flat (Turin)
RV 256; P 15; F –; R – in B flat (Österreichische National-bibliothek, Vienna) incomplete
RV 527; P 365; F I, 99; R 208 in B flat (Turin)
RV 528; P –; F –; R – in B flat (Uppsala) related to RV 381 and RV 383a
RV 529; P 391; F I, 42; R 111 in B flat (Turin)

Concerto for 2 'cellos, orchestra and basso continuo
RV 531; P 411; F III, 2; R 61 in G minor (Turin)

Concerto for 2 mandolines, orchestra and basso continuo
RV 532; P 133; F III, 2; R 104 in G (Turin)

Concerto for 2 flutes, orchestra and basso continuo
RV 533; P 76; F VI, 2; R 101 in C (Turin)

Concertos for 2 oboes, orchestra and basso continuo
RV 534; P 85; F VII, 3; R 139 in C (Turin)
RV 535; P 302; F VII, 9; R 264 in D minor (Turin)
RV 536; P 53; F VII, 8; R 263 in A minor (Turin)

Concerto for 2 trumpets, orchestra and basso continuo
RV 537; P 75; F IX, 1; R 97 in C (Turin)

Concertos for 2 horns, orchestra and basso continuo
RV 538; P 320; F x, 1; R 91 in F (Turin)
RV 539; P 321; F x, 2; R 121 in F (Turin)

Concertos for 2 different instruments, orchestra and basso continuo
RV 766; P –; F –; R – in C minor (Royal Academy of Music, London) for violin and organ. Related to RV 510

RV 540; P 266; F xii, 38; R 320 in D minor (Dresden) for viola d'amore and lute

RV 541; P 311; F xii, 19; R 95 in D minor (Turin) for violin and organ

RV 542; P 274; F xii, 41; R 353 in F (Dresden) for violin and organ. Of doubtful authenticity

RV 543; P 301; F xii, 35; R 265 in F (Turin) for violin and oboe. Related to RV 139

RV 544; P 308; F iv, 5; R 135 in F (Turin) *Il Proteo o sia il mondo al rovescio.* For violin and 'cello. Related to RV 572

RV 767; P –; F –; R – in F (Royal Academy of Music, London) for violin and organ. Related to RV 765

RV 545; P 129; F xii, 36; R 280 in G (Turin) for oboe and bassoon

RV 546; P 238; F iv, 6; R 146 in A (Turin) for violin and 'cello all'Inglese

RV 547; P 388; F iv, 2; R 35 in B flat (Turin) for violin and 'cello

RV 548; P 406; F xii, 16; R 73 in B flat (Turin) for violin and oboe

Concertos for 3 and 4 violins, orchestra and basso continuo
RV 551; P 278; F i, 34; R 88 in F (Turin) for 3 violins

RV 552; P 222; F i, 139; R 319 in A (Dresden) for echo violin and 3 others

RV 553; P 367; F i, 59; R 134 in B flat (Turin) for 4 violins

Concertos for various instruments, orchestra and basso continuo
RV 554; P 36; F xii, 34; R 250 in C (Turin) for violin, organ (or violin) and oboe

RV 554a; P 36; F –; R – in C (Turin) same as preceding, with 'cello instead of oboe

RV 555; P 87; F xii, 23; R 142 in C (Turin) for 3 violins, oboe, 2 recorders, 2 viole all'Inglese, salmoe (*see* p. 104), 2 'cellos, 2 harpsichords, and 2 trumpets in the third movement

RV 556; P 84; F xii, 14; R 54 in C (Turin) *Per la solennità di S. Lorenzo,* for 2 oboes, 2 claren (see p. 104), 2 recorders, 2 violins and bassoon

RV 557; P 54; F xii, 17; R 90 in C (Turin) for 2 violins, 2 oboes or bassoons, with recorders and bassoon in the second movement

RV 558; P 16; F xii, 37; R 318 in C (Dresden) for 2 violins in *tromba marina,* 2 recorders, 2 trumpets, 2 mandolines, 2 salmoe (see p. 104), 2 theorboes and 'cello

RV 559; P 74; F xii, 2; R 10 in C (Turin) for 2 clarinets and 2 oboes

RV 560; P 73; F XII, 1; R 3 in C (Turin) for 2 clarinets and 2 oboes

RV 561; P 58; F IV, 3; R 53 in C (Turin) for violin and 2 'cellos

RV 562; P 169; F XII, 47; R 380 in D (Dresden) for violin, 2 oboes, and 2 horns

RV 562a; P 444; F –; R – in D (University Library, Amsterdam) for violin, 2 oboes, 2 horns and drums

RV 563; P 210; F XII, 50; R 510 in D (Österreichische National-bibliothek, Vienna) for violin and 2 oboes

RV 564; P 188; F IV, 4; R 99 in D (Turin) for 2 violins and 2 'cellos

RV 564a; P –; F –; R – in D (Dresden) an anonymous version of the preceding for 2 violins, 2 oboes and bassoon

RV 566; P 297; F XII, 31; R 213 in D minor (Turin) for 2 violins, 2 recorders, 2 oboes and bassoon

RV 568; P 276; F XII, 39; R 388 in F (Dresden) for violin, 2 oboes, 2 horns and bassoon

RV 569; P 273; F XII, 10; 43 in F (Turin) for violin, 2 oboes, 2 horns, and bassoon with 'cello in third movement

RV 570; P –; F XII, 28; R 150 in F (Turin) *Tempesta di mare* for flute, oboe and bassoon (with violin in first movement). Related works are RV 98 and RV 433

RV 571; P 268; F XII, 40; R 350 in F (Dresden) for violin, 2 oboes, 2 horns, 'cello and bassoon. A related work is RV 99

RV 572; P –; F –; R –; in F (British Museum, London) *Il Proteo o il mondo al rovescio* for 2 flutes, 2 oboes, violin, 'cello and harp-sichord. A related work is RV 544

RV 573; P 265; F –; R – in F (Darmstadt) a lost work for 2 oboes, 2 horns and 2 bassoons

RV 574; P 319; F XII, 18; R 94 in F (Turin) dedicated to Pisendel (?), for violin, 2 *trombon da caccia*, 2 oboes and bassoon

RV 575; P 135; F IV, 1; R 26 in G (Turin) for 2 violins and 2 'cellos

RV 576; P 359; F XII, 33; R 249 in G minor (Turin) dedicated to the Prince of Saxony, for violin, oboe, 2 recorders, 2 oboes and bassoon

RV 577; P 383; F XII, 3; R 25 in G minor (Turin) *per l'Orchestra di Dresda*, for violin, 2 oboes, 2 recorders and bassoon

RV 579; P 385; F XII, 12; R 51 in B flat (Turin) *Concerto funebre*, for violin, oboe, salmoe and 3 viole all'Inglese

Concertos for double orchestra

RV 581; P –; F ɪ, 13; R 55 in C (Turin) *Per la SSma Assontione di M V.* A related work is RV 179

RV 582; P 164; F ɪ, 62; R 141 in D (Turin) *Per la SSma Assontione di M V*

RV 583; P 368; F ɪ, 60; R 136 in B flat (Turin) for violin with scordatura

RV 584; P 309; F –; R – in F (Turin) incomplete, for violin and organ as solo instruments in each orchestra

RV 585; P 226; F xɪɪ, 48; R 381 in A (Dresden) for 2 violins and 2 recorders in the first orchestra, and 'cello in the third movement. The basso continuo in the second movement is assigned to theorbo or organ. For the second orchestra, 2 violins and 2 recorders again as soloists, with organ and 'cello in the third movement

Sacred vocal music

RV 586 Mass (University Library, Warsaw)

RV 587 Kyrie for double choir (Turin)

RV 588 Gloria with Introduction (Turin) related works are RV 639 and RV 639a

RV 589 Gloria (Turin)

RV 590 Gloria (Kreuzherren catalogue) *a 5 voc. Oboe Trombae D♯*, a lost work

RV 591 Credo (Turin)

RV 592 Credo (University Library, Warsaw)

RV 593 *Domine ad adiuvandum me* (Psalm 69) for double choir (Turin)

RV 594 *Dixit Dominus* (Psalm 109) for double choir (Turin)

RV 595 *Dixit Dominus* (Psalm 109) (Narodny Museum, Prague)

RV 596 *Confitebor* (Psalm 110) (Turin)

RV 597 *Beatus vir* (Psalm 111) for double choir (Turin)

RV 598 *Beatus vir* (Psalm 111) (Turin)

RV 599 *Beatus'a 5 voc'* (Kreuzherren catalogue) a lost work, possibly another *Beatus vir* (Psalm 111)

RV 600 *Laudate pueri* (Psalm 112) (Turin)

RV 601 *Laudate pueri* (Psalm 112) (Turin)

RV 602 *Laudate pueri* (Psalm 112) for 2 sopranos, choir, oboe and double orchestra. There is an earlier version which Ryom denotes as RV 602a, and another version for 1 soprano, choir and double orchestra, RV 603 (Turin)

RV 604 *In exitu Israel* (Psalm 113) (Turin)

RV 605 *Credidi propter quod* (Psalm 115) (Turin) Ryom suggests that this is a parody of an anonymous *Lauda Jerusalem* (Psalm 147), also in Turin

RV 606 *Laudate Dominum* (Psalm 116) (Turin)

RV 607 *Laetatus sum* (Psalm 121) (Turin)

RV 608 *Nisi Dominus* (Psalm 126) (Turin)

RV 609 *Lauda Jerusalem* (Psalm 147) for double choir (Turin)

RV 610 *Magnificat* for 2 sopranos, alto and tenor with SATB chorus and orchestra. There is another version, RV 610a, for 2 sets of soloists, 2 choirs and 2 orchestras. Both are in Turin

RV 611 *Magnificat* for soprano and alto solo, SATB chorus and orchestra, incorporating 3 movements from RV 610

RV 612 *Deus tuorum militum* (Hymn) (Turin)

RV 613 *Gaude Mater Ecclesia* (Hymn) (Turin)

RV 614 *Laudate Dominum* ('Offertory') (University Library, Warsaw)

RV 615 *Regina coeli* (Antiphon) incomplete. (Turin)

RV 616 *Salve Regina* (Antiphon) for double choir. (Turin)

RV 617 *Salve Regina* (Antiphon) (Moravian Museum, Brno)

RV 618 *Salve Regina* (Antiphon) (Turin)

RV 619 *Salve* (Antiphon) probably a *Salve Regina* (Kreuzherren catalogue) a lost work

RV 620 *Sanctorum meritis* (Hymn) (Turin)

RV 621 *Stabat Mater* (Sequence) (Turin)

RV 622 *Te Deum* (reported in the *Mercure de France* in October 1727) a lost work

RV 623 *Canta in prato* (Motet) for soprano. (Turin)

RV 624 *Carae rosae respirate* (Motet) for soprano. (Royal College of Music, London)

RV 625 *Clarae stellae* (Motet) for alto. (Turin)

RV 626 *In furore* (Motet) for soprano. (Turin)

RV 627 *In turbato* (Motet) for soprano. (Dresden)

RV 628 *Invicti bellate* (Motet) for alto. (Turin)

RV 629 *Longe mala* (Motet) for soprano. (Turin)

RV 630 *Nulla in mundo* (Motte) for soprano. (Turin)

RV 631 *O qui coeli* (Motet) for soprano. (Turin)

RV 632 *Sum in medio* (Motet) for soprano. (Dresden)

RV 633 *Vestro principi* (Motet) for alto. (Turin)

RV 634 *Vos aurae* (Motet) for soprano. (Biblioteca Communale, Assisi)

RV 635 *Ascende laeta* ('Introduction') to a *Dixit*, for soprano. (Turin)

RV 636 *Canta in prato* ('Introduction') to a *Dixit*, for soprano. (Turin)

RV 637 *Cur sagittas* ('Introduction') to a *Gloria*, for alto. (Turin)
RV 638 *Filiae mestae* ('Introduction') to a *Miserere*, for alto. (Turin)
RV 639 *Jubilate o amaeni* ('Introduction') to a *Gloria*, RV 588, for alto. (Turin). RV 639a is a version for soprano, also in Turin
RV 640 *Longe mala* ('Introduction') to a *Gloria*, for alto. For another version see RV 629, which Ryom does not seem to connect. (Turin)
RV 641 *Non in pratis* ('Introduction') to a *Miserere*, for alto. (Turin)
RV 642 *Ostro picta* ('Introduction') to a *Gloria*, for soprano. (Turin)
RV 643 *Moyses Deus Pharaonis* (Oratorio) performed Venice 1714. The music is lost, but a copy of the anonymous libretto is in Rome
RV 644 *Juditha triumphans* (Oratorio) performed Venice 1716. There is a copy of J. Cassetti's libretto in Rome
RV 645 *L'adorazione delli tre re magi* (Oratorio) performed Milan 1722. The music is lost, but there is a copy of the anonymous libretto in Milan
RV 646 *Ad corda reclina* ('*concertus italicus*') (University Library, Warsaw)
RV 647 *Eia voces* ('*aria de sanctis*') (University Library, Warsaw)
RV 648 *Ihr Himmel nun* ('*concertus italicus*') (University Library, Warsaw)

Secular vocal works
Cantatas for soprano solo and basso continuo
RV 649 *All'ombra d'un bel faggio* (Turin)
RV 650 *All'or che lo sguardo* (Turin)
RV 651 *Amor hai vinto* (Turin)
RV 652 *Aure voi più non siete* (Turin)
RV 653 *Del suo natio rigore* (Turin)
RV 654 *Elvira, Elvira anima mea* (Turin)
RV 655 *Era la notte* (Turin)
RV 656 *Fonti di pianto piangete* (Turin)
RV 657 *Geme l'onda che parte* (Turin)
RV 658 *Il povero mio cor* (Turin)
RV 659 *Indarno cerca la tortorella* (Turin) there is a slight doubt about the authenticity of this work
RV 660 *La farfalletta s'aggira* (Turin)
RV 661 *Nel partir de te* (Turin)
RV 662 *Par che tardo* (Turin)

RV 663 *Scherza di fronda* (Dresden)
RV 664 *Seben vivono senz'alma* (Turin)
RV 665 *Si levi dal pensier* (Turin)
RV 666 *Si si luce adorate* (Turin)
RV 667 *Sorge vermiglia in ciel* (Turin)
RV 668 *T'intendo si mio cor* (Turin)
RV 669 *Tra l'erbe, i zeffiri* (Turin)
RV 753 *Prendea con mandi latte* (Bodleian Library, Oxford)

Cantatas for alto solo and basso continuo
RV 670 *Alla caccia* (Turin)
RV 671 *Care selve* (Turin)
RV 672 *Filli di gioia* (Florence Conservatory)
RV 673 *Ingrata Lidia* (Florence Conservatory)
RV 674 *Perfidissimo cor!* (Dresden)
RV 675 *Piango, gemo, sospiro* (Florence Conservatory)
RV 676 *Pianti, sospiri* (Dresden)
RV 677 *Qual per ignoto* (Dresden)

Cantatas for soprano, instruments and basso continuo
RV 678 *All'ombra di sospetto* (Dresden) with flute
RV 679 *Che giova il sospirar* (Staatliche Museum, Meiningen) with 2 violins and viola
RV 680 *Lungi dal vago* (Turin) with violin
RV 681 *Perche son molli* (St Michael's, Tenbury) with 2 violins
RV 682 *Vengo a voi luci adorate* (Turin) with 2 violins and viola

Cantatas for alto, instruments and basso continuo
RV 683 *Amor hai vinto* (Turin) with 2 violins and viola
RV 684 *Cessate omai cessate* (Turin) with 2 violins and viola
RV 685 *O mie porpore più belle* (Turin) with two violins and viola.
Dedication: in praise of Monsignor da Bagni, Bishop of Mantua
RV 686 *Qual in pioggia dorata* (Turin) with 2 horns, 2 violins and
viola. Dedication: in praise of Prince Philip of Darmstadt,
Governor of Mantua

Serenatas and similar extended vocal works
RV 687 *La Gloria e Imeneo* (Marriage cantata) Turin
RV 688 *Le gare del dovere* (Serenata) dedicated to Francesco
Querini. Performed Venice 1719. The music is lost, but there is a
copy of the anonymous libretto in Milan
RV 689 *Le gare della giustitia e della pace* (Serenata?) a lost work
RV 690 *Mio cor povero cor* (Serenata a 3) Turin

RV 691 *Il Mopso* (*Egloga pescatoria*) performed in Venice in 1740. A lost work

RV 692 *Questa Eurilla gentil* (Serenata a 4) performed in Mantua 1726 for the birthday of Philip of Hesse-Darmstadt. The music is lost, but there is a copy of the anonymous libretto in Milan

RV 693 *La Sena festeggiante* (Serenata a 3) written to celebrate the birth of the French princesses in 1729. Turin. The libretto is by D. Lalli, and Vivaldi used the sinfonia as the first movement of RV 117

RV 694 *L'unione della Pace e di Marte* (Serenata a 3) Venice 1727. The music is lost, but there is a copy of the libretto by A. Grossatesta in Milan

Operas (all in Turin unless otherwise mentioned)

RV 695 *Adelaide*, Verona 1735. The music is lost, but there is a copy of the anonymous libretto in Milan

RV 696 *Alvilda regina de' Goti*, Prague 1731. The music is lost, but there is a copy of the anonymous libretto in the University Library, Prague

RV 697 *Argippo*, Prague 1730. The music is lost, but there is a copy of the anonymous libretto in the University Library, Prague

RV 698 *Aristide*, Venice 1735. The music is lost, but there is a copy of the libretto by Goldoni (Calindo Grolo) in the Marciana Library, Venice

RV 699 *Armida al campo d'Egitto*, Venice 1718. There is a copy of the libretto by G. Palazzi in the Marciana Library, Venice. Vivaldi used the sinfonia for *Ercole sul Termondonte*, RV 710

RV 700 *Arsilda regina di Ponto*, Venice 1716. There is a copy of the libretto by D. Lalli in the Marciana Library, Venice. Vivaldi used the sinfonia for *Il Teuzzone*, RV 736

RV 701 *Artabano rè de' Parti*, Venice 1718. The music is lost, but there is a copy of the libretto by A. Marchi in the Marciana Library, Venice. The opera was a version of *La costanza*, RV 706

RV 702 *L'Atenaide*, Florence 1729. There is a copy of the libretto by A. Zeno in Milan

RV 703 *Bajazet* (*Tamerlano*), Verona 1735. Libretto by A. Piovene

RV 704 *La Candace*, Mantua 1720. The music is lost, but there is a copy of the libretto by F. Silvani and D. Lalli in Washington, Library of Congress

RV 705 *Catone in Utica*, Verona 1737. There is a copy of the libretto by P. Metastasio in Milan

RV 706 *La costanza trionfante degli amori e degli odii*, Venice

1716. The music is lost, but there is a copy of the libretto by A. Marchi in the Marciana Library, Venice. The opera was reworked as *Artabano*, RV 701, and *Doriclea*, RV 708

RV 707 *Cunegonda*, Venice 1726. The music is lost, but there is a copy of the libretto by A. Piovene in the Marciana Library, Venice.

RV 708 *Doriclea*, Prague 1732. The music is lost, but there is a copy of the libretto by A. Marchi in the University Library, Prague. The opera was a version of *La costanza*, RV 706

RV 709 *Dorilla in Tempe*, Venice 1726. There is a copy of the libretto by A. M. Lucchini in the Marciana Library, Venice. Vivaldi used the sinfonia for *Farnace*, RV 711

RV 710 *Ercole sul Termodonte*, Rome 1723. There is a copy of the libretto by G. F. Bussani in Florence, and the sinfonia (Paris Conservatoire) is also found in *Armida*, RV 699

RV 711 *Farnace*, Venice 1727. There is a copy of the libretto by A. M. Lucchini in the Marciana Library, Venice. Vivaldi used the sinfonia for *Dorilla*, RV 709

RV 712 *La fede tradita e vendicata*, Venice 1726. The music is lost, but there is a copy of the libretto by F. Silvani in the Marciana Library, Venice

RV 713 *Feraspe*, Venice 1739. The music is lost, but there is a copy of the libretto by F. Silvani in the Marciana Library, Venice

RV 714 *La fida ninfa*, Verona 1732. There is a copy of the libretto by S. Maffei in the Bibloteca Marucelliana, Florence

RV 715 *Filippo rè di Macedonia*, Venice 1721. The music is lost (though only the third act was by Vivaldi), but there is a copy of the libretto by D. Lalli in the Marciana Library, Venice

RV 716 *Ginevra principessa di Scozia*, Florence 1736. The music is lost, but there is a copy of the libretto by A. Salvi in Bologna

RV 717 *Il Giustino*, Rome 1724. There is a copy of the libretto by N. Berengani in Rome. Vivaldi used the first movement of the sinfonia as the first movement of RV 111 and RV 111a, and the second movement as the second movement of RV 693

RV 718 *Griselda*, Venice 1735. There is a copy of the libretto by A. Zeno and C. Goldoni in the Marciana Library, Venice

RV 719 *L'incoronazione di Dario*, Venice 1716. There is a copy of the libretto by A. Morselli in the Marciana Library, Venice

RV 720 *Gli inganni per vendetta*, Vicenza 1720. A version of *Armida*, RV 699. There is a copy of the libretto in Bologna

RV 721 *L'inganno trionfante in amore*, Venice 1725. The music is lost, but there is a copy of the libretto by M. Noris and G. M. Ruggieri in the Marciana Library, Venice

RV 722 *Ipermestra*, Florence 1728. The music is lost, but there is a copy of the libretto by A. Salvi in Bologna

RV 723 *Montezuma*, Venice 1733. The music is lost, but there is a copy of the libretto by G. Giusti in the Marciana Library, Venice

RV 724 *Nerone fatto Cesare*, Venice 1715. The music is lost (though only 12 arias were by Vivaldi), but there is a copy of the libretto by M. Noris in the Marciana Library, Venice

RV 725 *L'Olimpiade*, Venice 1734. There is a copy of the libretto by P. Metastasio in the Marciana Library, Venice

RV 726 *L'oracolo in Messenia*, Venice 1738. The music is lost, but there is a copy of the libretto by A. Zeno in the Marciana Library, Venice

RV 727 *Orlando finto pazzo*, Venice 1714. There is a copy of the libretto by G. Braccioli in the Marciana Library, Venice

RV 728 *Orlando furioso*, Venice 1727. There is a copy of the libretto by G. Braccioli in the Marciana Library, Venice

RV 729 *Ottone in villa*, Vicenza 1713. There is a copy of the libretto by D. Lalli in Milan

RV 730 *Rosilena ed Oronta*, Venice 1728. The music is lost, but there is a copy of the libretto by G. Palazzi in the Marciana Library, Venice

RV 731 *Rosmira*, Venice 1738. There is a copy of the libretto by S. Stampiglia in the Marciana Library, Venice

RV 732 *Scanderbeg*, Florence 1718. The music is lost, but there is a copy of the libretto by A. Salvi in Bologna

RV 733 *Semiramide*, Mantua 1732. The music is lost, but there is a copy of the anonymous libretto in Milan

RV 734 *La Silvia*, Milan 1721. The music is lost, but there is a copy of the anonymous libretto in Milan

RV 735 *Siroe rè di Persia*, Reggio 1727. The music is lost, but there is a copy of the libretto by P. Metastasio in Washington, Library of Congress

RV 736 *Il Teuzzone*, Mantua 1719. There is a copy of the libretto by A. Zeno in the Fondazione Cini, Venice. Vivaldi used the same sinfonia for *Arsilda*, RV 700

RV 737 *Tieteberga*, Venice 1717. The music is lost, but there is a copy of the libretto by A. M. Lucchini in Milan

RV 738 *Tito Manlio*, Mantua 1719. There is a copy of the libretto by M. Noris in the Studienbibliothek, Dillingen

RV 739 *La verità in cimento*, Venice 1720. There is a copy of the libretto by G. Palazzi and D. Lalli in the Marciana Library, Venice

RV 740 *La virtù trionfante dell'amore e dell'odi ovvero Il Tigrane*, Rome 1724. Only the second act is by Vivaldi. There is a copy of the libretto by F. Silvani in the Biblioteca Marucelliana, Florence Under RV 741–RV 750 inclusive, Ryom deals with various fragments and lost works about which it is impossible to be more specific, and his appendix lists several works, prefixed with Anh. for Anhang, referred to in the literature but whose authenticity is doubtful or about which too little is known to be of value

Select Bibliography

ADDISON, J. *Remarks on several parts of Italy in 1701; 2 and 3*, London, 1705

ARNOLD, D. 'Orphans and ladies: the Venetian conservatories (1680–1790)', in *Proceedings of the Royal Musical Association*, vol. LXXXIX (1962–3)
'Vivaldi's church music: an introduction', in *Early music*, vol. I, no. 2, April 1973

BETTIO, P. (ed.), *Lettere scelte di celebri autori all'Ab. Antonio Conti pubblicate per le nozze Da Ponte-Di Serego*, Venice, 1812

BOCAGE, MME DU, *Recueil des oeuvres de Mme du B.* (3 vols.), Lyons, 1764

DE BROSSES, C. *Lettres familières sur l'Italie* (2 vols.) Paris, 1931 ed.

BURNEY, C. *General history of music* (2 vols.) 1935 ed. *Music, men, and manners in France and Italy, 1770*, London, 1969 ed.

CAFFI, F. *Storia della musica sacra nella già Cappella Ducale di San Marco in Venezia dal 1318 al 1797* (2 vols.) Venice, 1854–5

DE CANDÉ, R. *Vivaldi*, Paris, 1967

CAVICCHI, A. 'Inediti nell'epistolario Vivaldi-Bentivoglio', in *Nuova Rivista Musicale Italiana*, vol. I, May/June 1967

CICOGNA, E. *Delle iscrizioni veneziane* (6 vols.) Venice, 1824–42

CORK and ORRERY, J., EARL OF, *Letters from Italy 1754–5*, ed. J. Duncombe, 1774

CORYATE, T. *Coryats crudities*, London, 1611

EINSTEIN, A. *Lebensläufe deutscher Musiker*, Leipzig, 1915 (?)

EVELYN, J. *Diary* (2 vols.) London, 1907 ed.

FRESCHOT, C. *Nouvelle relation de Venise* (3 vols. in 1) Utrecht, 1709

GALLO, R. 'Antonio Vivaldi, il Prete Rosso, la famiglia, la morte', in *Ateneo Veneto*, Venice, December 1938

GALVANI (SALVIOLI) L. N. *I teatri musicale di Venezia nel secolo XVII*, Milan, 1879

GIAZOTTO, R. *Tomaso Albinoni*, Milan, 1945
Antonio Vivaldi, Turin, 1973

GOLDONI, C. *Commedie*, Venice, 1761
Mémoires pour servir à l'histoire de sa vie (3 vols.) Paris, 1787

DE GOUDAR, A. *De Venise – Remarques sur la musique et la danse ou: lettres de Mr G[oudar] à Milord P[embroke]*, Venice, 1773

DE GOUDAR, A. or S. *Le brigandage de la musique italienne*, Paris (?), 1777

GROSLEY, P. J. *Nouveaux mémoires sur l'Italie* (3 vols.) Paris, 1764

GYROWETZ, A. *Biographie des A. Gyrowetz*, 1848, ed. A. Einstein (see above)

HAWKINS, J. *General history of the science and practice of music* London, 1776 (London, 1963 ed., 2 vols.)

HERIOT, A. *The castrati in opera*, London, 1956

HILLER, J. A. *Lebensbeschreibungen berühmter Musikgelehrten*, 1784

HONOUR, H. *Companion guide to Venice*, London, 1965

IVANOVICH, C. *Minerva al Tavolino* (2 vols.) Venice, 1688

KEYSLER, J. G. *Travels* (4 vols.) London, 1756–7

KOLNEDER, W. *Antonio Vivaldi, his life and work*, London, 1970

MAIER, A. *Discorso sulla origine e stato attuale della musica italiana*, Padua, 1821

MAIER, J. C. *Beschreibung von Venedig*, Leipzig, 1789

MALIPIERO G. F. 'Un frontespizio enigmatico', in *Bollettino biografico-musicale*, Milan, January 1930

MARPURG, F. W. *Historisch-kritische Beyträge*, Berlin, 1754

MARTELLO, P. J. *Della tragedia antica e moderna*, 1715 (Bologna, ed., 1735)

MENDEL, H. *Musikalisches Konversationslexicon*, 1870–83

MISSON, F. M. *A new voyage to Italy* (2 vols.) London, 1695

MOLMENTI, P. *Epistolari veneziani del secolo XVII*, Milan, 1914 *Venezia nella vita privata* (4 vols.) Bergamo, 1905–8

PAUL, E. 'La date de naissance d'Antonio Vivaldi', in *Convegno Vivaldiano*, Brussels, 1963

PAULY, R. G. 'Benedetto Marallo's satire on early 18th-century opera', in *Musical Quarterly*, vol. XXXIV (1948) and vol. XXXV (1949)

PINCHERLE, M. *Antonio Vivaldi et la musique instrumentale*, Paris, 1948
   Vivaldi, Paris, 1955, transl. as *Vivaldi, genius of the baroque*, New York, and London, 1955

POELLNITZ, K. L. VON *Memoirs* (2 vols.) London, 1737

PREUSSNER, E. *Die musikalischen Reisen des Herren von Uffenbach*, Kassel, 1949

QUANTZ, J. J. *Lebenslauf* (see Marpurg above)

RENIER-MICHIEL, G. *Origine delle feste veneziane* (6 vols. in 3) Milan, 1829

RINALDI, M. *Catalogo numerico tematico delle composizioni di Antonio Vivaldi*, Rome, 1945

ROUSSEAU, J. J. *Confessions*, Paris, 1964 ed.

RUDGE, O. 'Lettere e dediche di Antonio Vivaldi' in *Accademia Musicale Chigiana* XX (1942)

RYOM, P. *Verzeichnis der Werke Antonio Vivaldis, kleine Ausgabe*, Leipzig, 1974

SALVATORI, A. 'Antonio Vivaldi (il Prete Rosso) note biografiche', in *Rivista mensile della città di Venezia*, Venice, August 1928

SCHERING, A. *Geschichte des Instrumentalkonzerts*, Leipzig, 1905

SELFRIDGE-FIELD, E. *Venetian instrumental music from Gabrieli to Vivaldi*, Oxford, 1975

STEFANI, F. *Sei lettere di Antonio Vivaldi veneziano, maestro compositore di musica della prima metà del secolo XVIII*, Venice, 1871

STRAVINSKY, I. and CRAFT, R. *Conversations with Igor Stravinsky*, London, 1959

TALBOT, M. O. *The instrumental music of Tomaso Albinoni*, PhD. thesis, Cambridge University Library, 1968

THRALE, MRS (H. L. PIOZZI) *Observations and reflections made in the course of a journey through France, Italy and Germany*, Dublin, 1789

WESTRUP, J. A. 'Monteverdi and the orchestra', in *Music and Letters*, Vol. XXI, no. 3, July 1940

WHITE, D. MAXWELL. *Zaccaria Angelo Seriman* ... Manchester, 1961

WIEL, T. *Catologo delle opere in musica rappresentate nel secolo XVIII in Venezia*, in *Nuovo Archivio Veneto*, Venice, 1891–1921

WRIGHT, E. *Some observations made in travelling through France, Italy, etc. in the years 1720, 1721, and 1722* (2 vols.) London, 1730

Notes

CHAPTER ONE

1. A. Salvatori: 'Antonio Vivaldi (il Prete Rosso) note biografiche', in *Rivista mensile della città di Venezia* (Venice, August 1928). The date was reiterated by M. Pincherle in *Antonio Vivaldi et la musique instrumentale* (Paris, 1948), though in fact Pincherle had been working on Venetian music since before 1913, the year in which he completed his doctor's dissertation.

2. E. Paul: 'La date de naissance d'Antonio Vivaldi', in *Convegno Vivaldiano* (Brussels, 1963). The text is as follows:

> Antonio Lucio figliolo del Sig^r Gio. Batta qd. Agustin Vivaldi sonador et della Sig^{ra} Camilla figliola del qd. Camillo Calicchio sua consorte, nato li 4 marzo ult^o caduto, qual'hebbe l'acqua in casa per pericolo di morte della comare allevatrice Mad^{ma} Margarita Veronese, hoggi fu portato alla chiesa ricevè gli essorcismi et ogli SS^{mi} da me Giacomo Tornacieri piovano, a quali lo tene il Sig^r Antonio qd. Gerolemo Veccelio specier all'Insegna del Dose in Contrà.

Remo Giazotto, in *Antonio Vivaldi* (Turin, 1973), p. 15, gives a slightly different version which is hard to reconcile with the original document.

3. The text is as follows:

> S'ha da Cont^r Mat^o tra la Sig^{ra} Camilla figliola del qd. Sig Camillo Calicchio sartor sta nella n^{ra} [nostra] Contra in Campo Grando nelle case de Ca' Salamon, et il Sig^r Gio: Batta qd. Agostin Vivaldi sta nelli Forni in Contra di S. Martin.

Registri di stato libero, S. Giovanni in Bràgora, Venice, 6 June 1676

4. *Antonio Vivaldi*, p. 12 and p. 28n.1. Without any more specific reference, he cites Biblioteca Marciana, Venice, MS Ital, Clas. VII, 481

5. R. Gallo: 'Antonio Vivaldi, il Prete Rosso, la famiglia, la morte', in *Ateneo Veneto* (Venice, December 1938)

6. MS Ital. VII, 2447 (100 56), fols. 3–6

7. F. Caffi: *Storia della musica sacra nella già Cappella Ducale di San Marco in Venezia dal 1318 al 1797*, 2 vols. (Venice, 1854–5), *passim*

8. J. Westrup: 'Monteverdi and the orchestra', in *Music and letters*, Vol. XXI, no. 3 (July 1940)

9. *Storia della musica sacra*, II, 60

10. Archivio di Stato, Venice (afterwards cited as A.S.V.), *Basilica di S. Marco*, reg. 147, fol. 288v

11. All numbers quoted for works are given according to P. Ryom:

Verzeichnis der Werke Antonio Vivaldis, kleine Ausgabe (Leipzig, 1974). RV Anh. before a number denotes Ryom appendix

12. Archivio Patriarcale, Venice: *Registro sacre ordinazioni* 1688–1706, tonsure fol. 130, porter fol. 131, lector fol. 164, exorcist fol. 207, acolyte fol. 233, sub-deacon fol. 314, deacon fol. 381, priest fol. 464

13. F. Stefani: *Sei lettere di Antonio Vivaldi veneziano, maestro compositore di musica della prima metà del secolo XVIII* (Venice, 1871)

14. A.S.V., *Ospitali e luoghi pii*, Quaderno di Cassa, reg. 999, fols. 300–13, 316

15. P. Molmenti: *Venezia nella vita privata*, 4 vols. (Bergamo, 1905–8) (Eng. ed. London, 1906–8), VI, 80

16. Archivio di Stato, Florence (afterwards cited as A.S.F.), *Lettere die residenti, Del Teglia*, busta 3048, fol. 322

17. F. M. Misson: *A new voyage to Italy*, 2 vols. (London, 1695), I, 211

18. E. Wright: *Some observations made in travelling through France, Italy, etc. In the years 1720, 1721, and 1722*, 2 vols. (London, 1730) I, 79. Wright accompanied George, Lord Parker, Viscount Ewelme on this journey.

19. *A new voyage to Italy*, I, 177

20. C. Freschot: *Nouvelle relation de Venise*, 3 vols. in 1 (Utrecht, 1709), p. 306

21. *Antonio Vivaldi*, pp. 20–1

22. R de Candé: *Vivaldi* (Paris, 1967) p. 40

23. *A new voyage to Italy*, II, 5

24. *Some observations*, I, 99

25. C. de Brosses: *Lettres familières sur l'Italie*, 2 vols. (Paris, 1931), I, 176

26. T. Coryate: *Coryats crudities* (London, 1611), p. 250. In fact Coryate got his dates wrong. He gives the Assumption of the Blessed Virgin Mary as 5 August, when it is 15 August, and S. Roch as 6 August, when it is 16 August

27. J. Evelyn: *Diary*, 2 vols. (London, 1907), I, 195, 209–10

28. *Lettres familières sur l'Italie*, I, 237

29. P. J. Grosley: *Nouveaux mémoires sur l'Italie*, 3 vols. (Paris, 1764), II, 10

30. C. Burney: *Music, men, and manners in France and Italy, 1770*, BM Ad. MS 35122 (London, 1969), pp. 73, 76

31. Mrs Thrale (H. L. Piozzi): *Observations and reflections made in the course of a journey through France, Italy and Germany* (Dublin, 1789), p. 124

32. *Nouvelle relation de Venise*, p. 318

33. *Nouveaux mémoires sur l'Italie*, pp. 52–3

34. A. or S. (wife) de Goudar (?): *Le brigandage de la musique italienne* (Paris ?, 1777), pp. 53–4

35. *Some observations*, I, 99

36. *Diary*, I, 195–6

37. *Lettres familières sur l'Italie*, I, 188–9

38. *Storia della musica sacra*, I, 366
39. *Some observations*, I, 80
40. *Lettres familières sur l'Italie*, I, 173
41. *Some observations*, I, 62
42. *ibid.*, p. 63
43. *Storia della musica sacra*, I, 376
44. *Coryats crudities*, p. 249
45. *Nouveaux mémoires sur l'Italie*, II, 54–5

CHAPTER TWO

1. *Venezia nella vita privata*, VI, 29
2. *Observations and reflections*, p. 127
3. *Lettres familières sur l'Italie*, I, 189
4. *Nouveaux mémoires sur l'Italie*, II, 42
5. *Venezia nella vita privata*, IV, 121–2
6. Museo Correr, Venice, Schede Cicogna Ba 495
7. *Bilanci generali dal 1736 al 1755 pubblicati dalla reale commissione per la pubblicazione dei documenti finanziari della Republica* (Venice, 1903), vol. III
8. *ibid.*
9. A.S.F. *Lettere* etc. busta 3048, fol. 693
10. G. Renier-Michiel: *Origine delle feste veneziane*, 6 vols. in 3 (Milan, 1829), IV, 92
11. P. Bettio (ed.): *Lettere scelte di celebri autori all'Ab. Antonio Conti pubblicate per le nozze Da Ponti-Di Serego* (Venice, 1812), p. 76
12. *Diary*, I, 213
13. *Some observations*, I, 90
14. *ibid.*, p. 87
15. *A new voyage to Italy*, I, 190
16. *Observations and reflections*, p. 139
17. *New Cambridge modern history* (Cambridge, 1960–71), II, 282
18. D. Maxwell White: *Zaccaria Seriman 1709–84 . . .* (Manchester, 1961), p. 45
19. *Some observations*, I, 96
20. *ibid.*, p. 97
21. *ibid.*, p. 97
22. *Observations and reflections*, pp. 113–14
23. *Some observations*, I, 92–3
24. *Nouveaux mémoires sur l'Italie*, II, 19
25. *Observations and reflections*, pp. 134–5
26. H. Honour: *Companion guide to Venice* (London, 1965), p. 23
27. *Storia della musica sacra*, I, 316–17
28. *Sei lettre di Antonio Vivaldi*, 3 May 1737
29. *ibid.*, 6 November 1737
30. *ibid.*, 16 November 1737

CHAPTER THREE

1. *Coryats crudities*, p. 269
2. The text, as copied by the author of the present work, is as follows:

Fulmina il signor iddio maleditioni, e scomuniche contro quelli quali mandano, o permettano syno mandati il loro figlioli, e figliole si legittimi come naturali in questo hospedale della Pietà havendo il modo, e faculta di poterli allevare esseendo obligati al resarcimento diogni danno, e spesa fatta per quelli, ne possono esser assolti se non sodisfano, come chiaramente appare nella bolla di nostro signor Papa Paolo Terzo data ADL. 12 Novembre l'anno 1548.

3. A.S.V. *Ospitali* etc. busta 687, fol. 51
4. *ibid.*, fol. 141f
5. *ibid.*, Notatorio D, fol. 19
6. *ibid.*, Notatorio E, fol. 186
7. *ibid.*, busta 688, Notatorio G, fol. 102v
8. *Diary*, I, 213
9. *Antonio Vivaldi et la musique instrumentale*, p. 45
10. *ibid.*, pp. 45–6
11. K. L. von Poellnitz, *Memoirs*, 2 vols. (London, 1737), I, 414
12. A.S.V. *Ospitali* etc. busta 692, Notatorio R, fol. 4
13. A.S.V. *Ospitali* etc. reg. 1009, fol. 373
14. A.S.V. *Ospitali* etc. busta 662
15. *Lettres familières sur l'Italie*, I, 238–9
16. P. A. Tolstago, May 1698, quoted in W. Kolneder: *Antonio Vivaldi, his life and work*, Eng. ed. (London, 1970), pp. 10–11
17. *Some observations*, I, 79
18. J. G. Keysler: *Travels*, 4 vols. (London, 1756–7), III, 329
19. *Memoirs*, I, 414
20. *Lettres familières sur l'Italie*, I, 238
21. J. J. Rousseau: *Confessions*, Part II, Book 7. He uses the term *scuole*, but in Venice this meant the charitable institutions such as S. Rocco and S. Giorgio degli Schiavoni, which were suppressed by Napoleon in 1807 but subsequently revived.
22. *Venezia nella vita privata*, VI, 80–4 *passim*
23. *Music, men, and manners*, pp. 83–4
24. T. Wiel: *I teatri musicali veneziani del settecento* (Venice, 1897) Preface
25. A.S.V. *Ospitali* etc. Quaderno di Cassa, reg. 999, fols. 300–16, 333, 448, 518–93, 602–24
26. *ibid.*, busta 999
27. A.S.V. *Inquisitori di Stato*, busta 601, 602
28. *Vivaldi*, p. 51
29. *Antonio Vivaldi*, p. 105
30. M. O. Talbot: *The instrumental music of Tomaso Albinoni*, PhD. thesis, Cambridge University Library 1968, pp. 252–3
31. *Antonio Vivaldi*, pp. 121ff

32. A.S.V. *Ospitali* etc. busta 689, Notatorio H, fol. 182r
33. *Vivaldi*, p. 53
34. A.S.V. *Ospitali* etc. busta 689, Notatorio I, fol. 86

CHAPTER FOUR

1. *Antonio Vivaldi*, p. 20
2. C. Ivanovich published his *Minerva al Tavolino* (2 vols.), which is an invaluable account of the theatres of Venice at that time, in 1688
3. *A new voyage to Italy*, I, 193
4. *Venezia nella vita privata*, III, 154–5
5. *Minerva al Tavolino*, I, 401
6. *Diary*, I, 202
7. L. N. Galvani (Salvioli): *I teatri musicali di Venezia nel secolo XVII* (Milan, 1879)
8. *Venezia nella vita privata*, III, 159
9. See also T. Wiel, *Catologo delle opere in musica rappresentate nel secolo XVIII in Venezia*, published in parts in *Nuovo Archivio Veneto* (Venice, 1891–1921)
10. *Diary*, I, 202
11. *A new voyage to Italy*, I, 193
12. *Minerva al Tavolino*, I, 411–12
13. *Travels*, III, 264
14. A. Heriot: *The castrati in opera* (London, 1956), Ch. 4 *passim*
15. *A new voyage to Italy*, I, 191–2
16. J. Addison: *Remarks on several parts of Italy in 1701; 2 and 3* (London, 1705), pp. 96–7
17. P. J. Martello: *Della tragedia antica e moderna*, 1715 (Bologna ed. 1735, p. 144) quoted in *Musical Quarterly* Vol. XXXIV No. 2 (April, 1948), p. 225
18. C. Goldoni: *Mémoires pour servir à l'histoire de sa vie*, 3 vols. (Paris, 1787), Ch. 28
19. A.S.V. *Inquisitori di Stato*, busta 611
20. *Diary*, I, 213–14
21. *Nouvelle relation de Venise*, pp. 285–6
22. *Storia della musica sacra*, I, 342 and Giazotto: *Tomaso Albinoni* (Milan, 1945), *passim*
23. A.S.V. *Ospitali* etc. busta 689, Notatorio I, fol. 88v
24. A.S.V. *Notarile*, Notatorio Bianconi, fol. 1103

CHAPTER FIVE

1. *Antonio Vivaldi*, pp. 139–40
2. E. Preussner: *Die musikalischen Reisen des Herren von Uffenbach* (Kassel, 1949), *passim*

3. *Antonio Vivaldi et la musique instrumentale*, pp. 69–70

4. M. Pincherle: *Vivaldi* (Paris, 1955), pp. 75–6

5. C. Burney: *General history of music*, 2 vols. (1935 ed.), II, 445

6. *ibid.*, p. 451

7. *ibid.*, p. 637. Unfortunately it has not been possible to locate any music by Vivaldi in 'the collection mentioned above', which is in fact Dr Aldrich's Collection at Christ Church, Oxford. Ryom designates it Anh. 60

8. *Musical Quarterly*, Vol. XXXIV No. 3 (July 1948), p. 382

9. *Antonio Vivaldi, his life and work*, p. 180

10. *General history of music*, II, 733

11. *Verzeichnis der Werke Antonio Vivaldis*, p. 159

12. A.S.V. *Ospitali* etc. busta 690, Notatorio L, fol. 18v. On this occasion seven voted for Vivaldi, and five against him. At the second ballot, held the same day, there was a tie of six all. When it came to the next ballot on 24 May (fol. 26v), eleven voted for him and only one against him.

13. *Antonio Vivaldi et la musique instrumentale*, pp. 101–3, and *Vivaldi*, pp. 107–8

14. J. A. Hiller: *Lebensbeschreibungen berühmter Musikgelehrten* (1784), quoted in Pincherle: *Vivaldi*, p. 33

15. *Some observations*, I, 100

16. E. Selfridge-Field: *Venetian instrumental music from Gabrieli to Vivaldi* (Oxford, 1975), p. 221. The Ryom information was communicated in private correspondence, and the Strohm date is in 'Vivaldis Opern in Mantua', *Vivaldi informations* (1972), p. 85

17. *Some observations*, I, 86

18. *ibid.*, pp. 83–4

19. *ibid.*, p. 85

20. *Accademia Musicale Chigiana*, 'La Scuola Veneziana', Vol. XIX (1941), pp. 51–7

21. G. F. Malipiero: 'Un frontespizio enigmatico', in *Bollettino biografico-musicale* (Milan, January 1930). It is also treated at length in the same author's book *Antonio Vivaldi, il Prete Rosso* (Milan, 1958). See also *Musical Quarterly*, Vol. XXXIV (1948), pp. 371–403, and Vol. XXXV (1949), pp. 85–105, for articles and translations by R. G. Pauly.

22. *Antonio Vivaldi*, p. 133

23. *Travels*, III, 262

24. *Storia della musica sacra*, II, 212ff

25. *Antonio Vivaldi*, p. 198

CHAPTER SIX

1. J. J. Quantz: *Lebenslauf*, in F. W. Marpurg, *Historisch-kritische Beyträge* (Berlin, 1754), I, 223

2. A.S.V. *Ospitali* etc. busta 691, Notatorio N (Part 1), fol. 179

3. D. Arnold: 'Orphans and ladies: the Venetian conservatories (1689–1790)', in *Proceedings of the Royal Musical Association*, Vol. LXXXIX (89th session, 1962–3), p. 45

4. For example, the first recitative for Gloria refers to the '*Genio sempre augusto del gran rè che la Senna ognor' onora*', which is a reference to Louis XV, and in the second recitative Imeneo sings: '*O del Polona cielo bella più rara e grande vieni*' (referring to the Polish princess), and a little later there is a direct reference to Louis as '*gran Luigi*'.

5. *Storia della musica sacra*, I, 359–60

6. M. Rinaldi: *Catologo numerico tematico delle composizioni di Antonio Vivaldi* (Rome, 1945), p. 220

7. J. Hawkins: *General history of the science and practice of music* (London, 1776) (1963 ed., 2 vols.), II, 837

8. Biblioteca Marciana, Venice, MS Fr. append. 68–10102

9. O. Rudge: 'Lettere e dediche di Antonio Vivaldi', in *Accademia Musicale Chigiana*, XX (1942), p. 11

10. John, Earl of Cork and Orrery: *Letters from Italy 1754–5* (ed. J. Duncombe, 1774)

11. See note 8 above

12. *Verzeichnis der Werke Antonio Vivaldis*, p. 154. The MS in Vienna is no. 15.996

13. See note 8 above

14. *Travels*, III, 264

15. There is a copy in the Biblioteca Marucelliana, Florence.

16. H. Mendel: *Musikalisches Konversationslexicon* (1870–83), Vol. XI

CHAPTER SEVEN

1. Museo Correr, Venice, *Commemoriali Gradenigo*, Vol. II, fol. 36

2. C. Goldoni: *Commedie* (Venice, 1761), Vol, XIII, Preface by G. Pasquali

3. *Nouveaux mémoires sur l'Italie*, II, 6–7

4. A.S.V. *Ospitali* etc. busta 692, Notatorio Q, fol. 113r

5. All the known letters have now been published in *Nuova Rivista Musicale Italiana* Vol. I May/June 1967, pp. 45–79, ed. by Adriano Cavicchi

6. *ibid.*, p. 50

7. *ibid.*, p. 53

8. *ibid.*, pp. 55–6

9. *ibid.*, p. 58

10. *Antonio Vivaldi, passim*, but see, for example, Ch. 5

CHAPTER EIGHT

1. A. Cavicchi: 'Inediti nell' epistolario Vivaldi-Bentivoglio', in *Nuova Rivista Musicale Italiana* vol. I (May/June 1967), p. 60

2. See Ch. 7, n1
3. 'Inediti nell'epistolario . . .', pp. 65–7
4. A.S.V. *Ospitali* etc. busta 692, Notatorio Q, fol. 113r
5. *ibid.*, fol. 146r
6. *ibid.*, fol. 177
7. A.S.V. *Ospitali* etc. busta 692, Notatorio R, fol. 16
8. 'Lettere e dediche di Antonio Vivaldi', pp. 10–11
9. 'Inediti nell' epistolario . . .', p. 77
10. *ibid.*, p. 79
11. *Storia della musica sacra*, II, 218
12. *Lettres familières sur l'Italie*, I, 237–8
13. *ibid.*, p. 239
14. *Antonio Vivaldi*, p. 310
15. A.S.V. *Ospitali* etc. reg. 1009, fol. 541 and busta 704, reg. III, fol. 22
16. A.S.V. *Ospitali* etc. busta 692, Notatorio R, fol. 78v
17. A.S.V. *Ospitali* etc. reg. 1009, fol. 541
18. A.S.V. *Ospitali* etc. busta 704, reg. III, fol. 41
19. *Travels*, IV, 31–2
20. St Stephen's Cathedral, Vienna, register of deaths for 1741 and the account book for that year, fols. 177–8 (Vol. XXIII, fol. 63)

CHAPTER NINE

1. A.S.V. *Ospitali* etc. busta 692, Notatorio R, fol. 126v
2. *ibid.*, busta 693, Notatorio S, fol. 152
3. Madame du Bocage: *Recueil des oeuvres de Mme du B.*, 3 vols. (Lyons, 1764), III, 157–8
4. *Nouveaux mémoires sur l'Italie*, II, 53
5. *ibid.*, p. 55
6. *General history of music*, p. 78
7. *ibid.*, p. 85
8. 'Orphans and ladies', p. 47
9. A. de Goudar: *De Venise – Remarques sur la musique et la danse ou: lettres de Mr G[oudar] à Milord P[embroke]* (Venice, 1773), pp. 47–8
10. *Le brigandage de la musique italienne*, pp. 53–4
11. P. Molmenti: *Epistolari veneziani del secolo XVII* (Milan, 1914), p. 67
12. Biblioteca Marciana, Venice, MS 9314, fols. 89–91
13. A. Gyrowetz: *Biographie des A. Gyrowetz* (1848), ed. A. Einstein in *Lebensläufe deutscher Musiker* (Lepizig, 1915?), III–IV, 17–18
14. *Observations and reflections*, 123–4
15. J. C. Maier: *Beschreibung von Venedig* (Leipzig, 1789), II, 406
16. A. Maier: *Discorso sulla origine e stato attuale della musica italiana* (Padua, 1821), p. 157
17. E. Cicogna: *Delle iscrizioni veneziane*, 6 vols. (Venice, 1824–42) V, 331

CHAPTER TEN

1. A. Schering: *Geschichte des Instrumentalkonzerts* (Leipzig, 1905)
2. Quoted in Kolneder: *Antonio Vivaldi, his life and work*, pp. 113, 127
3. A.S.V. *Ospitali* etc. busta 690, Notatorio M, fol. 60v
4. A.S.V. *Ospitali* etc. busta 691, Notatorio Na, fol. 62. In fact this is dated 1721, but, since it is *more veneto*, is rightly 1722.
5. I. Stravinsky and R. Craft: *Conversations with Igor Stravinsky* (London, 1959), p. 76
6. *Lettres familières sur l'Italie*, II, 341
7. A.S.V. *Ospitali* etc. busta 691, Notatorio N, memorandum attached to fol. 216, dated 6 January 1724 (1723 *more veneto*)
8. N. Boulanger: *Le monde musical* 15–30 Jan. 1920

Index

251

253